THE LONG STRUGGLE FOR GENDER HARMONY IN AFGHANISTAN

Second Edition

WALE IDRIS

Paperback: 978-1-961438-43-9
eBook: 978-1-961438-44-6
Library of Congress Control Number: 2023911977

Ordering Information:

Prime Seven Media
518 Landmann St.
Tomah City, WI 54660

Printed in the United States of America

DEDICATION

Bismillah

Listen to the flute; it tells you a story
of nostalgia and separation.
-Mahmud Tarzi

A dedication to the brave and beautiful women of Afghanistan. May Allah grant the strength to overcome the challenges ahead and fulfill the highest, most truthful expression of yourself as the wonderful human being that you are.

-Author

"Either write something worth reading or
do something worth writing about."
-Benjamin Franklin

All glory be to God for the grace bestowed upon us all.

CONTENTS

ACKNOWLEDGMENTS

As a contributing member of the global alliance for world civilization, I acknowledge my responsibility as a part of the whole. I acknowledge all the parts and the role of each part, as well as the obligation and responsibility to foster a more congruous future for the advancement of humanity as a whole.

I am hereby acknowledging all who contributed directly by advising me or providing moral and material support while writing this book. I am grateful for the kindness and generous support from Funlola Jones and Beatrice de Salles for writing the foreword so generously and objectively. I am grateful to my daughters, Cherrelle, and Leni, for their support. Many thanks to my publisher, Simon Grant, for all his encouragement. Thanks to Sara Kazimi for taking the first edition of this book to Afghanistan.

I remain grateful to the late Professor Surendra Kaushik, a distinguished professor at Pace University Lubin School of Business, who, in honor of his paralyzed wife, whom he cared for until her death, founded the Mrs. Helena Kaushik Women's College in India. Dr. Kaushik taught me about the responsibility of males in gender issues.

I would like to take this time to thank Professors Donald Grunewald and Edward Yang, who privately taught me Harvard-level classes, for their encouragement and belief in me. My two younger American kids, Maya, and Soraya have been a terrific source of motivation. In addition to my late father, Muil Lekan Ajibade, who never stopped teaching me, I would like to dedicate this book to my late mother, Tai Ladun Ajibona, an ideal warrior queen mother. It is a celebration of their love and support. Finally, I would like to thank Funlola Jones for her important contributions and everlasting faith in my abilities.

FOREWORD

When I was invited to contribute to this book, I felt so honored due to the importance of current events involving all the radical changes in Afghanistan, including some personal friends in Kabul who have reached out asking for help. I am concerned not only for my friends but also for all the local people, some women and children, and people with disabilities. I wish somehow that I could understand the depth of their struggle and pain. As a linguist, culture enthusiast, and journalist, I enjoyed being away from "home," traveling and learning about other countries and cultures. Many countries that happened not to be on my bucket list are where I learned the most! Afghanistan has been of great interest to me because of its rich history and culture. This book has helped me understand the history and pinnacle of this profound culture. Reading this book and writing this foreword is like taking a journey throughout the country through its present world and throughout the past. Most of the roots of many of the causes of current events lie in old-time history, and the evolution of the events is narrated in this book with clarity and simplicity.

My multicultural heritage, multilingual professional career background, and being a resolute humanitarian activist give me the authority to appreciate the depth of research and analysis in this book. It met all my expectations. Dr. Wale's authority on the subject is unparalleled, and in this book, his passion for this subject truly shines. Few landscapes convey this society in all its untamed splendor like Pakistan & Afghanistan. Yet, sadly, this is a place to seek communion rather than dominance, as we must now bear witness and understand what took place so that catastrophes do not happen again. It is up to us. Let us not look away. Fear is our greatest oppressor, and this book is a simple testament of this world before it changes, maybe forever!

Beatrice de Salles is a Multi-Linguist journalist and a UN. Peace ambassador. She is a philanthropist serving on several organizations as Board Director, including African Views. She is the great-granddaughter of Campos Sales, the 4th and 5th president of Brazil, from 15 November 1898- 14 November 1902, and as minister of justice (1889-1891), senator, and governor of São Paulo (1896–1897).

PREFACE

The reason we support this book:

The girl on the book cover is Amina. We met her on November 18th, 2021, while surveying the starvation situation in Kochi Abad province in Kabul. She was 8 years old then. She only had potatoes to eat once a day. Her father was killed, and her mother sold firewood to provide for her five children. This type of story is why I keep going back to Afghanistan. We provided rice, lentils, beans, peas, and meat—enough for the 3 months of winter—along with coal to keep the little girl and her family warm and safe. This book captures Afghanistan's past, present, and future and highlights the extraordinarily complex and richly beautiful stories of the Afghan people's dreams, visions, and resilience. The author tells the stories differently from males' and females' views. He explains that conflict, suspicion, and betrayal are what drive the male perspective while beauty, romance, and tragedy are what drive the female perspective. Either way, it is a beautiful story about resilience. He says the females' perspective on the Afghans' story is worth telling.' The Long Struggle for Gender Harmony in Afghanistan is a complete history of women's suffrage and politics in Afghanistan,

as well as hypotheses on the future for girls like Amina. The book was beautifully written in honor of brave Afghan women like me. It is serendipity. I brought the book to Afghanistan and brought everyone to tears with this picture of Amina with the book. The book is very professionally researched and has very positive tones. I am happy to support it. Thank you so much, Dr. Wale Idris, for making such a difference!

Sara Kazimi, founder of LeoBella Inc. and the World Orphanage Foundation, embodies her passion for unity through art and personal life. After migrating from Afghanistan, she discovered freedom of expression and founded LeoBella, a luxury company featuring Swarovski crystals. Leobella organizes annual fundraising events for the foundation, which supports orphans and families in Afghanistan.

INTRODUCTION

This book delves into the multifaceted challenges faced by Afghan women, exploring the interplay of cultural traditions, social norms, and political dynamics that shape their lives. Through intimate narratives and personal accounts, we will witness their struggles for education, healthcare, and economic independence. We will learn about their aspirations, dreams, and the obstacles they overcome to carve out their own paths in a society that often seeks to confine them. We will also learn about the history of Afghanistan, the evoluti on of the political struggle of Afghan society, and the transformation of the religion that shaped and gripped the Afghanistan of our era. Moreover, this book is about the role and importance of Afghanistan in world development as well as a tribute to the countless unsung heroines who have defied societal expectations and made remarkable achievements by showing the capacity of women in leadership, arts, science, and technology, proving that humanity is limitless.

Through these stories, we aim to foster a deeper understanding of the Afghan women's journey, their resilience, and their enduring hope for a brighter future. By amplifying their voices, we strive to contribute to the ongoing global dialogue surrounding gender equality and human rights, highlighting the urgent need for support and empowerment. Unveiling Strength is a testament to the unbreakable spirit of Afghan women, reminding us of all that, despite adversity, their unwavering determination and resilience will continue to shape the path towards a more inclusive and equitable society. Join us on this transformative journey as we explore the challenges, triumphs, and aspirations of Afghan women and uncover the true strength that lies within them.

السلام عليكم

Peace be upon you

CHAPTER 1

The Golden Era of Afghanistan

Picture: A mixed-media illustration of the golden era of Afghanistan's direction in modern life and the illusion of strength and bravery against the odds.

Once upon a time, in Afghanistan, modernity, political stability, social progress, and economic prosperity were on the right track. Women were free to dress as they wished, and everyone had access to higher education. This period is commonly referred to as the "Golden Era" in Afghanistan. The period spans from the late 1930s to the late 1970s. Though every decade within this period saw a different form of progress as well as its challenges, it each laid the foundation for later advancements in women's rights, education, and modernization in Afghanistan. The most notable of the reforms enacted by King Zahir Shah was the approval of a new constitution in 1964 that gave women the right to vote and democratized the legislature, leading to increased representation and empowerment for women in Afghan politics.

During the golden era, Kabul became a major cultural center, attracting people from all over the world. Women became more visible in public life because of increased opportunities in the workforce and in higher education. The country's economy and infrastructure grew at a rapid rate. Cities like Kabul functioned as catalysts for women's empowerment, opening doors to higher education and professional careers. The country's historical and cultural significance drew foreign visitors and potential allies, opening numerous doors to prosperity. During the height of the Cold War, Afghanistan's neutrality attracted support from foreign communist and democratic countries, and their funding helped fuel economic growth, cultural development, and a soaring tourism industry.

Photo: A mixed-media illustration of the progressive era of Afghanistan's direction towards modern life.

Kingdom of Afghanistan was at peace during the reign of His Majesty Mohammed Zahir Shah (November 8, 1933–July 17, 1973). Women in Afghanistan were optimistic about the future. Afghanistan formally joined the League of Nations. By the 1930s and had established commercial ties with major powers in Asia and Europe. During World War II, King Zahir Shah maintained neutrality despite having close relations with the Axis powers. Afghanistan was one of the few countries that maintained neutrality throughout the conflict. Afghanistan already faced enough unrest from within its own tribal borders. King Zahir Shah advocated secularism because he saw the benefits of progress after World War II ended. The first modern university in Afghanistan was established at this time, and the country made other promising strides forward and underwent certain reforms. Afghan women were sophisticated, enlightened, free, and content with the direction of the country.

Afghan singer Rokhshana Hamida Assil (born around January 1, 1940; died December 20, 2020) photograph taken in the 1960s or 1970s in a jazz club in Kabul.

Queen Humaira Begum appeared in public without hijab, along with the King in western clothing, Afghan women could wear bikinis at picnics, and western music, and nightclubs were happening in Kabul. In a 1969 interview, Zahir Shah said that he is "not a capitalist. He also does not want socialism. "I don't want socialism to bring about the kind of situation [that exists] in Czechoslovakia. I don't want us to become the servants of Russia or China or the servant of any other place." King Zahir Shah wanted to be neutral to cooperate and trade with any country he wanted. Afghanistan was one of the few countries in the world to receive aid from both the Cold War enemies, though this would later turn out to be a tragedy of dilemmas in the fate of faith.

Photo: Mixed media composition of student life at the Kabul University, 1960s–80s

Prior to King Zahir Shah's modernization efforts, it was King Amanullah Khan who battled against the British and secured Afghanistan's independence in the Third Anglo-Afghan

War. On August 19, 1919, with the signing of the Treaty of Rawalpindi, Afghanistan became an independent nation. After years of isolation, King Amanullah Khan opened diplomatic contacts with other countries, most notably the Soviet Union and the Weimar Republic of Germany. After traveling through Europe and Turkey in 1927 and 1928, he returned to Afghanistan with ideas for modernizing the country. Mahmud Tarzi, a staunch advocate for girls' education, played a driving role in enacting these changes. He advocated for Article 68 of Afghanistan's constitution in 1923, which mandated that all children attend primary school. Queen Soraya Tarzi of Afghanistan was the daughter of Mahmud Tarzi and his wife, Amanullah Khan. Soraya Tarzi made a significant impact as queen, championing causes like women's education and suffrage.

Photo: Mixed media composition of Queen Soraya Tarzi, King Amānullāh Khān center, and together - Afghanistan- modernism

The history of Afghanistan is extraordinarily complex and rich, with beautiful stories of dreams, visions, and resilience. The stories are different from males' and females' views. Conflict, suspicion, and betrayal drive the male perspective, whereas beauty, romance, and tragedy drive the female perspective. Either way, it is a beautiful story about resilience. The females' perspective on the Afghans' story is worth telling. From the females' perspective, the history of Afghanistan is a testament to the strength and courage of women who have endured countless hardships. Their stories are filled with determination, sacrifice, and a fierce will to protect their families and communities. Despite the challenges they have faced, Afghan women have managed to find beauty amid chaos, and their resilience shines through their unwavering spirit. Their perspective sheds light on the untold narratives and highlights the vital role they have played in shaping Afghanistan's history.

CHAPTER 2

The Great Game

Picture: the great game illustration

Afghanistan was caught in the rivalry between Russia and Britain throughout the 19th century. This conflict was known as "The Great Game." The British were concerned about a Russian invasion of India, and the Russians were concerned by the expansion of British interests in Central Asia. Two of Europe's most powerful countries became embroiled in an atmosphere of suspicion and war threats. British protection of India's borders was prioritized while Russia proceeded in its conquest of Central Asia. The Great Game began when Britain decided to develop a new trade channel to the Emirate of Bukhara on January 12, 1830. Taking control of the Emirate of Afghanistan and turning it into a protectorate was part of a larger British imperialist strategy to utilize the Ottoman Empire, the Persian Empire, the Khanate of Khiva, and the Emirate of Bukhara as buffer states against Russian advance. This blockage would protect India and key British sea trade routes by stopping Russia from gaining a port in the Persian Gulf or the Indian Ocean, ensuring British dominance in the region. By establishing Afghanistan as a protectorate, the British would have direct control over its internal affairs, ensuring that no other power could influence or manipulate its government. This would also allow the British to maintain a strong military presence in the region, deterring any potential Russian aggression. Furthermore, the buffer states surrounding Afghanistan would serve as a physical barrier, making it difficult for Russia to infiltrate or expand its influence into British-controlled territories. This strategy would solidify British control over India and safeguard their vital trade routes, securing their economic and strategic interests in the region.

Photo: The first anglo-Afghan war

The rivalry between Britain and Russia grew as both powers tried to gain control over Afghanistan. Russia proposed Afghanistan as a neutral zone. The conflict led to the First Anglo-Afghan War (also known by the British as the Disaster in Afghanistan), fought between the British East India Company and the Emirate of Afghanistan from 1839 to 1842. This war was a devastating defeat for the British, as they were eventually forced to withdraw from Afghanistan.

Photo: British seized weapons at war times

This rivalry left a lasting impact on both Afghanistan and British foreign policy and shaped the geopolitical landscape of Central Asia for decades. The British initially resolved a succession conflict between emir Dost Mohammad (Barakzai) and former emir Shah Shujah (Durrani), whom they had installed after taking Kabul in August 1839. After several harsh winters, the main British Indian and Sikh force in Kabul and their camp followers almost perished in January 1842 as they fled.

The British then sent an Army of Retribution to Kabul to avenge their defeat, having demolished parts of the capital and recovered prisoners. They left Afghanistan altogether by the end of the year. Dost Mohamed returned from exile in India to resume his rule.

Sher Ali Khan of the Barakzai dynasty, the son of the previous Emir Dost Mohammad Khan, ruled Afghanistan from 1878 to 1880, during which time the British Raj and the Emirate of Afghanistan engaged in a military conflict. This war was part of the Great Game between the British and Russian empires.

Photo: Amir Yacoub Khan soldiers in 1878

The war was split into two campaigns; the first began in November 1878 with the British invasion of Afghanistan. The British were quickly victorious and forced Amir Sher Ali Khan to flee. Ali's successor, Mohammad Yaqub Khan, immediately sued for peace, and the Treaty of Gandamak was then signed on May 26, 1879.

British Colonial Army in Afghanistan in 1878

Major Cavagnari with Afghan Warlords, ca. 1879

Sir Louis Cavagnari, a British envoy, led a mission to Kabul, but on September 3, this mission was massacred, and Ayub Khan rekindled the fighting, forcing Yaqub to abdicate. As a result, Afghanistan plunged into a state of chaos, and power struggles ensued. The British government, outraged by the attack on their envoy, swiftly responded by sending a military expedition to Kabul. Their objective was to restore stability and extract retribution for the massacre. This marked a turning point in British-Afghan relations as they sought to assert their dominance and protect their interests in the region.

The Third Anglo-Afghan War, also known as the Afghanistan Independence War, began on May 6, 1919, when the Emirate of Afghanistan invaded British India, and ended with an armistice on August 8, 1919. Russia had recently undergone its Communist revolution, leading to strained relations with the United Kingdom. Amanullah Khan recognized the opportunity to use the situation to gain Afghanistan's independence over its foreign affairs. He led a surprise attack against the British in India on May 3, 1919, beginning the Third Anglo-Afghan War. After initial successes, the war quickly became a stalemate as the United Kingdom was still dealing with the costs of World War I. An armistice was reached, and Afghanistan became independent on August 19, 1919.

CHAPTER 3

The Loss of Innocence

Photo: The British's Afghanistan border crossing warning

After guiding Afghanistan to independence, Amanullah Khan rose to prominence as a leader and utilized his position to develop the nation. Amanullah reformed long-standing customs, including severe clothing standards for women, and established new, modern schools for both boys and girls in the area. He expanded business in both Europe and Asia. With the help of his father-in-law and Foreign Minister Mahmud Tarzi, he also supported a modernist constitution that included individual freedoms and equal rights. After Afghanistan gained independence, Mahmud Tarzi, and his daughter Soraya Tarzi—who was married to Amanullah Khan—played a significant role in shaping the country's pro-women policies.

Photo: welcome procession for Afghan royalties in England

This rapid modernization created a backlash and a reactionary uprising known as the Khost Rebellion, suppressed in 1925. He also met with many Bahá'ís in India and Europe, where he brought back books that are still to be found in the Kabul Library. These associations haunted him and served as one of the accusations when he was overthrown. Amanullah strengthened the army and established a limited Afghan Air Force consisting of donated Soviet planes. During Amanullah's visit to Europe, opposition to his rule increased, an uprising in Jalalabad culminated in a march to the capital, and much of the army deserted rather than resisted. In early 1929, Amanullah abdicated and went into temporary exile in then-British India. His brother, Inayatullah Khan, became the next king for a few days until Habibullah Kalakani took the power from him, becoming the new king of Afghanistan. Habibullah Kalakani's reign, however, was short- lived as he faced opposition from various factions within Afghanistan.

During the "Saqqawist period," Habibullah Kalakani, whose nickname was "Bacha-ye Saqao," which translates to "son of the water carrier," ruled Kabul. The Afghans did not like him because he was of Tajik descent. Mohammed Nadir Shah defeated him and had him put to death.

Photo: King Amanullah and the religious subjects

Image: a timeline in mixed media of Queen Soraya and King Amanullah's reign

As Afghan new king, Mohammed Nadir Shah swiftly undid most Amanullah Khan's reforms and empowered the tribal and religious leaders to quell the rife rural uprisings. Nadir Khan advocated for a constitution that put a focus on authentic Islamic denominational values. He strayed from a constitutional monarchy and changed the constitution to establish a royal oligarchy that excludes participation from the public. In a far more subdued manner than Amanullah, Nadir Khan also made efforts to materially modernize Afghanistan. He enhanced communication channels, particularly the Great North Road over the Hindu Kush, and contributed to the establishment of Kabul University, Afghanistan's first university, in 1931. However, Kabul University did not begin accepting students until 1932.

Photo: Afghan women in the 1920s

Photo: King Nadir Khan and his entourage

King Shah developed business ties with the same foreign nations that Amanullah had built diplomatic ties with in the 1920s. Under King Shah's leadership, Afghanistan experienced a period of economic growth and stability. The central banking system he established played a crucial role in attracting foreign investment and managing the country's finances effectively. King Shah's long-term economic planning laid the groundwork for Afghanistan's future prosperity and development.

While King Nadir Khan was attending a high school graduation ceremony in Kabul on November 8, 1933, one of the students by the name of Abdul Khaliq assassinated him. Khaliq shot Nadir Khan from closer range with a handgun of 22 caliber. Three bullets struck Nadir: two in the heart and one in the lung. Nadir took a bullet to the mouth in the opening exchange. As the guards ran towards Khaliq, a fourth gunshot injured one of them. Khaliq was caught as he threw the gun and tried to escape.

Image: condemnation of Khaliq and his martyrdom in Hazara history is depicted in a mixed media

Image: School group picture with Abdul Khaliq

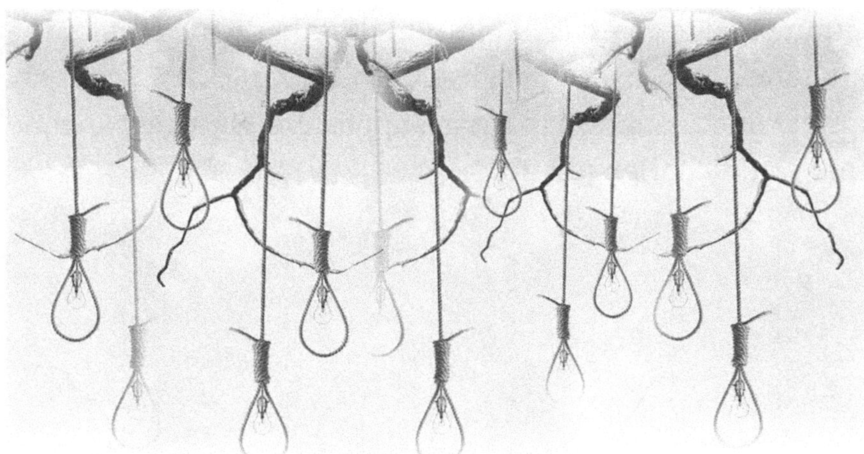

Image: mixed media: execution of Khaliq and his relatives

At the location of the execution, sixteen nooses were made. Khaliq was called over and questioned about which finger he used to push the trigger. As soon as he lifted his index finger, it was amputated. After asking him which eye he used to shoot with, they proceeded to gouge out that eye with a dagger. Instead of hanging Khaliq, the authorities eventually tortured him to death. Security personnel forced his family and friends to witness the torture of Khaliq, which included severing his tongue and piercing his eyes, before soldiers executed him with bayonets.

Nadir Khan may have been murdered in retaliation for the Hazaras' unfair taxation and executions, or perhaps Ghulam Nabi Charkhi's actions, a former Afghan ambassador to Moscow who fought in the 1928–1929 Afghan civil war for reformist Amanullah Khan. Khaliq saw King Nadir Khan's 1929 rise and intellectual and political killings in Afghanistan. Nadir, a general of King Amanullah Khan, was summoned to combat Habibullah Kalakani and restore the kingdom, but instead declared himself king. He selectively impris oned Amanullah Khan supporters. He killed anyone that could challenge him.

CHAPTER 4

The Ripples of Elitism and Classism

Photo: Zahir Shar and Queen Elizabeth of England

Mohammed Zahir Shah, the last King of Afghanistan, was King (Shah) on November 8, 1933, after the assassination of his father, Mohammed Nadir Shah. Following his ascension to the throne, he was given the regnal title "He who puts his trust in God, follower of the firm religion of Islam." He did not effectively rule for the first thirty years, ceding power to his paternal uncles, Mohammad Hashim Khan, and Shah Mahmud Khan. This period fostered growth in Afghanistan's relations with the international community, as in 1934, he reigned from November 8, 1933, until he was deposed on July 17, 1973. During his four decades of rule, Zahir Shah became a prominent Afghan figure in the world. He established friendly relations with many countries and modernized his country. While in Italy receiving medical treatment, Zahir Shah was overthrown in a surprise coup by his cousin and former prime minister, Mohammed Daoud Khan. He remained in exile near Rome until 2002, returning to Afghanistan after the fall of the Taliban. He was given the title Father of the Nation, which he held until his death in 2007.

Picture: Mixed media - JFK, Zahir Shar, Queen Humaira, and Queen Elizabeth of England

After WWII ended, Zahir Shah brought in various international advisors to help modernize Afghanistan. Potential reforms and advancements during this time of factionalism were thwarted by political infighting and In 1963, Zahir Shah gained full executive power. Afghanistan became a contemporary democratic state with universal suffrage, civil rights, women's rights, and free elections in 1964, despite internal political strife and a new constitution. However, this period of progress and stability was short-lived. In the following years, Afghanistan faced increasing external pressures and internal conflicts. The rise of the Soviet Union and its influence in the region, coupled with growing opposition from conservative factions within the country, led to a gradual erosion of the democratic reforms implemented by Zahir Shah. In 1978, a communist coup overthrew the monarchy and plunged Afghanistan into a prolonged period of turmoil and violence.

Over the course of their history, the Afghans have fought numerous conflicts against various empires and peoples. During the War of Independence of the First East Turkestan Republic founded by Muslim Uighurs and Kirghiz in 1934, King Zahir Shah supported them with aid, arms, and Afghan fighters.

The fight of the Turkestan State with moderate help from Pakistan, Afghanistan, Tajikistan, Kyrgyzstan, and Kazakhstan -- against China

Photo: Rural dwellers in Afghanistan, Jalalabad (late 19th century)

At the confrontation that took place in April 1934 in Yarkand and the Battle of Yangi Hissar in 1934 in Xinjiang, China, Gen. Ma Zhancang's Chinese Muslim army defeated the Uighurs and Kirghiz secession movement and killed them all. The emir Abdullah Bughra was killed and beheaded; his head being put on display at the Idgah mosque marked the end of the First East Turkestan Republic and reinstated Chinese government rule over the territory. The Uyghurs and other Kyrgyz minority tribes are still a minority seeking recognition and autonomy in China, to no avail. This situation widened the gap in classism compared to rural inhabitants whose cultural practices are deeply rooted in traditions of fundamental Islam and were vehemently against these changes in the capital.

The advent of rural Islamic Communist protests in Afghan revolutionary

Their agitations gave rise to the development of various political and ideological protests. They include the Islamic fundamentalists who want to revive Islamic tradition in Afghanistan and the Communist movement, which succeeded in overthrowing the monarch through a coup d'état under the leadership of Mohammed Daoud Khan, a former prime minister and member of the royal family. Mohammed Daoud Khan declared Afghanistan a republic and became its first president, ruling from 1973–1978. The event marks the beginning of the end of centuries of continuous Afghan monarchical governance and the beginning of Afghanistan's descent into political chaos.

CHAPTER 5
The Cold War Era in Afghanistan

Photo: Sardar Mohammed Daoud Khan who served as the Prime Minister of Afghanistan from 1953 to 1963 and, as leader of the 1973 Afghan coup d'état

Mohammed Daoud Khan (July 18, 1909–April 28, 1978) served as Prime Minister under the monarch regime of Afghanistan from 1953 to 1963. He led the 1973 Afghan coup d'état, which overthrew the monarchy, and became the first President of Afghanistan in 1973, establishing an autocratic one-party system. Born into the Afghan royal family, Khan started as a provincial governor and later a military commander before being appointed prime minister by King Mohammed Zahir Shah. Having failed to persuade the King to implement a one-party system, he planned rebellion for more than a year before he, on July 17, 1973, seized power from the King in a bloodless coup, backed by a large number of army officers who were loyal to him, facing no resistance. Departing from tradition, and for the first time in Afghan history, he did not proclaim himself Shah, establishing a republic instead as President. The role of pro- communist Parchamite officers coupled to him earned him the nickname "Red Prince."

Picture: Mixed Media: The Genesis of US-Afghan Relations, Officially in 1953-1973; here in picture: Daoud Khan, Zahir Shar, Nixon, and Kissinger, mixed media

He used autocratic rule and educational and progressive social reforms to quell communist inclinations during his rule. Under his regime, he led a purge of communists in the government. Many of his policies also dissatisfied religious conservatives, liberals who favored restituting the multiparty system that existed under the monarchy, and ethnic minorities who resented what they perceived as favoritism towards Pashtuns. Social and economic reforms implemented under his rule were relatively successful, but his foreign policy led to tense relations with neighboring countries.

The Daoud regime was an overtly anti-communist government, though they had helped him to power.

Akbar (Khyber) Khaibar, a prominent Afghan communist intellectual and a leader of the Parcham faction of the People's Democratic Party of Afghanistan (PDPA), was assassinated outside his home on April 17, 1978. His assassination by an unidentified person or people led to the overthrow of Mohammed Daoud Khan's republic and the advent of a socialist regime in Afghanistan, the Democratic Republic of Afghanistan.

Mixed Media: Khyber mourned by the comrades, led by Taraki.

Daoud Khan's government attempted to blame Khyber's death on Gulbuddin Hekmatyar's Hezbi Islami, but Nur Mohammad Taraki of the PDPA charged that the government was responsible for a belief that was shared by much of the Kabul intelligentsia. A fervent anti- communist interior minister named Mohammed Issa Nuristani, according to American historian and Afghanistan expert Louis Dupree, ordered the execution. Several sources, including fellow Parchamites Babrak Karmal and Anahita Ratebzad, claimed that Hafizullah Amin, the head of the opposition

Khalq movement, had planned the assassination. However, a number of former Khalq ministers claim that Karmal and the Soviet Union were responsible for ordering the assassination. Abdul Samad Ghaus, Daoud's confidant, speculated on a heated rivalry between Amin and Khyber as they attempted to penetrate the military for their different factions. According to communist sources, Khyber's attempts to unify Khalq and Parcham cells within the military would have endangered Amin's control. Mr. Ghaus claims that Amin's henchmen, Siddiq Alamyar and his brother, were in charge of Khyber and Inamulhaq Gran (mistakenly assumed to be Karmal) under Amin's orders. Alamar was appointed Minister of Planning by Amin and President of the General Transportation Authority by his brother.

Picture: public support for Communist government on 19th April 1978 funeral of Khyber

At Khyber's funeral on April 19, about 15,000 PDPA sympathizers gathered in Kabul and paraded through the streets chanting slogans against the CIA and the SAVAK, the Shah of Iran's secret police. People's Democratic Party of Afghanistan (PDPA) overthrew General Mohammed

Daoud Khan on April 27–28, 1978. Daoud Khan, who had himself taken power in the 1973 Afghan coup d'état and established an autocratic one-party system in the country, was assassinated. The coup d'etat was ordered by PDPA member Hafizullah Amin, who claimed that the event was not a coup but a revolution by the "will of the people." There were heavy casualties. Daoud ordered a crackdown on the PDPA leadership in response to this display of communist strength, which prompted the PDPA to launch a military coup known as the Saur Revolution.

People's Democratic Party of Afghanistan (PDPA) overthrew General Mohammed Daoud Khan on April 27–28, 1978. Daoud Khan, who had himself taken power in the 1973 Afghan coup d'état and established an autocratic one-party system in the country, was assassinated. Hafizullah Amin, a PDPA member, ordered the coup de tat and claimed that the event was not a coup but rather a revolution driven by the "will of the people." There were heavy casualties. The Saur Revolution marked the end of the monarchy in Afghanistan and the onset of decades of conflict. Saur, or Sowr, is the Dari (Persian) name of the second month of the Solar Hijri calendar, the month that the uprising took place.

The communist People's Democratic Party of Afghanistan (PDPA) seized power in a bloody coup d'état against Mohammed Daoud Khan, killing 23 members of his family in the Saur Revolution. When a single-party communist republic took power, a war began that would change the face of the country. The PDPA initiated various social, symbolic, and land distribution reforms that provoked strong opposition and brutally oppressed political dissidents. Muslim clerics were the first targets of repression; several arrests were made, and there were frequent disappearances.

After the PDPA murdered Daoud Khan and most of his family members at the presidential palace, they formed a Soviet-aligned government with Nur Muhammad Taraki as President (General Secretary of the Revolutionary Council). In August 1978, Taraki and Amin claimed to have uncovered a plot and executed or imprisoned several cabinet members, even imprisoning General Abdul Qadir, the military leader of the Saur Revolution. Amin overthrew Taraki in September 1979, and he then executed him. The PDPA government then denied that it was communist. “What is most ridiculous is the branding of Afghan National and Democratic Revolutionaries as communists.” The Chairman of the Revolutionary Council of the Democratic Republic of Afghanistan, Nur Muhammad Taraki, has openly and boldly declared that the reactionary press has deformed and twisted the facts. No political party ever existed in Afghanistan as a communist party. The Kabul Times, May 6, 1978. However, the It took 30 years and the relative stability and freedom under President Hamid Karzai for the former officer, Pacha Mir, to reveal the unmarked mass grave secret of the bodies of Afghanistan’s first president, Sardar Mohammad Daoud Khan, and his family had been buried. The victims included the president’s wife and her sister; his brother, Naim Khan; his three sons; three daughters; a son-in-law and a daughter-in-law; and four grandchildren, one of whom was only 18 months old. Eighteen members of the Daoud family were killed that night in the presidential palace, along with his officers and aides. reality was quite different.

Photo: Mawla Gul, left, and his brother marked the site on their land near Kabul where an Afghan leader and his family were buried

The government identified the remains of the former president and his family and did a state funeral. "If you ask any Afghan when did it all start? They would say it the assassination of Daoud Khan was the turning point." "The last day that Afghanistan was independent was April 27, 1978." Mr. Daoud was the founder of the Republic of Afghanistan and a towering figure in the development of the modern state. He overthrew his cousin, the last king of Afghanistan, Mohammad Zahir Shah, in a coup in 1973, but it was his assassination five years later that plunged the country into bloodshed and turmoil.

The popular account of the massacre was that the family was slain between 4 a.m. and 5 a.m. on April 28, 1978. After a day of fierce fighting, an army captain named Emamuddin entered the palace with a unit of men to arrest Mr. Daoud. The president refused to go with him and fired a pistol at the men. The mutinous soldiers responded with a withering hail of gunfire. Immediately, the president's assassination unleashed 20 months of bloodletting by the Communists. Many victims were buried in unmarked graves on or near a military firing range at Pul-i-Charkhi, an area on the eastern side of the capital, Kabul. That is where government investigators began searching.

A local farmer, Mawla Gul, 16 at the time, also learned the secret when he came upon soldiers camped on his family's land in the days after the Communist coup. He told his mother. She urged him to mark the grave with stones and plant a martyr's flag there, which he did three months later after the soldiers had left. Gul led them to the spot after he had kept the secret for 30 years until he met the government commission searching the area near his village. Mr. Daoud was eventually recognized using dental molds and a little golden Koran pinned to his inside breast pocket and gifted to him by the King of Saudi Arabia.

Photo: Daoud Khan State funeral on March 17, 2019

Daoud Khan's funeral was meant to close one of the bloodiest chapters in Afghan history and may bring some peace to his surviving relatives, some of whom were wounded in the shootings 30 years ago. Mr. Ghazi and Mr. Naeem, Daoud's grandsons, said they hoped that a new burial might also open the way for a process of national reconciliation or even a truth commission to address the war crimes committed under every Afghan government since 1978. "We have not come back for revenge," said Mr. Ghazi, whose father, Mohammed Nizam, a son-in- law of the president and a Foreign Ministry official, was killed along with his grandfather. "The truth has to be discovered and put at the disposal of the Afghan people." For the family, the discovery has come as a relief. "As Muslims," Mr. Ghazi said, "we need a grave and place to pray. If we can have that, we can rest."

CHAPTER 6

Evolution of Afghanistan

A string of crises that the Afghans have faced may be to blame for the country's unsteadiness. Afghanistan has had many wars in its history, including the First Anglo-Afghan War (1838–1842) and the Second Anglo-Afghan War (1878–1880). The Third Anglo-Afghan War began in May 1919 and lasted for a month, resulting in the Treaty of Rawalpindi, also known as the Anglo-Afghan Treaty, a peace treaty recognizing the independence of Afghanistan that was signed in Rawalpindi (now Pakistan) on August 8, 1919, in Rawalpindi, Punjab, by the United Kingdom and the Emirate of Afghanistan. The Treaty formally brought an end to the Third Anglo-Afghan War, a brief war that started on May 4, 1919, when Afghanistan invaded British India.

August 19, 1919, marked a significant turning point in Afghanistan's history as King Amanullah Khan boldly declared the nation's independence, breaking free from British influence and embarking on a path of sovereignty and self-determination. The nation's name, "Afghanistan," is recent. In ancient times, the land was known as Ariana and Bactria, and it was named Khorasan in the Middle Ages.

Archaeological evidence indicates that urban civilization began in the region occupied by modern Afghanistan between 3000 and 2000 B.C. The first historical documents date from the early part of the Iranian Achaemenian Dynasty, which controlled the region from 550 B.C. until 331 B.C. Between 330 and 327 B.C., Alexander the Great defeated the Achaemenian emperor Darius III and subdued local resistance in the territory that is now Afghanistan. Alexander's successors, the Seleucids, continued to infuse the region with Greek cultural influence. Shortly thereafter, the Mauryan Empire of India gained control of southern Afghanistan, bringing with it Buddhism. In the mid-third century B.C., nomadic Kushans established an empire that became a cultural and commercial center. From the end of the Kushan Empire in the third century A.D. until the seventh century, the region was fragmented and under the general protection of the Iranian Sassanian Empire. During this time, the region experienced frequent invasions and struggled to maintain stability.

After defeating the Sassanians at the Battle of Qadisiya in 637, Muslims began a 100-year process of conquering the Afghan tribes and introducing Islam. The land spans across southern Asia, the north and west of Pakistan, and the east of Iran. Its capital is Kabul, and most of the country is sparsely populated. Like all nations, Afghanistan's geography has played a significant role in its history. The landlocked, mountainous nation is relatively inaccessible and bordered by Pakistan, Iran, Turkmenistan, Uzbekistan, Tajikistan, and China. Additionally, its rugged terrain has made it difficult for outside forces to conquer.

The founder of the Afghan Empire was an Afghan prince by the name of Ahmad Shah Durrani (in picture), a member of the Sadozai tribe. The name The term Durrani was an abbreviation for 'Durr-i-Durran, Pearl of Pearls,' which was his regnal title, and his entire tribe took on that moniker, Durrani. The name Durrani symbolized the significance and grandeur of Ahmad Shah Durrani and his tribe, reflecting their power and authority. He became the Durrani Empire's sultan and is acknowledged to be the "Father of the Nation" of modern Afghanistan. The Hotak dynasty was an Afghan monarchy founded by Ghilji Pashtuns that briefly ruled portions of Iran and Afghanistan during the 1720s. Although the Hotak Empire has existed since the 17th century, the Durrani Empire is seen as the founding entity of the modern nation-state of Afghanistan. After a long series of battles, the Durrani-Afghan Empire came to power and replaced the Hotak Empire in 1747.

After throwing off Persian rule earlier in the 1700s, leaders of the Pashtun people of Afghanistan gathered and elected Ahmad Shah Durrani to be their leader, or emir, in 1747. This marked the beginning of the Durrani Empire. Ahmad Shah Durrani led the Pashtun people for over twenty years. Over the course of his reign, he focused on securing

Afghanistan's sovereignty through military campaigns; he waged wars against the Mughal Empire of India and the various principalities of Persia, as well as other Central Asian peoples. Over the course of this campaign, the Durrani Empire came to dominate the crumbling Mughal Empire, even forcing the empire to pay tribute and sacking the capital of Delhi in 1757.

In 1761, the Durrani Empire scored a major victory against the ascendant Maratha Empire of India in the Third Battle of Panipat. This indirectly resulted in the colonization of India by Britain, as both the Maratha and Mughal empires were deeply weakened by the conflict. In one of the last campaigns before his death in 1772, Durrani and his men sacked the Sikh holy city of Amritsar, killing thousands and destroying their holy temple (though it was soon rebuilt). As Ahmad Shah Durrani died, his sons feuded for the throne. Timur Shah Durrani won by killing his brothers. Like his father, he ruled for over twenty years. Also like his father, Timur Shah conducted campaigns against the Sikh people of India and other neighbors.

The Sadozai Kingdom was another name for the Durrani. The people were governed by strict Islamic religion agenda. The empire's sphere of influence encompassed the Indian subcontinent, the Iranian plateau, and Central Asia. In its prime, it ruled over a sizable portion of what is now Afghanistan, a good portion of Pakistan, a small portion of northeastern and southeast Iran, a good portion of eastern Turkmenistan, and a small portion of northern India. One of the two most potent Islamic nations of the eighteenth century was the Durrani Empire, which shared power with the Ottoman Empire. The Barakzai dynasty came to rule Afghanistan in the 19th and 20th centuries after two brothers, Dost Muhammad Khan, and Barakzai, overthrew the Durrani dynasty in Kabul.

EVOLUTION OF THE AFGHAN CULTURAL HERITAGE

516-330 BC

ACHAEMENID DYNASTY
Darius I invades Afghanistan, makes it part of the Achaemenid Empire.

330-327 BC

HELLENISTIC DYNASTY
Alexander the Great of Macedonia defeated the Achaemenian emperor Darius III. Afghanistan becomes part of the Seleucid Empire after Alexander.

327-320 BC

SELEUCID DYNASTY
Seleucus I Nicator was the successor of Alexander the Great. He found the eponymous Seleucid Empire, led by the Seleucid dynasty.

320-303 BC

MAURYA DYNASTY
Chandragupta Maurya, founder of the Maurya Empire, after defeating Seleucus I. Introduced Buddhism alongside zorostrian

300 BC-1 A.D.

ARSACID DYNASTY
Arsaces I was the first king of Parthia, and the founder and eponym of the Arsacid dynasty of Parthia. The Parthian Empire re-established the Persians as a major power in late antiquity

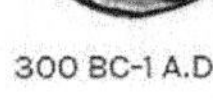

1-335 AD

KUSHAN DYNASTY
Heraios, was the first king to call himself "Kushan". The Kushan dynasty lasted for about three centuries,, until the invasions of the Kidarites.

335-460 AD

KIDARA HUNS DYNASTY
"lord Uglarg, the King of the Huns, the great Kushanshah, ruled Central and South Asia. Buddhas of Bamiyan were built during this period.

460-637 AD

SASANIAN DYNASTY
Ardashir I established the Sasanian dynasty, and was the last pre-Islamic Iranian empire after losing the Battle of Qadisiya to the Muslims in 637.

637-665 AD

RASHIDUN CALIPHATE
Abd al-Raḥmān ibn Samura was the general of the Rashidun who defeated the Sassanid King. The Rashidun Caliphs successors of the Prophet who spread Islam.

666-1111 AD

TURK SHAHIS DYNASTY
Kabul Shahis were a dynasty of Western Turk that ruled from Kabul and Kapisa to Gandhara. Defeated by the Arab Abbasid Caliphate and forced to convert.

1200-1368 AD

MONGOL DYNASTY
Genghis Khan founded the largest contiguous empire ever. Conquered China, Central Asia, and Eastern Europe.

1370-1507 AD

TIMURID DYNASTY
Timurid dynasty was a Sunni Muslim dynasty or clan of Turco-Mongol origin descended from the warlord Timur from the line of Genghis Khan.

The Barakzai dynasty played a crucial role in shaping Afghanistan's structure and historical trajectory. The Barakzai brothers ruled Afghanistan and effectively divided it in two in 1826. Dost Mohammad Khan ascended to power in about 1837, marking the beginning of the dynasty. Barakzai monarchs included Dost Mohammad Khan, Mohammad Afzal Khan, Yaqb Khan, Abd al-Ramn Khan, Habibullah Khan, Amanullah Khan, Mohammad Nader Khan, Mohammad Zahir Shah, and many others until 1929.

King Amanullah Khan abdicated the throne to his junior brother, Inayatullah Khan, due to the pressure of the civil war. Habibullāh Kalakāni, Bacha-ye Saqao, who did not belong to a dynasty, contested the throne during the 1928–29 civil war and removed Inayatullah Khan. But Habibullah did not last either before he was deposed and executed. Mohammad Nader Khan and the Barakzai dynasty ruled in direct succession. King Zahir Shah, Nader Khan's son, reigned from 1933 (after his father's assassination) until 1973. Mohammad Daoud Khan's coup d'état that overthrew King Mohammad Zahir Shah on July 17, 1973, ended his 40-year reign, and established a republic. This marked the beginning of a time of unrest in the country. The relative peace of modern Afghanistan is over.

The Saur Revolution in 1978 resulted in the overthrow of the Republic of Afghanistan and the establishment of the Democratic Republic of Afghanistan, which signaled the start of the country's first significant conflict. The People's Democratic Party of Afghanistan (PDPA) overthrew President Mohammad Daoud Khan and the Afghan Republic. The constitutionalizing of the Soviet-backed, socialist Democratic Republic of Afghanistan (1978–1992) led to widespread resistance and opposition from various factions within the country. Political rivalry brought about factions that were often divided along ethnic and ideological lines. Afghanistan experienced rapid changes in political leadership and uncertainty about its future direction. Abdul Qadir served as president for only two days, from April 28 to April 30, 1978. Nur Muhammad Taraki served from 30 April 1978 till 14 September 1979, 1 year, 137 days. He was assassinated on the orders of Hafizullah Amin. Hafizullah Amin served from September 14 to December 27, 1979, for a total of 104 days. During Operation Storm-333, Soviet special forces assassinated him. Babrak Karmal was president for 6 years and 332 days, from December 27, 1979, to November 24, 1986.

HISTORY OF THE AFGHAN GOVERNANCE SYSTEM

(1709-1738)

HOTAK DYNASTY
Mirwais Khan Hotak, considered a hero of his people, established the Hotak dynasty in 1709.

(1747-1823)

DURRANI DYNASTY
Ahmad Shah Abdali established the Durrani dynasty, He is considered the founder of modern Afghanistan in 1747.

1823-1926

BARAKZAI DYNASTY
Muhammad Khan Telai established the Emirate Afghanistan with the Barakzai dynasty ruled Afghanistan for 150 years.

1926-1929

KINGDOM OF AFGHANISTAN
Amanullah Khan became the first King to establish a constitutional monarchy and was deposed.

1929-1973

KINGDOM RESTORED
Mohammad Nadir Shah establish Afghanistan's first university in 1931. He was killed by a student.

1933-1973

THE LAST KING
Mohammad Zahir is the last King and was considered the father of the nation. His ouster brought an end to monarchy in Afghanistan.

1973-1978

REPUBLIC OF AFGHANISTAN
Mohammad Daoud Khan, first president of the Afghans having served as PM under the Monarch which he ended.

1978-1992

DEMOCRATIC REPUBLIC OF AFGHANISTAN
Nur Muhammad Taraki was a revolutionary communist politician, journalist and writer.

1992-2002

ISLAMIC STATE OF AFGHANISTAN
Sibghatullah Mojaddedi led Mujahideen against the USSR. He served as President after the fall of Najibullah.

1996-2001

ISLAMIC EMIRATE OF AFGHANISTAN
Mullah Omar founded the Taliban. He ordered the destruction of the Bamiyan Budha statues.

2002-2014

TRANSITIONAL ISLAMIC STATE OF AFGHANISTAN
Hamid Karzai was the first elected president of the Islamic Republic of Afghanistan

2014-2021

ISLAMIC REPUBLIC OF AFGHANISTAN
Was the last democratically elected president of Afghanistan. He lost the country to the Taliban in August 2021.

Haji Mohammad Chamkani served from November 24, 1986, to September 30, 1987, for 310 days. Mohammad Najibullah served from September 30, 1987, to April 16, 1992, for 4 years, 199 days. After Mohammad Najibullah, the Communist regime in Afghanistan ended. The Soviet Union's armed forces intervened in Afghanistan from

1979 to 1989 to aid the PDPA in its fight against widespread insurrection. The major combatants were the Afghan mujahideen, who had backing from the United States, the United Kingdom, Pakistan, Saudi Arabia, China, and Iran. Finished off in 1989 when the Soviet Union pulled out of Afghanistan. The Soviet Union intervened militarily on the side of the government after the revolution, which sparked the Soviet Afghan War in the 1980s.

Following the Soviet withdrawal at the end of the Cold War, Mujahideen forces continued fighting against the government, which collapsed in 1992. Unable to come to agreement on a governing coalition, a multifactional war broke out between various mujahideen groups, with grave atrocities committed by many of the factions. Abdul Rahim Hatif served as acting president from April 16–28, 1992, until April 28, 1992.

The era of the Islamic State of Afghanistan (1992–2002) started with Sibghatullah Mojaddedi, who also served as acting president from April 28, 1992, until June 28, 1992, for 61 days. Burhanuddin Rabbani served from June 28, 1992, to June 22, 2001, for 9 years and 177 days. He fled Kabul following its fall to the Taliban on September 27, 1996, but continued to serve as president in areas controlled by the Northern Alliance during the 1996–2001 Civil War until being fully reinstated following the recapture of Kabul on November 13, 2001. Between 1996 and 2001, the Islamic State remained the internationally recognized government, despite only controlling about 10% of Afghan territory. Hamid Karzai ruled from December 22, 2001, to July 13, 2002, for 203 days.

By 1996, Kabul and the rest of Afghanistan were under the control of the Taliban, a militant group. They later declared Afghanistan an Islamic Emirate, but it was not widely recognized. However, the Northern Alliance still controlled the majority of northern Afghanistan, and fighting between the two sides was ongoing.

The Taliban and al-Qaeda, who were later largely in their place, and all received support from Pakistan; Hezb-e Wahdat, who received support from Iran; and Junbish-i Milli Islami, who received support from Uzbekistan, later took over. Mujahideen loyal to the Islamic State of Afghanistan received support from Saudi Arabia. It ended with the Taliban seizing control of Kabul and most of the country in 1996, establishing the first Islamic Emirate of Afghanistan (IEA).

The Taliban's rule lasted until 2001, when the Transitional Islamic Republic of Afghanistan (2002–2004) installed Hamid Karzai as transitional president from July 13, 2002, to December 7, 2004—2 years, 147 days. Hamid Karzai then ruled from December 7, 2004, to September 29, 2014, for 9 years, 296 days, as the first democratically elected head of state; he was elected in 2004 and re-elected in 2009. Ashraf Ghani served as president from September 29, 2014, to August 15, 2021, for 6 years, 320 days. His presidency marked the first peaceful transition of power; he was elected in 2014 and re-elected in 2019; he was deposed during the fall of Kabul in 2021.

The American-led assault toppled the Taliban administration and installed a transitional one after the September 11 attacks on the United States. The government and a NATO-led coalition then faced a Taliban insurgency that lasted for over twenty years. After NATO soldiers left Afghanistan, the Taliban were able to retake most of the country.

A reconstructed Taliban and occasionally other Islamist terrorist groups, including al-Qaeda, the Haqqani network, Hezb-e Islami Gulbuddin, and the Islamic State of Khorasan Province, have been fighting the Afghan government and NATO-led coalition troops for years. During the 2021 Taliban attack, which resulted in the fall of the Islamic Republic and the establishment of the second Islamic Emirate of Afghanistan, the Taliban and the United States came to an agreement that allowed American and NATO soldiers to withdraw.

Conflict between the Islamic State and the Taliban (2015–ongoing): It all started in 2015, during the post-9/11 fighting, when a faction of the Taliban decided to build its own Islamic state (not to be confused with the old Islamic state of Afghanistan). The Taliban and NATO troops were targets, although civilians were the primary focus of the group's attacks. There is still an active insurrection.

In 2021, people who remained faithful to the overthrown Islamic Republic founded a new group in the Panjshir Valley called the National Resistance Front of Afghanistan. The Panjshir Valley succumbed to the Taliban in September 2021, and the leadership of the National Resistance Front withdrew to Tajikistan. The freshly constituted Taliban military and the widely scattered National Resistance

Front are currently engaged in combat in the provinces of Panjshir and Baghlan.

Mullah Mawlawi Hibatullah Akhundzada is the incumbent Supreme Leader of the Taliban, who has ruled over the Islamic Emirate of Afghanistan since August 25, 2021. The Islamic Emirate is currently not internationally recognized, despite controlling all Afghan territory.

CHAPTER 7

Ripples of the Saur Revolution

Photo: Afghan communist government in 1978
Third from left: Kamal, Nur Taraki in the middle, and Hafizullah right next to him.

In September 1979, suspicion between political protégé prime minister Hafizullah Amin and PDPA General Secretary Mohammed Nur Taraki turned their close relationship sour. Hafizullah Amin and Mohammed Taraki had participated in the previous coup d'état that ousted Daoud Nur in April 1978 during the Saur Revolution. Hafizullah Amin had adored Taraki and set out to construct a cult-like personality around him. In party and government meetings, Amin would refer to Taraki as "The Great Leader," "The Star of the East," or "The Great Thinker" among other titles, while Amin was given such praises in honest admiration and mentorship, as a true disciple, Mohammed Taraki believed him.

Amin soon realized that Taraki became overly arrogant with the belief in his own ingenuity, had several rallies organized with his praises and pictures everywhere carried by school children for self- aggrandizement. Amin had created political idolatry and cult-like personality in Nazi Germany, North Korea, China, Russia, and Uganda. It was often thought that this kind of situation was endemic to communism or despotic leaders of third-world countries until the advent of the 45th president of the United States, whose idolatry was compared to Kim Il-sung-style. This type of idolatry is considered haram in Islam.

Picture: mixed media: USSR Secretary General Leonid Brezhnev (R) meets Nur Muhammad Taraki (middle) with pictures reflecting Soviet influence on Afghan women.

The Arabic word haram means “forbidden.” The Quran and the Sunnah prohibit certain behaviors, known as haram. No matter how pure one’s motives, if Islam forbids anything, it cannot be done. At political rallies, communist ladies would parade around with images of Taraki, further inflaming Muslim animosity toward the government. Amin and Taraki's relationship quickly deteriorated as they grew increasingly resentful of one another. There was a fight for the leadership of the Afghan National Army. Their relationship hit a snag after Amin accused Taraki of nepotism, and Taraki countered with claims of Amin's ineptitude.

Taraki had signed a Twenty-Year Treaty of Friendship with the Soviet Union on December 5, 1978, which expanded Soviet aid to his regime. Following the Herat uprising, Taraki contacted Alexei Kosygin, chair of the USSR Council of Ministers, and asked for "practical and technical assistance with men and armament." Kosygin was unfavorable to the proposal, citing the negative political repercussions such an action would have for his country. Kosygin rejected all further attempts by Taraki to solicit Soviet military aid in Afghanistan. Taraki went directly to the top and requested aid from Leonid Brezhnev, the general secretary of the Communist Party of the Soviet Union and Soviet head of state. Brezhnev warned him that full Soviet intervention "would only play into the hands of our enemies— both yours and ours." Brezhnev also advised Taraki to ease the drastic social reforms and seek broader support for his regime.

Brezhnev referred to the USSR's rivalry from 1945 to 1991, the Cold War, which dominated international affairs. The global competition between the United States and the Soviet Union took different forms: political, economic, ideological, and cultural. At times, the constant arms race burst into armed conflict. But overshadowing all was the threat of nuclear war.

Afghanistan shares borders with the Soviet Union. All Afghan leaders had some form of good relationship with the Soviets. Daoud Khan said he was happiest when he could light his American cigarettes with Soviet matches. The relationship between Afghanistan and the Soviet Union was inevitable. Afghanistan's international policy of neutrality has always been strategically non-alliance: why take the chance? Taraki's regime, however, leaned far left with the Soviets. Brezhnev was happy with Taraki, and the United States was not. Both President Carter and President Reagan resented the idea of communism in Afghanistan.

The rivalry between Taraki and Amin intensified, suspicion grew, and various killings occurred. Taraki tried but failed to eliminate Amin. Amin, who had gained control of the army, retaliated by taking over the government and arresting Taraki. After Taraki's arrest, Amin discussed the incident with Brezhnev, in which he said, "Taraki is still around. What should I do with him?" Brezhnev replied that it was his choice. Amin, who now believed he had the full support of the Soviets, ordered the death of Taraki. Taraki was suffocated with pillows by three men under Amin's orders. Taraki did not resist nor say anything as the men instructed him to lie down on a bed to be suffocated. The men secretly buried his body at night. The news shocked Brezhnev, who had vowed to protect Taraki. This incident was the most crucial factor in the Soviet invasion of Afghanistan in December of 1979.

President is tried, executed

From Tribune Wire Services

PRESIDENT Hafizullah Amin of Afghanistan was overthrown in a military coup, Afghanistan radio reported Thursday. Broadcasts monitored in Washington and London said he had been executed.

Soviet troops, part of a contingent of 6,000 flown into the country in recent days, were believed to be fighting in support of the coup. Heavy fighting was reported in the center of Kabul, the Afghan capital.

Babrak Karmal, a former deputy premier, proclaimed himself in control of the government and announced that he would release political prisoners and extend what he called democratic freedoms to the Afghan masses.

"I announce to the world that the last link of the chains of the Amin regime has been broken. . . ." Karmal, speak-

Amin Karmal

gents who have fought for 19 months against pro-Soviet administrations in the nation. In his statement, Karmal denounced the former government as a "fascist regime."

THE OFFICIAL Afghan radio also an-

In Moscow, the Soviet news agency Tass praised the takeover and denounced the Amin regime, calling it a dictatorship and an agent of American imperialism.

State Department officials said they had received accounts that Soviet troops led an assault on the Radio Afghanistan building and were involved in heavy fighting elsewhere in the capital. One report said Soviet troops were seen taking some Afghans prisoner.

KABUL RADIO said Amin was executed after being convicted at a revolutionary trial of crimes against the Afghan people.

The terse broadcast said, "Hafizullah Amin has been tried and sentenced to death. The sentence has been carried out."

Karmal, who was forced out of Afghanistan by Amin, is believed to have

President executed. This picture prepares readers for the shape of things to come.

Picture: Mixed media-Darul Aman Palace, Kabul: Participants of the Operation "Storm 333"

On December 24, 1979, the Soviet Union invaded Afghanistan, deploying an assault unit against Tajbeg Palace, and quickly defeating the Afghan army loyal to Hafizullah Amin. Amin trusted the Soviet Union until the very end, despite the deterioration of official relations, and was unaware that the tide in Moscow had turned against him since he ordered Taraki's death. He kept a portrait of Joseph Stalin on his desk. When Soviet officials criticized his brutality, Amin replied, “Comrade Stalin showed us how to build socialism in a backward country. The Soviet invasion of Afghanistan in December 1979 marked the beginning of a long and bloody conflict.

When the Afghan intelligence service handed Amin a report that the Soviet Union would invade the country and topple him, Amin claimed that the report was a product of imperialism. Earlier, concerned for his safety, five days before the Soviet invasion, Amin had moved from the Presidential Palace to the Tajbeg Palace, which had previously been the headquarters of the Central Corps of the Afghan Army. The palace was formidable, with walls strong enough to withstand artillery fire. The Soviets had launched propaganda that Amin was a “CIA agent” who had betrayed the Saur Revolution to encourage mutiny within Amin’s inner circle and the Soviet forces to move against him. The Soviets had tried to poison him on a few occasions before resorting to brute force.

Picture: Mixed media - Hafizullah Amin with Fidel Castro.

Amin still believed the Soviet Union was on his side during the attack and told his adjutant, “The Soviets help us.” The adjutant replied that it was the Soviets who were attacking them; Amin initially replied that this was a lie. Only after he tried but failed to contact the Chief of the General Staff, he muttered, “I guessed it. It’s all true.”

There are various accounts of how Amin died; he was either killed by a deliberate attack or died from random gunshots. His son was fatally wounded and died shortly after. His daughter was wounded but survived. The men of Amin’s family were all executed, while the women, including his daughter, were imprisoned at Pul-e-Charkhi prison until President Najibullah took over in early 1992.

Photo: Mural in memory of Hafizullah in Afghanistan

After Amin’s death on December 27, 1979, Radio Kabul broadcast Babrak Karmal’s pre-recorded speech to the Afghan people, saying, “Today the torture machine of

Amin has been smashed." The Soviets installed Karmal as Afghanistan's new head of government, while the Soviet Army began its intervention in Afghanistan, which would last for nine years.

General Secretary of the CPSU, Chairman Leonid Brezhnev, President Kamal, and Anahita Ratebzad

Babrak Karmal was made Chairman of the Revolutionary Council and Chairman of the Council of Ministers on December 27, 1979, by the Soviets. He released people imprisoned during Nur Mohammad Taraki's and Amin's rule. Karmal also replaced the red Khalqist flag with a more traditional one. These policies failed to increase the PDPA's legitimacy in the eyes of the Afghan people and the Afghan mujahideen rebels; he was widely seen as a Soviet puppet, which he was by self-acknowledgment amongst the populace. Despite his position, Karmal followed advice from Soviet advisers and was not permitted to make critical decisions. The Soviet control of the Afghan state was so overbearing that Karmal himself admitted to a friend of his unfree life, telling him: "The Soviet comrades love me boundlessly, and for the sake of my personal safety, they don't, and tongue had been tied, and he had no right to speak without the permission of his personal friends" - Zia Majid, a friend of Babrak Karmal.

Karmal's government granted concessions to religious leaders and the restoration of confiscated property. Certain properties that were confiscated during earlier land reforms were also partially restored. All these measures, except the general amnesty of prisoners, were introduced gradually. The introduction of more Soviet-style institutions led the Afghan people to distrust the communist government even more. When Karmal took power, leading posts in the Party and government bureaucracies were taken over by Parchamites.

The People's Democratic Party of Afghanistan was formed in 1967 by Babrak Karmal. The basic ideology of the Parchamites was one of a gradual move towards socialism in Afghanistan. The Parcham faction supported this idea because they felt that Afghanistan was not industrialized enough to undergo a genuine proletarian revolution, as stated in the Communist Manifesto. The Parcham faction had more urban-based members who belonged to the middle and upper-middle classes. Opposed to the more moderate Parchamis were the radical Khalq faction. The Khalq (meaning "people") developed a more active line, advocating an immediate and violent government overthrow and establishing a Soviet-style communist regime.

The opposition Khalqists mockingly referred to the Parcham as the "royal communist party" because of its ties to the Kingdom of Afghanistan and initial desire to preserve the constitutional monarchy. In 1977, Parcham reunited with Khalq, and following the Saur Revolution of 1978, many Parchamites were represented in the initial government. Very soon after the revolution, Parchamites were purged from the government by the Khalqist leadership of Nur Muhammad Taraki, and the regime eventually went into a reign of terror, jailing and executing Parchamites. The Parcham faction gained back power after the replacement of Hafizullah Amin with Babrak Karmal in December 1979 by the Soviet Union's Operation Storm-333. Under Mikhail Gorbachev, the Soviet Union deposed Karmal in 1986 and replaced him with Mohammad Najibullah. In June 1990, the Parcham-led PDPA converted itself into the Watan Party of Afghanistan (Homeland Party), with references to Marxism-Leninism removed.

THE
KABUL TIMES

Remnants of monarchy wiped

First radio announcement

Karmal elected vice-chairman of Revolutionary Council

Taraki elected Chairman of Revolutionary Council

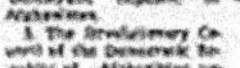

ARMED FORCES COUNCIL DECREE

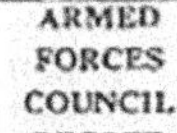

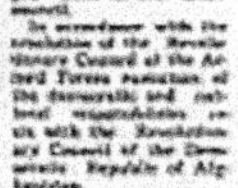

Foreign reactionary mass media propaganda blasted

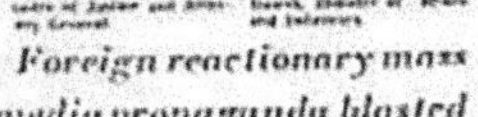

Remnants of Monarch wiped announcement by Kabul Times

Years after the end of his leadership, Babrak Karmal denounced the Saur Revolution of 1978, in which he took part, aiming at the Khalq governments of Taraki and Amin. He told a Soviet reporter:

> *It was the greatest crime against the people of Afghanistan. Parcham's leaders were against armed action because the country was not ready for a revolution. I knew that people would not support us if we decided to keep power without such support.*

In early December 1996, Karmal died in Moscow's Central Clinical Hospital from liver cancer. Karmal was the most powerful politician in Kabul under the leadership of Parcham. However, he could not make peace with the Mujahideen rebels, who despised him for being a Soviet stooge.

Photo: Mujahideen resistance against the Afghan Soviets military campaign

The Soviet Afghans were stationed in Afghanistan during the Karmal regime. About 100,000 Soviet troops were deployed to control the cities, larger towns, and major garrisons, and the mujahideen moved with relative freedom throughout the countryside. Soviet troops tried to crush the insurgency with various tactics, but the guerrillas eluded their attacks. The Soviets then attempted to eliminate the Mujahideen's civilian support by bombing and depopulating the rural areas. These tactics sparked a massive flight from the countryside; by 1982, around 2.8 million Afghans had sought asylum in Pakistan, and another 1.5 million had fled to Iran. The Mujahideen eventually neutralized Soviet airpower through shoulder-fired antiaircraft missiles supplied by the Soviet Union's Cold War adversary, the United States.

CHAPTER 8

The Soviet Agenda

Picture: Mixed media- soviet agenda

The British started the great game; the Russians played American Billiard; the Americans played Russian Roulette; the Afghans played poker; and the U.N. was the croupier. This inference explains the Afghan Saga in its entirety, but it is not the focus of this book. However, it is vital to mention it because everyone involved in the Afghan war has only done so for selfish interests. There is nothing wrong with self-interest, which is often described openly as national interest, except deceit and hypocrisy that cost the life of a nation. Joanne Herring, a longtime political activist, and philanthropist, deserves a great deal of credit for helping break the back of the Soviet Union in Afghanistan in the 1980s. Joanne argued that the Soviet Union's agenda was to take over Afghanistan to control the Strait of Hormuz, the passage today for one-fifth of the world's crude oil exports. She figured it all out while she was in Afghanistan along the border with Pakistan and had witnessed the Soviet tanks heading into Kabul. Herring became politically engaged in the Middle East in the 1970s.

> *I thought, "Why do the Soviets want Afghanistan? Why are they invading this little country that does not have a blade of grass, 90 degrees in the summer and below 30 in the winter? What are they doing here?" And then I saw Pakistan, and I said, "Oh! And they are going to invade Pakistan? Why?" Because of Pakistan, you could control the Strait of Hormuz. - Joanne Herring*

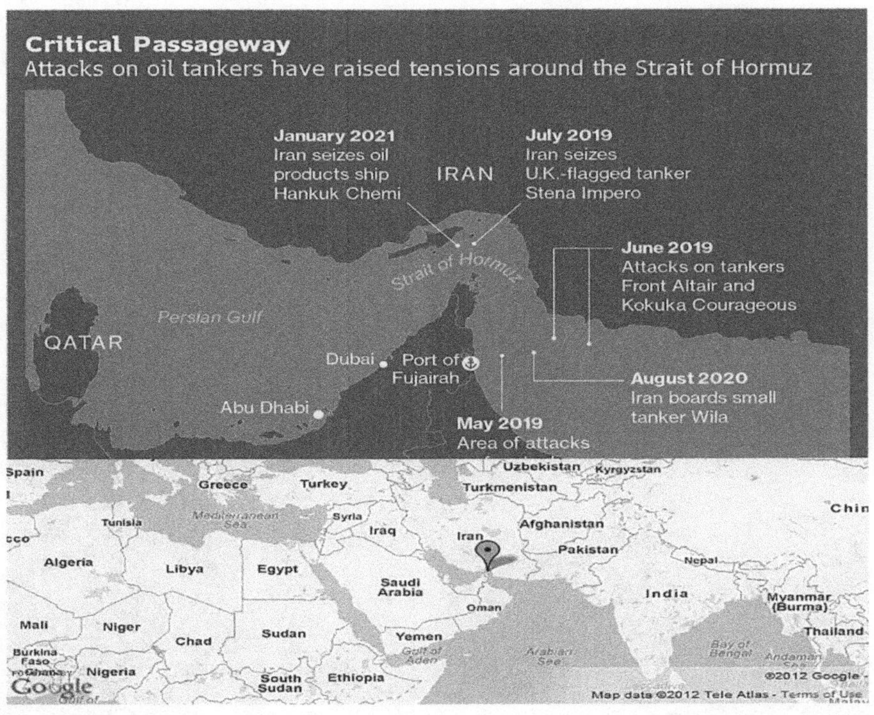

The Strait of Hormuz is a strait between the Persian Gulf and the Gulf of Oman. It provides the only sea passage from the Persian Gulf to the open ocean and is one of the world's most strategically important choke points. On the north coast lies Iran, and on the south coast are the United Arab Emirates and Musandam, an exclave of Oman.

For years, maritime traffic in the strait has facilitated the smooth conveyance of goods, arms, and services across the gulf. In the 1980s, during the Iran-Iraq War, both sides fought a so-called "tanker war," targeting each other's oil exports. That conflict eventually dragged on in the United States, which protected oil tankers and led to several run-ins with Iranian forces, resulting in a pair of damaged U.S. Navy vessels. On July 3, 1988, 290 people were killed when an Iran Air Airbus A300 was shot down over the strait by the United States Navy guided-missile cruiser USS Vincennes (CG-49), which was wrongly identified as a jet fighter.

Joanne Herring

As part of the settlement, even though the U.S. government did not admit legal liability or formally apologize to Iran, it agreed to pay $61.8 million on an ex-gratia basis in compensation to the families of the Iranian victims. The shootdown was the deadliest aviation disaster involving an Airbus A300 as well as the deadliest aviation disaster in 1988. It was also the deadliest airliner shootdown incident until 2014 when Malaysia Airlines Flight 17 was shot down over Ukraine.

In the Strait of Hormuz, every day, 80 million barrels of oil pass. The United States was not energy independent. I said, "Oh, my goodness! It is not our air conditioners and cars that are threatened, but our factories, jobs, defenses, airplanes, and boats. We don't have the means of keeping them working until we have enough petroleum to make them work."

Photo: Charlie Wilson in Mujahideen clothes during operation cyclone

Herring also discussed her philanthropic work in Afghanistan, which she called Marshall Plan Charities, and how one Afghan village was revitalized by empowering the people with the tools they needed to survive. Herring made a documentary move with the help of the former President of Pakistan, Muhammad Zia-ul-Haq, which was used to convince the late Rep. Charlie Wilson, D-Texas, to work together to get the Afghan people the resources they needed to defeat the USSR and move America one giant step closer to winning the Cold War. Together, they convinced Congress that it was the United States' economy that the USSR was targeting. We have managed to save the Strait of Hormuz. When I took this to Charlie Wilson, and the other people in the United States who had told me Afghanistan was not important, and [President Ronald] Reagan—see, this got to Reagan, too, and he understood it quickly.

And that's why Charlie, with the Republicans voting solidly behind him, got money for helping Afghanistan. And it started with little money, and they had to do all kinds of machinations to get the armaments for them because they could not be marked "made in the USA." And this was not easy, but they managed to get it through connections in Egypt and Saudi Arabia and Charlie's connections in Israel. And this all came together, and under the radar, they were starting to help the Afghans fight the war, and they did. "What Charlie and I did there didn't involve one American soldier. All we did was help the Afghans help themselves," she said. "We gave them the tools; they did the rest through free enterprise." Joanne Herring In 1983, Charlie Wilson and Joanne Herring secured funds for anti-aircraft weapons to shoot down Mil Mi-24 Hind helicopters.

The year after, CIA officer Gust Avrakotos directly approached Wilson, breaking the CIA's policy against lobbying Congress for money and asking Wilson for $50 million more. Wilson agreed and convinced Congress, saying, "The U.S. had nothing whatsoever to do with these people's decision to fight... but we'll be damned by history if we let them fight with stones." Later, Wilson succeeded in giving the Afghans $300 million of unused Pentagon money before the end of the fiscal year.

Thus, Wilson directly influenced the level of United States government support for the Afghan Mujahideen. Wilson has said that the covert operation succeeded because "there was no partisanship or damaging leaks." Michael Pillsbury, a senior Pentagon official, used Wilson's funding to provide Stinger missiles to the Afghan resistance in a controversial decision. The Stinger missile was a deciding factor in the Afghan-Soviet war. The Mujahideen never won a battle against the Soviets before they got the Stinger missiles, and they never lost a battle against the Soviets after that.

Charlie Wilson and Joanne Herring convinced the CIA to support their cause, and a Hollywood movie called Charlie Wilson's War was made to commemorate their efforts. Together, they waged a secret war that would change the cause of history. For Charlie Wilson, it was an opportunity to take revenge on Moscow for the USSR's support of North Vietnam against the United States. The Soviets had helped the North Vietnamese to deliver a blow to the Americans in Vietnam. In addition to the Hollywood Movie starred by Tom Hanks, Julia Roberts, and Timothy Seymour Hoffman, a documentary titled the true story of Charlie Wilson recounts more accurately the totality of the American involvement in the Afghan defeat of the USSR.

Photo: Joanne Herring and Charlie Wilson

First sting (a decisive weapon against the Soviet helicopters)

The injustice during communist rule caused unrest and quickly expanded into a state of civil war by 1979. The mujahideen guerrilla (and smaller Maoist guerillas) rose against regime forces countrywide, which quickly turned into a proxy war. The Pakistani and United States governments began to support the Afghan rebels with covert training through Pakistan's Inter-Services Intelligence (ISI). The Soviet Union sent military advisers to support the PDPA regime. Meanwhile, there is increasingly hostile friction between the dominant Khalq and the more moderate Parcham, which are competing factions within the PDPA. After the overthrow of President Mohammad Daoud Khan in April 1978, power was shared by two Marxist-Leninist political groups, the People's (Khalq) Party and the Banner (Parcham) Party, which had earlier emerged from a single organization, the People's Democratic Party of Afghanistan, which had reunited in an uneasy coalition shortly before the coup.

Photo: Afghanistan Political prison gate during the communist era

The new government had little populace support, forged close ties with the Soviet Union, launched ruthless purges of all domestic opposition, and began extensive land and social reforms and religious clampdowns that the devoutly Muslim groups bitterly resented.

Between April 1978 and the Soviet invasion of December 1979, Afghan communists executed 27,000 political prisoners at the sprawling Pul- i-Charki prison, six miles east of Kabul. Many of the victims were village mullahs and headmen who were obstructing the modernization and secularization of the intensely religious Afghan countryside. By Western standards, this was a salutary idea in the abstract. But it was carried out in such a violent way that it alarmed even the Soviets. Robert D. Kaplan, Soldiers of God: With Islamic Warriors in Afghanistan and Pakistan.

The brutal execution of political prisoners at Pul-i-Charki prison by the communists not only targeted those who opposed modernization and secularization but also instilled fear and terror among the Afghan population. The excessive violence employed during these executions, however, caused concern and unease even among the Soviets, who had initially supported the communist regime. The harsh methods used by the communists highlighted the extent to which they were willing to go to enforce their ideology, leaving a lasting impact on the Afghan people.

CHAPTER 9

The Afghan Resistance

Photo: Afghans prepared to resist the soviets with gas masks and automatic rifles

During the Communist era and the Soviet occupation of Afghanistan, the military used many scare tactics to force the rural population into cities where they could be controlled. They confiscated land and property, which forced many people to flee Afghanistan to Iran, Pakistan, and other places. They used landmines and other brutal methods to force farmers from the opium plantations. Women and children fled from their houses, and the men old and brave enough to fight stayed behind to defend their homes. When the Soviet army arrived, they brought their overwhelming military superiority to the battle, and the Afghan government military was better equipped and better trained than the peasants they were facing. So, the rural inhabitants resorted to the guerrilla style of attack as their resistance strategy. Robert D. Kaplan stated that the Saur Revolution and its harsh land reform program, rather than the December 1979 Soviet invasion "as most people in the West suppose," "ignited" the mujahidin revolt against the Kabul authorities and prompted the refugee exodus to Pakistan.

The rural resistance did not begin with trained soldiers. They took advantage of their knowledge of their habitats. They knew the terrain and the harsh mountainous climate conditions of the areas. So, they hid where Soviet tanks could not reach and used patterns of flying birds to avoid attacks by incoming bomber planes while fighting only in areas where they had a tactical advantage. The situation forced a large group of men to bond together while fighting and praying to defend their homes. Disgruntled farmers and landowners were farmers living simple lives before the war, now disconnected from their families and in the constant company of other men in unimaginable harsh conditions.

Picture: Hekmatyar Massoud and other mujahideen who turned out as politicians after the war

This war changed the nature of men and worsened the perception of the role of women in Afghanistan. The inhabitants were initially fighting for their homes and dignity without any specific political goal. It was about survival and resistance to the Russian efforts in rural Afghanistan. The groups were decentralized without sophisticated military intelligence. The insurgencies were sporadic and spontaneous until international interest groups such as the U.S., Pakistan, Saudi Arabia, and the U.N. intervened on humanitarian grounds. The spokesperson for the movement and the allies echoed the reference to the movement as Mujahideen (fighters of the Holy War).

During The influence of the interest groups began to take political and religious direction and shape as the Mujahideen Islamic revolution against the Communist government. Mujahideen fighters stated specific goals, among which are: to exterminate domestic infidels, defeat and drive out foreign occupation, and establish the purest form of fundamental Islamic governmental system in a free and independent Afghanistan. One of the most outspoken and charismatic Mujahideen leaders was Gulbuddin Hekmatyar. Gulbuddin Hekmatyar wore many hats, including being a Mujahideen guerrilla warlord, among politicians accused of genocide, a CIA operative, a criminal, a high-profile drug trafficker, and the prime minister of Afghanistan. The drug warlord allegation leads to a critical history of drug trafficking in Afghanistan.

Photo: Afghan rural farmers

Farmers in Afghanistan suffered greatly as a result of the Soviet War with the Mujahideen. Russian-built roads, livestock, and American- built irrigation systems from the 1950s and 1960s were all wiped off. The country's agricultural output and distribution channels collapsed. Afghan farmers, desperate for cash to pay for expensive food imports, turned to opium, which had long been a key cash crop in the country. Even after the warlords of Afghanistan succeeded the Soviets and the Taliban in power in 1995, poppy continued to be their preferred crop.

Afghanistan has a long history of opium poppy cultivation. Food production fell, but opium output increased. There was evidence that puppy seeds may survive and even flourish in arid environments with minimal watering. Their sticky sap is used to make opium paste; hence, they are farmed for that purpose. Hundreds of shady labs in Afghanistan transform some of the paste into heroin, while the remainder is smuggled out of the country through Pakistan, Iran, and Tajikistan.

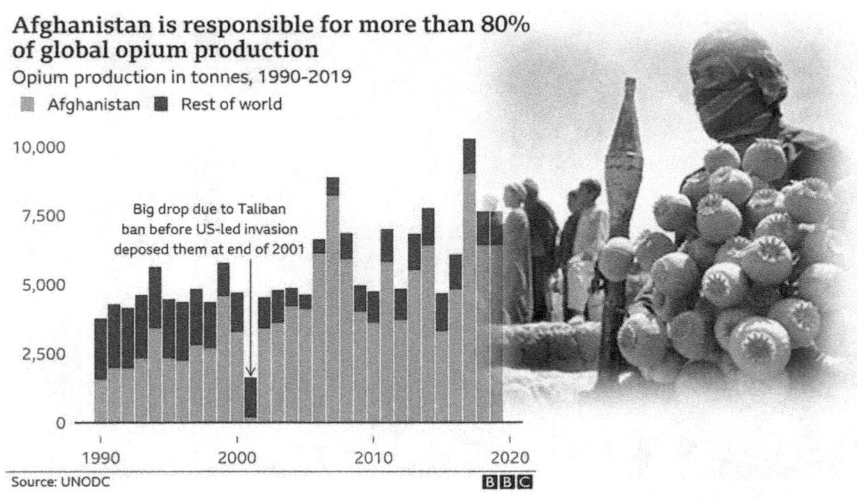

During the 1920s and 1930s, when opium addiction was widespread in China, it was discussed in the League of Nations. Afghanistan borders China and was a major player in the opium trade in the early 20th century. This problem had been the primary source of tension between rural Afghans and the government.

Photo: Hippies in Afghanistan

Afghanistan was a significant tourist destination for hippies looking for adventure, drugs, and spiritual connections. Locals Afghans became increasingly wary of Western travelers – notably in the region between Kabul and Peshawar, by the significant presence of unkempt hippies drawn to the region for its famed Opium and wild cannabis. Part of the attraction was also a quasi-religious dimension. The Hippies associated “the East” with spiritual enlightenment and were on a quest to share in its insights and experiences. For some, that meant India and an ashram, with Afghanistan simply a stop along the way. For others, the entire trip into alien worlds filled with people who prayed and thought so differently was part of what they were seeking. Presumably because it, too, was very focused on regimentation and rules - precisely what they were seeking to escape - Islam offered little attraction, with many more being drawn instead to Hinduism or Buddhism, or at least some elements associated with those such as meditation, incense, bells and other accouterments of mental elevation, especially by the ancient Bamiyan Buddhas “Solsol” and “Shahmama” built-in 507 CE. The Buddhas of Bamiyan were one of the oldest world historical relics, before the Taliban destroyed them. On orders from Taliban founder Mullah Omar, the statues were destroyed in March 2001, after the Taliban government declared that they were idols. International and local opinion strongly condemned the destruction of the Buddhas.

A Buddha of Bamiyan, before and after its demolition

Opium and heroin have a prominent place in the Afghan conflict, as they served as a reliable asset for farmers due to their durability and as an asset-backed guarantee for loans and credit and forward contracts. The United Nations Office on Drugs and Crime (UNODC) estimates that Afghanistan produced more than 90 percent of the world's Opium. When Afghanistan's pro-Communist coup in 1978, Afghan farmers produced an estimated 300 tons of Opium annually, enough to satisfy local and regional demand and supply a handful of heroin production labs that sold their product to Western Europe.

The hippie trail ended in the late 1970s everywhere. In 1979, both the Iranian Revolution and the Soviet invasion of Afghanistan closed the overland South Asian route to Western travelers, and Chitral and Kashmir became less inviting due to tensions in the area. The Yom Kippur War also put strict visa restrictions for Western citizens in Syria, Iraq, and Lebanon on the Middle Eastern route. The Lebanese civil war broke out in 1975.

Afghanistan produced 4,500 tons of opium in 1999, roughly 15 times the output of 20 years earlier. The considerable increase sent heroin cascading across Europe and the former Soviet Union, leading to pressure on the Taliban to reduce production. Eager to end its virtual isolation by the international community and profit from its own stockpiles of opium, the Taliban announced a ban on poppy cultivation in late 2000. The United States and other countries praised the shift, but when the U.S. ousted the Taliban, it had the unintended consequence of eliminating the ban on cultivation. Poppy farmers were eager to plant more crops to recoup losses incurred when the Taliban stopped most production. According to the UNODC, production jumped more than 16-fold to 3,400 tons for the harvest in the fall of 2002. Afghanistan was back in the opium business. The dramatic rebound in just a year demonstrated the resilience of poppy farmers, who had few other ways to feed their families.

Another factor influenced the escalation of opium production. After the invasion, the Central Intelligence Agency and U.S. Special Forces put regional and local warlords and militia commanders on their payroll to undermine the Taliban regime and go after Al Qaeda operatives. This pattern repeats itself as a stubborn, short-term solution to U.S. policy. Despite alliances with the opium trade, many of these warlords later traded on their stature as U.S. allies to take senior positions in the new Afghan government, laying the groundwork for the corrupt nexus between drugs and authority. Gulbuddin Hekmatyar was exemplary of such a pervasive power structure, which empowered and enriched warlords who continue to benefit as allies with the United States. Total income from producing, processing, and trafficking opium in 2003 had soared to $2.3 billion, roughly half of the country's legal and illegal gross domestic product. Zalmay Khalilzad, the previous administration's special envoy and ambassador to Afghanistan, acknowledged at the time that, rather than getting better, it had gotten worse. There is a potential for drugs to overwhelm the institutions—a sort of narco-state.'

Little Afghan heroin makes it to the United States, but Afghan heroin floods British streets, so the British took the lead on developing a counternarcotics strategy for Afghanistan. But their effort suffered from chronic personnel shortages and contradictory policies among ISAF members. [Senate Prints 111–29] [From the U.S. Government Printing Office] 111th Congress (Breaking the link between drug traffickers and insurgents)

Mujahideen declaration

The resistance was not about a specific political ideology but rather about the religious and economic freedom threatened by the government. The pace of imposing western civilization is not as determinant as the inclination of Western doctrine and Western rules. These efforts by the government were considered inimical and destructive to the wellbeing of the Islamic faith, which had been the pride of Afghanistan since the 9th century. Those believed to perpetrate such acts against the peaceful practice of Islam are called infidels. However, this rhetoric can be debated endlessly. Nevertheless, this is a religious belief that is protected under the U.N. Declaration of Human Rights.

Photo: Mujahideen fighters' profile

The Mujahideen quickly built-up insurgencies against the communist government in tribal and urban areas. Mujahideen, as these armed resistance groups were collectively known in Arabic, mujāhidūn, are "those who engage in jihad." The literal meaning of Jihad is struggle or effort, and it means much more than holy war. Muslims use the word jihad to describe three distinct kinds of struggle:

A believer's internal struggle to live out the Muslim faith as well as possible The struggle to build a good Muslim society The Mujahideen's cause was purely a struggle or war against the enemies of Islam. So, Mujahideen was formed under the premise of the declaration of Jihad against the infidels.

This call to action for all Muslims to rise against the identified infidel (threat to Islam) led to several uprisings financed by the mujahideen and a fragmented handful of independent groups, and their military efforts remained random and uncoordinated throughout the war. However, the quality of their arms and combat organization gradually improved due to organized training and lots of arms supplied to the rebels via Pakistan, by the United States and other countries, and by sympathetic Muslims worldwide. In addition, an indeterminate number of Muslim volunteers—popularly termed "Afghan Arabs," regardless of their ethnicity—traveled from all parts of the world to join the opposition.

President Reagan meeting with Mujahideen leader Rabbani

President Reagan met several times with the Mujahideen Islamic movement from 1981 to 1988. There ought to be no question about his dedication to the Afghan cause. He utilized the Afghan occupation by the Soviets as the reason to end the Cold War. The pullout of the Soviets from Afghanistan was a military defeat orchestrated covertly by Charlie Wilson and Joanne Herring, but also a diplomatic agreement, unquestionably the outcome of President Ronald Reagan's leadership and his mobilization of U.N. support. His friendship with Mikhail Gorbachev was also crucial to the successful, peaceful withdrawal of the Soviets. Ince Afghanistan was the key to ending the Cold War, and the end of the Cold War marked a turning point in world civilization as it allowed scientists to cooperate and share intelligence between the east and the west. A new world was born, and Afghanistan was the key to it. It is without question that Ronald Reagan was the architect of it.

Reagan friendship of substance with Gorbachev

Here is an excerpt from Ronald Reagan's Remarks Following a Meeting with Afghan Resistance Leaders and Members of Congress on November 12, 1987. The speech at the White House revealed the U.S. technical strategy and political altruism of the Americans in the future of Afghanistan.

> *Well, we have just held a very useful and, I might say, brief, but I also had a very moving discussion with Chairman Yunis Khalis of the Islamic Union of Mujahidin of Afghanistan and other members of his distinguished delegation. I expressed our nation's continued strong support for the resistance and our satisfaction with the Afghan resistance's significant step toward unity in choosing a chairperson for the first time. This new political milestone demonstrates that the people of Afghanistan speak with one voice in their opposition to their homeland's Soviet invasion and occupation. This increasing unity has already made itself felt on the battlefield. During the past 18 months, the Mujahidin fighting improved their weapons, tactics, and coordination. The result has been a string of severe defeats for the Soviet elite units and many divisions of the Kabul army.*
>
> *Chairman Khalis and his delegation are visiting Washington following the November 10 U.N. General Assembly vote, which, with a record vote, once again called overwhelmingly for the withdrawal of all foreign troops from Afghanistan. This is the eighth time since the December 1979 invasion that the General Assembly has decisively called upon the Soviet Union to pull its forces out of Afghanistan. And let there be no mistake about it: the withdrawal of Soviet forces is the key to resolving the*

Afghan crisis. Other issues raised to divert attention from this fact only extend the combat and prolong the suffering of the Afghan people.

General Secretary Gorbachev has publicly stated his readiness to withdraw. In April and September of 1987, I asked the Soviet Union to set a date this year when that withdrawal would begin. I also stated that when the Soviet Union showed convincing readiness for a genuine political settlement, the United States would be helpful. After all, the Soviet presence in Afghanistan is a major impediment to improved U.S.-Soviet relations, and we would like to remove it. The Soviets should want to do so as well. The Soviet's answer on a date for rapid withdrawal has been silent. Instead, we have seen the Kabul regime announce a phantom cease- fire and propose a transitional government that would leave this discredited and doomed group in control. These gambits have been rejected by the only voice that really counts that of the Afghan people, speaking through their resistance representatives. Any proposal unacceptable to the resistance is destined to fail.

And as the resistance continues to fight, other responsible governments and we will stand by it. The support that the United States has been providing for the resistance would be strengthened rather than diminished to continue fighting effectively for freedom. The just struggle against foreign tyranny can count on worldwide support, both political and material. The goal of the United States remains a genuinely independent Afghanistan, free from external interference, an Afghanistan whose people choose the type of government they wish, an Afghanistan to which the four million refugees from Soviet aggression may return in safety and, yes, in honor. On behalf of the American people, I salute Chairman Khalis, his delegation, and the people of Afghanistan themselves. You are a nation of heroes. God bless you.

Photo: President Reagan meets with Mujahideen leader Rabbani

President Reagan met with representatives of the Afghan Resistance Alliance: Professor Burhanuddin Rabbani, who was the current spokesperson for the Alliance, and his colleagues on November 9, 1988.

Burhānuddīn Rabbānī (September 1940 – September 20, 2011) was an Afghan politician and teacher who served as President of Afghanistan from 1992 to 2001 (in exile from 1996 to 2001). He formed the Jamiat- e Islami (Islamic Society) at the university, which attracted then- students Gulbuddin Hekmatyar and Ahmad Shah Massoud, who would eventually become the two leading commanders of the Afghan mujahideen in the Soviet Afghan War in 1979. Rabbani was chosen to be the President of Afghanistan after the end of the former communist regime in 1992. Rabbani and his Islamic State of Afghanistan government were later forced into exile by the Taliban. He then served as the political head of the Northern Alliance, an alliance of various political groups that fought against the Taliban regime in Afghanistan. Sponsored by various rebel factions, a transitional government proclaimed an Islamic republic, but jubilation was short- lived. President Burhanuddin Rabbani, leader of the Islamic Society (Jamʿiyyat-e Eslāmī), an influential mujahideen group, refused to leave office following the power-sharing arrangement reached by the new government. Other mujahideen groups, particularly the Islamic Party (Ḥezb-e Eslāmī), led by Gulbuddin Hekmatyar, surrounded Kabul, and began to barrage the city with artillery and rockets. These attacks continued intermittently over the next several years as the countryside outside Kabul slipped into chaos.

Photo: A memorial for Rabbani

Hekmatyar declined to form part of the new government and, with other warlords, engaged in the Afghan Civil War, leading to the deaths of around 50,000 civilians in Kabul alone. Hekmatyar was accused of bearing the most responsibility for the rocket attacks on the city. After the Taliban government was toppled during Operation Enduring Freedom, Rabbani returned to Kabul and served briefly as President from November 13 to December 22, 2001, when Hamid Karzai was chosen as his succeeding interim leader at the Bonn International Conference.

Rabbani was killed on his 71st birthday at his home in Kabul on September 20, 2011, by suicide bombing. Two men posing as Taliban representatives approached him to offer a hug and detonated their explosives. The suicide bomber claimed to be a Taliban comma nder, said he bore a "crucial and positive message" from Taliban leaders in Pakistan, and wanted to "discuss peace" with Rabbani. Four other members of Afghanistan's High Peace Council were also killed in the blast. As suggested by the Afghan parliament, Afghanistan's President Hamid Karzai gave him the "Martyr of Peace" title. His son, Salahuddin Rabbani, was chosen in April 2012 to forge peace in Afghanistan with the Taliban.

Afghanistan has never conducted a complete census, and it is thus challenging to gauge the number of casualties suffered in the country since the outbreak of fighting. The best estimates indicate that about 1.5 million Afghans were killed before 1992, although the number killed during combat and the number killed as an indirect result of the conflict remain unclear. Several thousands were killed due to factional fighting; hundreds or thousands of prisoners and civilians were executed by tribal, ethnic, or religious rivals; and many combatants—and some non-combatants—were killed during the U.S. offensive. Moreover, tens of thousands died of starvation or various diseases, many of which could have been easily treated in less troubled times, and hundreds of thousands were killed or injured by the numerous land mines in the country. (Afghanistan was, by the end of the 20th century, one of the most heavily mined countries in the world, and vast quantities of unexploded ordnance littered the countryside.) The number of Afghan refugees living abroad fluctuated over the years with the fighting and peaked at six million people in the late 1980s. This number could be rivaled in 2021.

Photo: (L-R) Former Afghan president Hamid Karzai, Afghan warlord Gulbuddin Hekmatyar, former Jihadi leader Abdul Rabb Rasool Sayyaf, and former VP

Gulbuddin Hekmatyar became one of the former Mujahideen guerillas to serve as an Afghan politician. He is the founder and current leader of the Hezb-e-Islami Gulbuddin political party and has served twice as Prime Minister during the 1990s. Hekmatyar became Prime Minister of Afghanistan from 1993 to 1994 and again briefly in 1996 before the Taliban takeover of Kabul forced him to flee to Iran's capital, Tehran. Hekmatyar joined the Muslim Youth organization as a student in the early 1970s, where he was known for his Islamic radicalism, which was rejected by much of the organization. He spent time in Pakistan before returning to Afghanistan when the Soviet Afghan War began in 1979. His group was one of the primary recipients of the CIA and Pakistani intelligence service, ISI, training, and U.S. grants. His rapidly growing Hezb-e Islami organization was one of the largest of the Afghan mujahideen. He received more CIA funding than any other mujahideen leader during the Soviet Afghan War.

Hekmatyar became Prime Minister of Afghanistan from 1993 to 1994 and again briefly in 1996 before the Taliban takeover of Kabul forced him to flee to Iran's capital, Tehran. Sometime after the Taliban's fall in 2001, he went to Pakistan, leading his paramilitary forces into an unsuccessful armed campaign against Hamid Karzai's government and the international coalition in Afghanistan. In 2016, he signed a peace deal with the Afghan government and could return to Afghanistan after almost 20 years in exile.

Following the collapse of the Islamic Republic of Afghanistan, on August 17, 2021, Hekmatyar met with Hamid Karzai, former President of Afghanistan, and Abdullah, Chairman of the High Council for National Reconciliation, and former Chief Executive, in Doha, seeking to form a government.

Reports emerged on August 25 that a 12- member council would govern the de facto newly reinstated Islamic Emirate of Afghanistan. Seven members were already agreed upon: Hekmatyar himself, Karzai, Abdullah, Abdul Ghani Baradar, Mohammad Yaqoob, Khalil-ur-Rehman Haqqani, and Hanif Atmar.

CHAPTER 10

End of the Cold War

Picture: Mikhail Gorbachev and Ronald Reagan, ending the cold war. The INF Treaty of December 1987 eliminated all nuclear and conventional missiles.

The war in Afghanistan became a quagmire for what, by the late 1980s, was the disintegrating Soviet Union. (The Soviets suffered some 15,000 deaths and many more injuries.) In 1988, the United States, Pakistan, Afghanistan, and the Soviet Union signed an agreement by which the latter would withdraw its troops (completed in 1989), and Afghanistan returned to nonaligned status. On April 16, 1992, a Mujahideen rebel group, led by Gulbuddin Hekmatyar, took Kabul, and overthrew Najibullah's communist president. Days later, various rebel groups, together with newly rebellious government troops, stormed the besieged capital of Kabul, which had succeeded

Karmal in 1986. Leonid Ilyich Brezhnev (December 19, 1906 – November 10, 1982), the Soviet Union leader serving as General Secretary of the governing Communist Party (1964–1982), increased Soviet troops in more substantial numbers to support Karmal, marking the beginning of the Soviet Afghan War. American Ambassador Adolph Dubs was killed, and the United States cuts off assistance to Afghanistan. The 39th U.S. President Jimmy Carter (January 20, 1977–January 20, 1981) initiated a covert program through the CIA to financially support the Afghan rebels, the mujahideen, in July 1979.

When Brezhnev authorized the Soviet invasion of Afghanistan in 1979, Carter, following the advice of his National Security Adviser Zbigniew Brzezinski, denounced the intervention, describing it as the "most dangerous to peace since 1945". The U.S. stopped all grain exports to the Soviet Union and boycotted the 1980 Summer Olympics held in Moscow. Brezhnev responded by boycotting the 1984 Summer Olympics held in Los Angeles.

Although President Carter was primarily focused on Iran during the months before the Soviet invasion of Afghanistan, the CIA expanded the program, codenamed Operation Cyclone, and began providing weapons and money to the mujahideen through the Pakistani intelligence services. Operation Cyclone was one of the most protracted and expensive covert CIA operations ever undertaken. More than $20 billion in U.S. funds was funneled into the country to train and arm Afghan resistance groups with support from Pakistan, Saudi

Arabia, and China. By 1980, Afghanistan had become the epicenter of the Cold War.

The Cold War was an ideological rivalry between capitalism and communism, with significant benevolent and detrimental repercussions for their allies worldwide. It was a war of superiority between principles and cultural doctrines between two directions of civilization and governance systems. The Truman Doctrine (1947) pledged aid to governments threatened by communist subversion.

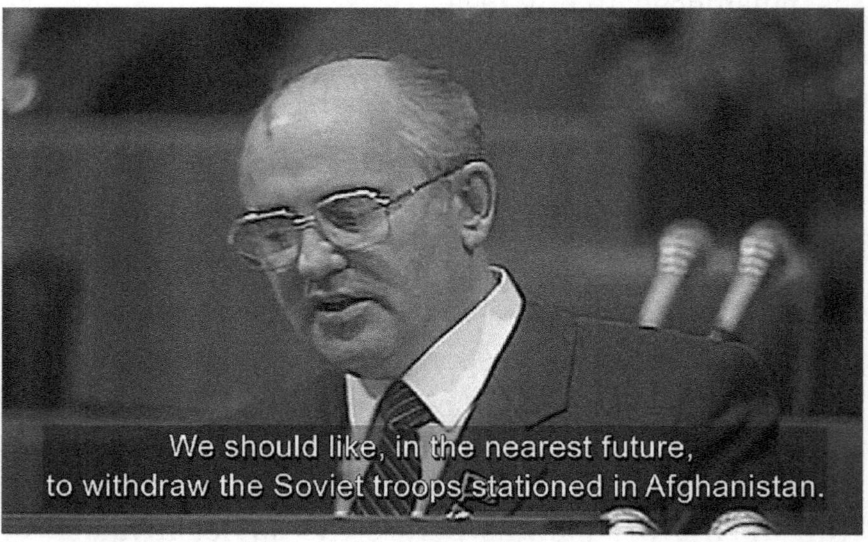

Photo: Mikhail Sergeyevich Gorbachev, the General Secretary of the Communist Party of the Soviet Union from 1985 until 1991.

The Marshall Plan (1947) provided billions of dollars in economic assistance to eliminate the political instability that could open the way for communist takeovers of democratically elected governments. The American government emphasized the dangers of communism, portrayed communist countries as oppressive regimes, and depicted communist leaders as evil dictators. The Western allies had always looked towards Russia with distrust and disdain, especially after the 1917 October Revolution in Russia, when the Bolsheviks engaged and defeated one of the strongest European empires, executed the imperial family in 1918, and consequently established a "dictatorship of the proletariat that became the Soviet Union in 1922. Bolshevik is a revolutionary Marxist ideology and a rigidly centralized and cohesive communist party founded by Vladimir Lenin.

In 1918, Britain provided money and troops to support the anti- Bolshevik "White" counterrevolutionaries. This policy was spearheaded by Minister of War Winston Churchill, a committed British imperialist and anti-communist. France, Japan, and the United States invaded Russia to topple the new Soviet government. The Bolshevik government succeeded in defeating all opposition and took complete control of Russia and breakaway provinces such as Ukraine, Georgia, Armenia, and Azerbaijan. Western powers started isolating the Soviet government. Vladimir Lenin stated that a "hostile capitalist encirclement surrounded the Soviet Union." He set up an organization to promote sister revolutions worldwide, the Comintern, and held seven World Congresses in Moscow between 1919 and 1935. Joseph Stalin, leader of the Soviet Union, dissolved the Comintern in 1943 to avoid antagonizing his allies in the later years of World War II, the United States, and the United Kingdom. It was replaced with, which lasted from 1947 to 1956.

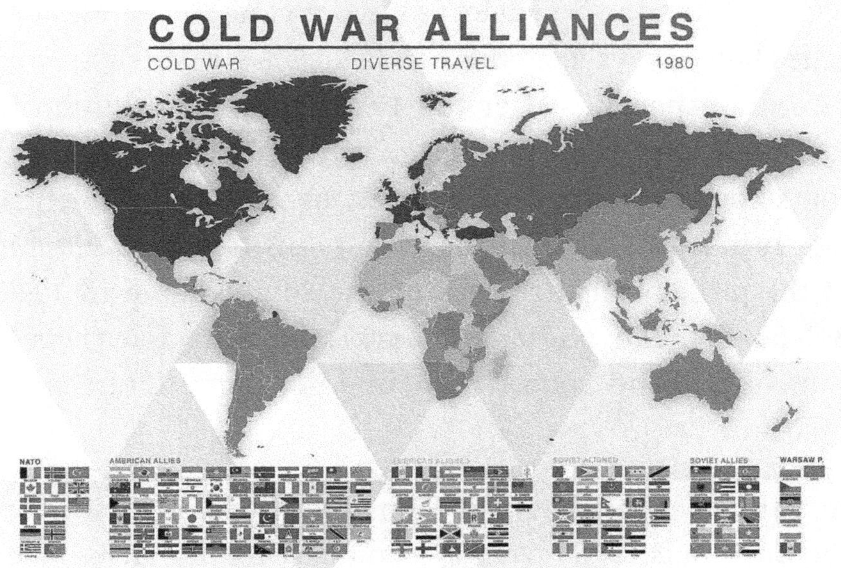

Cold War alliances ca. 1980

The real threat was the possibility of uprisings by the proletariat against the bourgeoisie and the aristocrats. A threat to capitalism, arguably inciting rabid revolutions, anarchy, and a world of chaos where power would be in the hands of the uneducated belligerent despot and feudal groups. A perfect example is the Taliban. This threat was why communism frightened the West, and the East turned it into a game of paranoia. The suspicion of malicious inclinations from East and West civilizations led to superpowers engaging in espionage, using many spies, double agents, and innovative technologies such as tapping telephone cables. The most prominent and active organizations were the American CIA, the Soviet KGB, and the British MI6.

Many leaders around the world have met their fates in this tug of war between communism and capitalism. The ideology that separated them has taken a toll on so many lives around the world. These are the simplest ways of understanding and differentiating these political systems. We would see that every country and state conceptually have a bit of each system, except leaning towards one more than another. This is often due to the cultural heritage of the country or the experience of its development into what it is through intervention or hegemony.

> *Socialism is a political system that prioritizes the interests of "all" the people. (Pro: choice of the people; Con: people have conflicting choices.) Capitalism is a political system that prioritizes the interests of individuals and organized groups. (Pro: choice of the individuals; con: individuals are not equally strengthened or equally powerful to make decisions or act.)*

> *Communism is a political system that prioritizes the interests of the state. (Pro: cannot argue with the state; con: cannot argue with the state, plus a clan of loyalists runs the state. Democracy may not be perfect, but it remains the best governance system for any progressive society. Democracy is a tool that requires skills and an understanding of the concept. It ultimately depends on how it is conducted. It is not an end in itself but an instrument that must be used toward an end.*

> *"Totalitarianism is never content to rule by external means, namely, through the state and a machinery of violence; thanks to its peculiar ideology and the role assigned to it in this apparatus of coercion, totalitarianism*

has discovered a means of dominating and terrorizing human beings from within." —Hannah Arendt

	Capitalism	Socialism
Ownership	Assets owned by private firms	Assets owned by government/ co-operatives
Equality	Income determined by market forces	Redistribution of income
Prices	Prices determined by supply and demand	Price controls
Efficiency	Market incentives encourage firms to cut costs	Government owned firms have fewer incentives to be efficient
Taxes	Limited taxes/ limited government spending	High progressive taxes / Higher spending on public services
Healthcare	Health care left to free-market	Healthcare provided by government free at point of use
Problems	Inequality, market failure, monopoly	Inefficiency of state industry, less incentives,
Advantages	Dynamic economy, incentives for innovation and economic growth	Promotion of equality. Attempt to overcome market failure.

Picture: Capitalism vs Communism

Attempting to change these systems is always challenging and often results in a dramatic and unnecessary conundrum. Some communist regimes were formed in the second half of the 20th century, including Angola, Cuba, North Korea, China, Vietnam, Mozambique, Ethiopia, Cambodia, Nicaragua, and Afghanistan. This was the basis of the U.S. war in the Korean and Vietnam Wars. Talks at the U.N. ushered in a détente, easing Cold War tensions between the U.S. and the Soviet Union from 1967 to 1979. The era was a time of increased trade and cooperation with the Soviet Union, which signed the Strategic Arms Limitation Talks (SALT) treaties. Thus, the Soviet Afghan War in 1979 halted Détente to a degree. In the mid-1980s, the new Soviet leader Mikhail Gorbachev introduced the liberalizing reforms of glasnost ("openness," c. 1985) and perestroika ("reorganization, c. 1987), which consequently ended Soviet involvement in Afghanistan. Whether democracy or socialism, the purpose of governance is to cater to the people's interest in one's sovereignty and observe international ethical standards.

The Taliban has not acted in the interest of the people of Afghanistan. It was neither selected nor elected. It has thus imposed itself on the people of Afghanistan, which is against the concept of self- determination. Any government that imposes itself on its subjects cannot last. It is just a matter of time. The Soviet Union provided a case in point. In 1989, the fall of the Iron Curtain after a peaceful wave of revolutions (except Romania and Afghanistan) overthrew almost all communist governments in the Eastern Bloc.

The Communist Party of the Soviet Union itself lost control of the Soviet Union and was banned following an abortive coup attempt in August 1991. This led to the USSR's formal dissolution in December 1991, the declaration of independence of its constituent republics, and the collapse of communist governments across much of Africa and Asia. The United States was left as the world's only superpower, and China became the next undesirable contender. The game has changed.

President Reagan's Speech on the Afghanistan Day Proclamation with Comments by Nahid Mojadidi who speaks of the Soviet domination and Presents President

Reagan with an Afghanistan Flag in the East Room on March 10, 1982:

710 PROCLAMATION 4908—MAR. 10, 1982

Proclamation 4908 of March 10, 1982

Afghanistan Day

By the President of the United States of America
A Proclamation

In December 1979, the Soviet Union invaded Afghanistan without provocation and with overwhelming force. Since that time, the Soviet Union has sought through every available means, to assert its control over Afghanistan.

The Afghan people have defied the Soviet Union and have resisted with a vigor that has few parallels in modern history. The Afghan people have paid a terrible price in their fight for freedom. Their villages and homes have been destroyed; they have been murdered by bullets, bombs and chemical weapons. One-fifth of the Afghan people have been driven into exile. Yet their fight goes on. The international community, with the United States joining governments around the world, has condemned the invasion of Afghanistan as a violation of every standard of decency and international law and has called for a withdrawal of the Soviet troops from Afghanistan. Every country and every people has a stake in the Afghan resistance, for the freedom fighters of Afghanistan are defending principles of independence and freedom that form the basis of global security and stability.

It is therefore altogether fitting that the European Parliament, the Congress of the United States and parliaments elsewhere in the world have designated March 21, 1982, as Afghanistan Day, to commemorate the valor of the Afghan people and to condemn the continuing Soviet invasion of their country. Afghanistan Day will serve to recall not only these events, but also the principles involved when a people struggles for the freedom to determine its own future, the right to be free of foreign interference and the right to practice religion according to the dictates of conscience.

NOW, THEREFORE, I, RONALD REAGAN, President of the United States of America, do hereby designate March 21, 1982, as Afghanistan Day.

IN WITNESS WHEREOF, I have hereunto set my hand this tenth day of March, in the year of our Lord nineteen hundred and eighty-two, and of the Independence of the United States of America the two hundred and sixth.

RONALD REAGAN

Editorial Note: The President's remarks of Mar. 10, 1982, on signing Proclamation 4908 are printed in the *Weekly Compilation of Presidential Documents* (vol. 18, p. 280).

Proclamation of Afghanistan Day with Nahid Mojadidi in 1982

I take satisfaction in signing today the proclamation authorized by Joint Resolution No. 142, which calls for the commemoration of March 21 as Afghanistan Day throughout the United States.

This resolution testifies to America's deep and continuing admiration for the Afghan people in the face of brutal and unprovoked aggression by the Soviet Union. A distinguished former Secretary of State, William P. Rogers, coordinated the observance of Afghan Day in the United States. He not only has my strong support that of former Presidents Carter, Ford, and Nixon and former Secretaries of State Muskie, Vance, Kissinger, and Rusk. The Afghans wish nothing more than to live their lives in peace, practice their religion in freedom, and exercise their right to self-determination. Consequently, they now find themselves struggling for their very survival as a nation. Nowhere are fundamental human rights more brutally violated than in Afghanistan today.

The Soviet Union bears a grave responsibility for the continuing suffering of the Afghan people, the massive violations of human rights, and the international tension which has resulted from its unprovoked attack. The Soviet Union must understand that the world would not forget, as it has not forgotten the peoples of the other captive nations from Eastern Europe to Southwest Asia -- who have suffered from Soviet aggression.

This is the meaning of Afghanistan Day that the Afghan people will ultimately prevail.

Coincidentally, the day after Afghanistan Day, this country plans to launch the third Columbia space shuttle. Just as the Columbia, we think, represents man's finest aspirations in science and technology, so too does the struggle of the Afghan people represent man's highest aspirations for freedom. The people of Afghan daily demonstrate the fact that freedom is the most vital force in the world. Accordingly, I am dedicating on behalf of the American people the March 22 launch of the Columbia to the people of Afghanistan. And in that same spirit, I call on all Americans to observe Afghanistan Day in their thoughts, their prayers, their activities, and in their own renewed dedication to freedom. With the help of those assembled here today, the unanimous backing of the Congress, and the support of the American people, I am confident that this day marked a true celebration, and not just for freedom in Afghanistan, but for freedom wherever it is threatened or suppressed the world over. Now, I shall sign the proclamation. – President Ronald Reagan

Withdrawal of the Soviet troops, 1989

Beginning on May 15th, 1988, and finishing on February 15th, 1989, under the command of Colonel-General Boris Gromov, all Soviet combat units withdrew from Afghanistan. The Congress of People's Deputies of the Soviet Union criticized the decision to invade as a blunder, and the withdrawal of Soviet forces was hailed as the long- awaited end to a brutal battle. The Soviet invasion of Afghanistan began on December 24, 1979, and ended on February 15, 1989. The nine-year conflict resulted in the deaths of 562,000 to 2 million Afghans and the displacement of over 6 million others, most of whom went to Pakistan and Iran. The aerial bombardment of numerous rural villages, the placement of millions of landmines, and the destruction of towns like

Herat and Kandahar left them in ruins. The Soviets left without leaving any soldiers behind, marking the end of their military presence in the region.

The end of the Cold War had a significant impact on global development, particularly in the fields of computers, the internet, and other technological advancements. As geopolitical tensions subsided, a conducive atmosphere for global collaboration was created, resulting in a rise in information exchange and collaborative research endeavors. Following the Cold War, economic liberalization increased market demand and investment, which fueled technological advancement. Moving money from military to civilian R&D accelerated technology, and the unrestricted flow of information and the global transmission of previously illegal technologies made the internet possible. Additionally, at this time, authoritarian regimes began to fall, which aided in the spread of information technologies. The rapid expansion of businesses like Apple and Microsoft is evidence that the tech sector prospered because of the ensuing political stability and globalization. To put it simply, the end of the Cold War sparked technological advancement and created the network, digital world we live in today.

CHAPTER 11

The End of the Mujahideen

Ahmad Shah Massoud, mujahideen powerful guerrilla commander who served as the Minister of defense from June 1992 – 2001 with Mujahideen

Ahmad Shah Massoud was posthumously named "National Hero" by order of President Hamid Karzai after the Taliban were ousted from power. The date of Massoud's death, September 9, is a national holiday known as "Massoud Day." His followers call him Amer Sāhib-e Shahīd, which translates to "(our) martyred commander." Massoud has been described as one of the most outstanding guerrilla leaders of the 20th century. He has been compared to Josip Broz Tito, Ho Chi Minh, and Che Guevara, notably because he successfully defended his local Panjshir Valley from capture by the Soviets and later the Taliban. His younger brother, Ahmad Zia Massoud, served as the First Vice President of Afghanistan from 2004 to 2009.

Mujahideen militia gives the scope of recruitment.

Following the rise of the Taliban in 1996, Massoud, who rejected the Taliban's fundamentalist interpretation of Islam, returned to armed opposition until he was forced to flee to Kulob, Tajikistan, strategically destroying the Salang Tunnel on his way north. He became the military and political leader of the United Islamic Front for the Salvation of Afghanistan, or Northern Alliance, which by 2000 controlled only between 5 and 10 percent of the country. Massoud traveled to Europe and urged European Parliament leaders to pressure Pakistan to stop supporting the Taliban in 2001. He also asked for humanitarian aid to combat the Afghan people's gruesome conditions under the Taliban. Massoud was assassinated at the instigation of al-Qaeda and the Taliban in a suicide bombing on September 9, 2001.

AHMAD SHAH MASSOUD AND SON AHMAD

Assassinated at age 48, known as the Lion of Panjshir (Afghanistan)

1980s	Celebrated Tajik commander who led **resistance** to the **Soviet occupation**
1996-2001	Led the strongest **resistance against the Taliban** from his stronghold in Panjshir Valley, a mountainous redoubt in the Hindu Kush region
2001	**Assassinated by Al-Qaeda** two days before the 9/11 attacks

- Declared national hero in Afghanistan by presidential decree
- Still seen as a unifying figure who could have led the country to a Taliban-free future, were it not for his murder
- Still emblazons billboards, blast walls, car windows and even coffee mugs across the country

Aged 32, claims to command a militia force in Panjshir Valley, which neither the Soviets nor the Taliban ever conquered

1989	Born July 10, **only son of Massoud**
From 2001	After his father's murder, he finished schooling in Iran then moved to England to **train at Sandhurst military academy**
2015-2016	Completed two degrees in London
2016	Returned to Afghanistan, appointed as chief executive officer of the Massoud Foundation
Aug 2021	**Says he has forces to mount an effective resistance against the Taliban**, in an op-ed in the Washington Post Calls on US for "more weapons, more ammunition and more supplies"

- Wears the same sort of beige pakol (Afghan woolen hat) that his father sported

CHAPTER 12

The Advent of the Taliban

Mohammad Najibullah, President of Afghanistan 1987-1992

After the Soviet withdrawal, the Civil War ensued until the communist regime under People's Democratic Party leader Mohammad Najibullah collapsed in 1992. Mohammad Najibullah Ahmadzai (August 6, 1947– September 27, 1996) served as the President of Afghanistan from 1987 until his resignation in April 1992, shortly after the mujahideen took over Kabul. After a failed attempt to flee to India, Najibullah took refuge at the United Nations complex in Kabul. He lived at the United Nations headquarters from 1992 to 1996.

Najibullah was at the U.N. compound when the Taliban soldiers came for him on September 26, 1996. They abducted him from U.N. custody, tortured him and his brother

(Shahpur Ahmadzai) in the most gruesome ways, and shot them to death. Their bodies were dragged behind a truck through the streets of Kabul and were hung from a traffic light pole outside the presidential palace the next day to show the public that a new era had begun. The Taliban prevented Islamic funeral prayers for Najibullah and Shahpur in Kabul. However, the International Committee of the Red Cross later arranged for their bodies to be sent to Gardez in Paktia Province, where both were given a proper burial with the Islamic funeral prayers by their fellow Ahmadzai tribesmen.

One of the last pictures taken of Ex-president Dr. Najibullah Ahmadzai and his brother General Ahmadzai, circa the mid-1990s

The death of Najibullah was met with great outrage from the international community, especially within the Muslim community. The United Nations also harshly criticized the Taliban Act. Many Afghans believe that the Taliban were successful in ending the civil conflict between warlords. However, they halted the advancements made by the

Afghan people, especially the women, and limited their freedom. Dostum, Massoud, and Burhanuddin Rabbani served in the Afghan government from 1996 until their assassination in 2001. They were members of the United Front (Northern Alliance), an opposition group that fought the Taliban.

CHAPTER 13

The Taliban

Picture: mixed media composition of the Taliban children grooming in Pakistan

The Taliban is a militant nationalist organization based on fundamental Pashtunwali and Deobandi beliefs. The word, Taliban, is from Pashto language, meaning student or seeker of knowledge. The Deobandi Islamist religious and political movement and military organization operates in Afghanistan. Deobandi is an Islamic revivalist movement within Sunni Islam formed during the late 19th century around the Darul Uloom Islamic seminary in Deoband, India, from which the name derives. It was founded in September 1994 in Kandahar, Afghanistan, under the leadership of Mohammed Omar (1994–2013), Akhtar Mansour † (2015–2016), and Hibatullah Akhundzada (2016–present). Deobandi teachings are based on principles and doctrines under the control of "a hardline sect," whose leading preacher loathed Western values, called on Muslims to "shed blood" for Allah, and preached contempt for Jews, Christians, and Hindus.

Abdul Ghani Baradar and Mohammed Omar started ultra-conservative madrassas, which gave birth to the Taliban. Almost 80% of all domestically trained Ulema were trained in these hardline seminaries.

Since the early days of communism and the Soviet invasion of Afghanistan, many people have fled and taken refuge in Pakistan. The refugee camp became an incubator of radical Islamic teaching. Mullah Mohammad Omar formed the Taliban in September 1994 in his hometown of Kandahar with 50 students. Omar himself had studied in the Sang-i-Hisar madrassa in Maiwand (northern Kandahar Province) since 1992. He was appalled by the warlords competing for power after ousting the Soviet-backed communist rule in Afghanistan. He believed the Mujahideen were incompetent and covetous jihadists and needed a thoroughbred of Islamic fundamentalists created to get rid of infidelity. Omar assumed leadership of the First Islamic Emirate in 1996 after the Taliban defeated the Northern Alliance in the 1996– 2001 Afghan Civil War and took control of much of the nation. Omar fled into hiding after an American invasion of Afghanistan overthrew the Taliban administration, shortly after al-Qaeda's September 11 attacks. He managed to avoid being apprehended by the coalition commanded by the United States until he passed away in 2013 from tuberculosis.

The children at the refugee camps have witnessed an unspeakable disaster: family members torn to pieces, rape, killings, and many other atrocities. Within months, in Pakistan, 15,000 students, often Afghan refugees, from religious schools or madrasas—one source calls them Jamiat Ulema-e-Islam-run madrasas—joined the group. The infamous Osama Bin Ladin was part of this grooming program for youth and children in the anti-Soviet insurgency. The U.S. government covertly provided schoolbooks promoting militant Islamic teachings and included images of weapons and soldiers to inculcate hatred of foreign invaders in children. The Taliban used American textbooks but scratched out human faces in keeping with strict fundamentalist interpretation. The United States Agency for International Development gave millions of dollars to the University of Nebraska at Omaha in the 1980s to develop and publish textbooks in local languages.

ZABIULLAH MUJAHID, AGE NOT KNOWN
■ Chief spokesperson; mysterious voice of the Taliban for at least a decade before he revealed himself before cameras at a news conference in Kabul on Tuesday.

SHER MOHAMMAD ABBAS STANIKZAI, 60
■ Chief negotiator at Doha; led day-to-day talks with the Americans before Mullah Baradar appeared on the scene after some progress had been made.

ABDUL SALAM HANAFI, AGE NOT KNOWN
■ Negotiator and member of the Taliban office in Doha; sometimes briefed reporters, was the first Taliban leader to announce a deal in early 2020; of Uzbek origin.

MILITARY COMMANDERS

SIRAJUDDIN HAQQANI, 48, DEPUTY LEADER
■ Son of Jalalauddin Haqqani and leader of the Haqqani network; has led much of the Taliban's recent military push.

MULLAH MUHAMMAD YAQOOB, 31, DEPUTY LEADER
■ Backed by the formidable pedigree of being the son of Mullah Omar, but considered much less dogmatic.

THE OLD TALIBAN

MULLAH MUHAMMAD OMAR
■ Founder of Taliban and leader of its 1996-2001 government.

JALALUDDIN HAQQANI
■ Founder of the Haqqani network, aligned himself with Taliban; died 2018.

WALI AHMED MUTTAWAKIL
■ Foreign minister and best known face of first Taliban regime.

MULLAH MOHAMMAD FAZL
■ Deputy defence minister of Taliban; was in Guantanamo.

KHAIRULLAH KHAIRKHWA
■ Taliban interior minister; part of 'Guantanamo Five'.

Photos: AP, Reuters, The NYT, FBI handout; Text: The NYT, AP, Reuters

Pictures of Taliban of Old and New Military commanders

The Taliban were the new breed of Jihadists, motivated by their traumatic experiences and sophisticated military training with Slavic adherence to the colonial appetite under the codes of Islam; in their religious schools, they had been taught beliefs in strict Islamic law. The Taliban operated like a secret society in infiltrating the Afghan society and easily recruited a great number of the populace based on shared disdain of foreign infiltration ruining their cultural and spiritual values.

CHAPTER 14

History of American and Afghan Relations

A mixed media illustration of the US-Afghans Relations

The first American to travel to Afghanistan was Josiah Harlan, a Pennsylvania Quaker. He worked as a surgeon for the Maharaja of Punjab and was a revolutionary ally of the exiled Afghan king. Dost Mohammed, in 1838. However, official bilateral relations between Afghanistan and the United States began under the leadership of King Amanullah Khan and President Warren G. Harding, following Afghanistan's independence from the British. The Afghan mission visited the United States to establish diplomatic relations after the Treaty of Rawalpindi was signed between Afghanistan and British India in January 1921. The envoys returned to Kabul with a greeting letter from US President Warren G. Harding. Following the establishment of diplomatic relations, the United States' policy of assisting developing countries in raising their standard of living was a key factor in preserving and improving relationships with Afghanistan.

After World War II, the United States replaced the United Kingdom as the "paramount" power in Afghanistan's affairs. Arnold Fletcher of the University of Southern California summarized the situation of this country in the United States in a 1950 publication as follows:

Few Americans realize Afghanistan's potential political importance; to most Westerners, it is a faraway land noted for nomads, dogs, and rifle-packing tribesmen. Actually, it is a solid Central Asian state the size of Texas, with a virile population of 12 million and a long history of ardent nationalism. For three thousand years, it has been Asia's highway.

Afghan American relations grew in importance as the Cold War between the United States and the Soviet Union began. Prince Mohammed Naim, King Zahir Shah's cousin, was appointed as the country's chargé d'affaires in Washington, D.C. At the time, US President Harry S. Truman stated that the presence of senior ambassadors in each capital would "preserve and strengthen" the two countries' friendship. Habibullah Khan Tarzi was the first formal Afghanistan Ambassador to the United States, serving until 1953.

William Harrison Hornibrook served as a non-resident United States Envoy (Minister Plenipotentiary) in Tehran from 1935 to 1936. Louis G. Dreyfus served from 1940 until the Kabul Legation was formed in 1942. The first

military attaché to Kabul was Colonel Gordon B. Enders of the American Army, and from 1942 to 1945, Cornelius Van Hemert Engert and later Ely Eliot Palmer represented the American Legation. Despite strong ties to Nazi Germany, Afghanistan remained neutral and did not participate in World War II. On May 6, 1948, the US Kabul Legation was raised to the US Embassy Kabul. From 1949 until 1951, Louis Goethe Dreyfus, who had previously served as Minister Plenipotentiary, was the United States' Ambassador to Afghanistan.

Richard Nixon, the United States' Vice President at the time, paid an official diplomatic visit to Kabul in 1953 and made a brief tour of the city, engaging with Afghan residents. In 1958, Prime Minister Daoud Khan became the first Afghan to speak before the United States Congress in Washington, D.C. His presentation focused on a number of issues, but most importantly, it underscored the importance of U.S.-Afghan relations. While in the U.S. capital, Daoud met with President Eisenhower, signed an important cultural exchange agreement, and reaffirmed personal relations with then-Vice President Richard Nixon that had begun during the latter's trip to Kabul in 1953. On December 9, 1959, US President Dwight D. Eisenhower paid a state visit to Afghanistan, which marked a watershed event in the two countries' diplomatic relations. Following this visit, the US presumed that Afghanistan was safe from becoming a Soviet satellite state.

During an eleven-nation tour of Asia, Vice President Spiro Agnew visited Kabul with Apollo 10 astronauts Thomas Stafford and Eugene Cernan. The American team presented the King with a piece of lunar rock, a small Afghan flag carried on the Apollo 11 journey to the Moon, and images of Afghanistan shot from space at a special supper held by the Royal Family. This ceremony would be outdone by the USSR, when Abdul Ahad Mohmand was chosen as the Afghan among a group of 400 volunteers to join a Soyuz crew for a nine-day mission to the Mir space station to participate in Interkosmos, a USSR program that sent men from non-Soviet countries to space on August 29, 1988. Mohmand took an Afghan flag and two copies of the Koran with him. However, Sultan bin Salman al Saud, a Saudi who had entered space with an American crew three years prior, claimed the title of "first Muslim in space. Mohmand was appointed Afghanistan's deputy minister of civil aviation, a position he held for six months before leaving for Germany when the civil war broke out in 1992 amongst various groups of the Mujahideen.

The nation was split up, with a province belonging to each warlord, who waged war on one another as directed by their separate foreign supporters who meddled in Afghan politics, much as they do now. Many people died, and they destroyed the nation," he declared.

In April 2013, he returned to Afghanistan at the invitation of former President Hamid Karzai to commemorate the 25th anniversary of his space expedition. He read the peace message he had delivered to the Afghan people in 1988 from orbit once more during the welcome. It holds the same significance now as it did back then.

President Eisenhower reviewing an Afghan honor guard at Bagram Airfield, Afghanistan, 1959.

Mohmand (right) joined by Russian and Ukrainian cosmonauts in 1988.

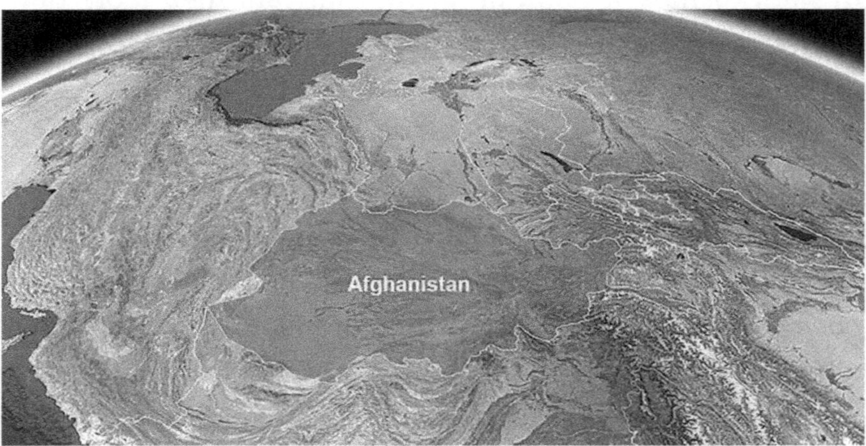

Picture of Afghanistan from space.

By the 1970s, a large number of American teachers, engineers, medics, scholars, diplomats, and explorers had traveled across Afghanistan's mountainous terrain, where they lived and worked. From the 1950s to 1979, the United

States provided more than $500 million in loans, grants, and surplus agricultural commodities to Afghanistan in order to develop transportation infrastructure, increase agricultural production, expand the educational system, stimulate industry, and improve government administration.

The Kajaki Dam project started in the rocky, rural north of Helmand Province in the 1950s, during America's first drive to modernize and ally Afghanistan. The dam's final studies began in 1946, and a preliminary design was completed in 1950. Between 1951 and 1953, the American Morrison-Knudsen Corporation built the dam as a part of the Helmand Valley Authority project. In the 1970s, the United States converted it into a hydroelectric power station but abandoned it before its completion when the Russians invaded in 1979. As part of Operation Kryptonite in February 2007, the Kajaki Dam was the site of a battle between coalition forces and Taliban fighters. According to Asadullah Wafa, the governor of Helmand province, over 700 Taliban terrorists from neighboring Pakistan (including Pakistanis, Chechens, and Uzbeks) fought against over 300 coalition troops. The majority of the coalition forces were Dutch and British. As of 2022, over 9 million people in Afghanistan are using the internet, which is accessible in all 34 of its provinces. The internet officially became available in 2002, during the presidency of Hamid Karzai. 97% of the population has access to electricity. The availability of electricity has significantly improved since the installation of power plants and infrastructure by international organizations.

During the 1970s, the Soviets too were apprehensive that the United States was turning Afghanistan into a satellite state. The Soviet Union saw Afghanistan as an opportunity to expand its influence and counter the United States' presence in the region. The Soviet Union, along with other countries, was a direct supporter of the Afghan communist party that took over the first Afghan republican government in a bloody coup de tat in April 1978, referred to as the Saur Revolution. The Saur Revolution marked the beginning of a decade-long conflict in Afghanistan, leading to extensive involvement by both the United States and the Soviet Union. The United States government's foreign aid program ended before the 1978 Saur Revolution.

On February 14, 1979, armed militants impersonating police stopped US Ambassador to Afghanistan Adolph "Spike" Dubs and his driver in their automobile on their way to the embassy. They were kidnapped and taken to the Kabul Hotel. The kidnappers demanded the release of a political prisoner. Despite US pleas to keep the situation quiet as they attempted to negotiate the ambassador's release, Afghan police, under the command of Soviet officials, launched a rescue operation that resulted in a barrage of gunfire, and Ambassador Dubs was killed during the rescue effort. The only physical evidence that the Americans would find was Dubs' body and clothing. An autopsy at Walter Reed in Washington found Dubs died of "at least 10 wounds inflicted by small-caliber weapons."

Ambassador Dubs in Afghanistan. Collection of the National Museum of American Diplomacy.

None of the weapons taken from the gang were produced for U.S. investigators. It would be three weeks before the regime permitted the Americans back into the room. By then, it had been completely repaired. The regime and their Russian backers vanquished all evidence, including bullet casings, clothing, and personal items.

The State Department's final investigation report slated the Kabul regime's account as "incomplete, misleading, and inaccurate," in part because it made "no mention of the Soviets involved in the incident." The report found evidence of "serious misrepresentation or suppression of the truth" by the regime. U.S. investigators concluded nine central questions remained unanswered, including: "What was the involvement of the Soviets in the decision-making process" that led to the assault?"

Adolph "Spike" Dubs was a career Foreign Service Officer and a specialist in the Soviet Union. He was charge d'affaires at the US Embassy in Moscow in 1973–74, and he was appointed US Ambassador to Afghanistan in 1978.

Spike Dubs was well known to the KGB operatives' most senior bosses in Moscow. Following his first posting to Ottawa, Dubs' Russian language skills placed him at the U.S. embassy in the Soviet capital during the 1962 Cuban Missile Crisis. By the time President Jimmy Carter posted Dubs to Afghanistan in 1978, he was well known to the KGB. He had already served at the US consulate in Moscow. In Kabul, the Soviets' intelligence column had their client regime "wired," according to former C.I.A. officers working there at the time. Easily, the KGB would have been aware Dubs was a frequent visitor to the Communist regime's foreign minister, Hafizullah Amin. The two had met at least 14 times by February of 1979. Amin was fluent in English, having studied at Wisconsin and Columbia universities. This worried the Russians, as did Amin's mercurial, egomaniacal nature. Just months later, KGB special forces troops murdered Amin and his family in the opening hours of the December 1979 Soviet invasion.

Six years before Dubs' assassination, a terrorist gang kidnapped and killed US Ambassador to Sudan Cleo Noel. On March 3, 1973, Ambassador Dubs wrote to Lindsay, including his opinions on the tragedy. His statements foreshadowed the scenario he would find himself in in Kabul. He stated:

> *"We cannot afford to give in to the ransom demands made by thugs who direct such organizations as the*

> *Black September Group. I personally don't like to think of myself as any kind of martyr, but if I were ever taken into a situation such as that which occurred in Khartoum, I would want Washington to understand that I would rather sacrifice my life than have someone capitulate to the demands of terrorists."*

The Soviet invasion of Afghanistan in 1979 was a turning point in the Cold War when the United States started to financially support the Afghan resistance. The country, under both the Carter and Reagan administrations, committed $3 billion in financial and diplomatic support to the anti-Soviet Mujahideen forces. Beginning in 1980, the United States began admitting thousands of Afghan refugees for resettlement and provided money and weapons to the Mujahideen through Pakistan's Inter-Services Intelligence (ISI).

After the Soviet Union invaded Afghanistan in late 1979, bin Laden began providing financial and logistical support to Islamic fighters fighting the Soviets. Al Qaeda, also known as "the Base," was founded by Osama bin Laden in 1988 to pursue the cause of jihad (holy war) through violence and murder after Soviet forces were routed and forced to retreat from Afghanistan. Al Qaeda quickly began gathering funds, establishing training camps, and giving military and intelligence training in places like Afghanistan, Pakistan, and Sudan. Al Qaeda began launching attacks and bombs in several countries under bin Laden's guidance in order to achieve its murderous goals. Bin Laden was getting increasingly antagonistic toward the United States at the time. He was particularly hostile to the United States' military involvement in Saudi Arabia and Somalia, and he wanted to force American troops out of these countries.

Bin Laden and other al Qaeda members proclaimed an open war on the United States and began attacking the United States and its inhabitants. Ramzi Yousef, a young radical who had trained in one of bin Laden's camps, staged the first major Middle Eastern terrorist strike on American soil on February 26, 1993, by putting a truck bomb beneath the World Trade Center. Although the operation to bring down both towers failed, six people were killed and over a thousand were injured.

Yousef was apprehended, and multiple terrorist operators were arrested and imprisoned for the World Trade Center bombing, intensifying bin Laden's contempt for America. Meanwhile, the Taliban government provided a secluded safe haven for al Qaeda to train recruits and plan attacks. On August 7, 1998, al Qaeda operatives bombed U.S. embassies in Dar es Salaam, Tanzania, and Nairobi, Kenya. The near simultaneous attacks killed more than 200 American, Kenyan, and Tanzanian citizens and wounded another 4,500 people. The attacks led to ramped-up anti-terror efforts by the U.S. and the FBI, which created its first Counterterrorism Division in 1999, consolidating its many anti-terrorism efforts and capabilities. On June 7, 1999, the FBI placed Osama bin Laden on its Ten Most Wanted Fugitives list, citing his connection to the 1998 attacks in East Africa.

As a new century dawned, al Qaeda continued its violent attacks. Some major plots failed, including a scheme to bomb the Los Angeles airport on the eve of millennial celebrations. However, on October 12, 2000, terrorists detonated an explosive-laden small boat adjacent to the USS Cole during a fuel stop in Yemen. The attack claimed the lives of 17 Navy personnel, injured over 40 others, and seriously destroyed the ship. Terrorists hijacked four planes in the eastern United States on September 11, 2001. They crashed three planes into buildings: the World Trade Center twin towers in New York and the Pentagon in Arlington, Virginia. After passengers valiantly resisted, they crashed the fourth jet in a field in rural Pennsylvania. Nearly 3,000 people were killed in the attacks, and thousands more were injured. The attacks prompted far-reaching changes in the FBI, which made terrorist strike prevention its top goal and purposefully set out to be more predictive and intelligence-driven in handling all key national security and criminal concerns.

In response to the terrorist attacks on September 11, 2001, Operation Enduring Freedom commenced on October 7, 2001, with American and British bombing raids against al-Qaeda and Taliban troops in Afghanistan. Initially, the Taliban were deposed, and al-Qaeda was severely weakened, but forces had to contend with a tenacious Taliban insurgency, infrastructure rehabilitation, and corruption among the Afghan National Army, Afghan National Police, and Afghan Border Police.

On May 2, 2011, U.S. Navy SEALS (Sea, Air, Land) launched a raid on Osama Bin Laden's compound in Abbottabad, Pakistan, killing the al- Qaeda leader and mastermind of the September 11th terrorist attacks. Operation Enduring Freedom officially ended on December 28, 2014, although coalition forces remained on the ground to assist with training Afghan security forces. The United States Armed Forces completed its withdrawal from Afghanistan on August 30, 2021, marking the end of the 2001–2021 war.

In August 2010, U.S. intelligence agencies developed information that Osama bin Laden was likely living in a compound in northern Pakistan. On May 2, 2011, under orders from President Obama, a special operations unit raided the compound and killed bin Laden. In announcing the successful operation, President Obama said, "Bin Laden was not a Muslim leader; he was a mass murderer of Muslims. Indeed, al Qaeda has slaughtered scores of Muslims in many countries, including our own. So, his demise should be welcomed by all who believe in peace and dignity." The Taliban leadership persisted in hiding throughout Afghanistan, largely in the southeast, and launched guerrilla attacks against forces of the United States, its allies, and the government of President Ashraf Ghani.

In February 2020, the United States and the Taliban reached a deal known as the Doha Agreement, under which the Trump administration agreed to withdraw all U.S. forces from Afghanistan by May 2021. The Intelligence Community's assessment in early 2021 was that Taliban advances would accelerate across large portions of Afghanistan after a complete U.S. military withdrawal and potentially lead to the Taliban's capturing Kabul within a year or two.

Over his last 11 months in office, President Trump ordered a series of drawdowns of U.S. troops. Chairman of the Joint Chiefs of Staff Milley testified that, on November 11, he had received an unclassified, signed order directing the U.S. military to withdraw all forces from Afghanistan no later than January 15, 2021. One week later, that order was rescinded and replaced with one to draw down to 2,500 troops by the same date. During the transition from the Trump administration to the Biden administration, the outgoing administration left the new administration with a date for withdrawal, but it provided no plans for how to conduct the final withdrawal or to evacuate Americans and Afghan allies. Indeed, there were no such plans in place. By the time that President Biden took office on January 20, 2021, the Taliban were in the strongest military position that they had been in since 2001, controlling or contesting nearly half of the country.

After four years of neglect—and, in some cases, purposeful deterioration by the outgoing Trump administration—critical systems, offices, and agency activities required for a safe and orderly exit were in disarray. When President Biden took office, the Special Immigrant Visa (SIV) program for Afghans who had served alongside our soldiers and diplomats required a 14-step procedure based on a legislative framework involving numerous government agencies. Because of the Trump Administration's apathy, if not hostility, toward the US commitment to Afghan friends, there is a large backlog of over 18,000 SIV applicants. Despite pulling down troops and committing to a thorough departure, the Trump administration effectively halted SIV interviews. Refugee support services had been gutted and personnel drastically cut, resulting in historic low admissions and the closure of more than 100 refugee resettlement institutions in the United States. In addition, the federal career workforce had been depleted. The Department of State employed 13% fewer personnel in November 2020, as President Biden prepared to take office, than it had four years earlier, leaving serious shortages.

In accordance with that strategy, President Biden requested military assets be deployed and pre-positioned in the area to assist with an emergency evacuation. It was this decision that later enabled the US to respond and deploy in a timely manner. President Biden followed the advice of his military leaders on tactical decisions surrounding the actual withdrawal of US forces from Afghanistan and ensured the safe departure of nearly 124,000 American citizens, permanent Afghan partners and allies, as well as locals, including the dates on which facilities were shuttered, and he frequently asked them if they needed anything extra.

On August 18, 2021, Avril Haines, Director of National Intelligence, claimed, "[the collapse] unfolded more quickly than [the intelligence community] anticipated." In fact, the collapse was faster than either the Taliban or the Afghan government had anticipated.

Americans anticipated that the Afghan National Defense and Security Forces (ANDSF) would defend Kabul. Chairman Milley stated on September 28, 2021, that "even during that time, there was no intelligence assessment that says the government's going to collapse and the Taliban will take over so quickly."

That tragic August 26th evening, at Abbey Gate, a suicide bomber set off an explosion that claimed the lives of 170 Afghans and 13 service members, wounded 45 more, and left a trail of casualties in her wake. The following day, August 27, the US military performed a drone hit in Nangarhar Province, killing two high-profile ISIS-K members. On August 29, a US drone strike killed ten civilians by accident in Kabul.

President Biden stated unequivocally that the US is committed to aiding our Afghan allies. The administration accelerated the SIV program and resumed SIV interviews that the previous administration had suspended. Finally, the US administration evacuated around 120,000 people from Kabul, Afghanistan, including 6,000 Americans. Many questioned if President Biden would be able to keep his promise, but he did. From August 14 to August 31, US military and civilian personnel worked nonstop to conduct the largest noncombatant airlift in US history. The US government went to remarkable lengths to fulfill this pledge, and it continues to be committed to providing major humanitarian aid, advocating for the rights of Afghan women and girls, and condemning and isolating the Taliban for its abysmal human rights record.

The speed and ease with which the Taliban took control of Afghanistan suggests that there was no scenario—except a permanent and significantly expanded U.S. military presence—that would have changed the trajectory after more than twenty years, more than $2 trillion dollars, and standing up an Afghan army of 300,000 soldiers. "When I hear that we could've, we should've continued the so-called low-grade effort in Afghanistan, at low risk to our service," President Biden said on August 31, 2021. Members are available at a modest cost. I do not think enough people realize how much we have asked of the one percent of Americans who put on that uniform and are willing to put their lives on the line in defense of our country. Any battle is anything but low-grade, low-risk, or low-cost.

Two-thirds of Americans believe the Afghan war was not worth waging; 65% of Democrats and 63% of Republicans concur. Afghanistan has become one of the world's biggest humanitarian catastrophes, with more than 28 million people—more than two- thirds of the population—in desperate need of assistance. According to the UN, four million people are acutely malnourished, including 3.2 million children under the age of five.

In his report to the UN General Assembly, Richard Bennett, the Special Rapporteur on the situation of human rights in Afghanistan, stated that "Afghanistan is facing a convergence of challenges, including a deteriorating human rights situation due to the Taliban's repressive policies and practices, a culture of impunity, an ongoing humanitarian and economic crisis, recent deadly earthquakes, and the possibility of massive involuntary returns. All of which require urgent action to avoid further suffering and potential instability in the country and the region."

The security situation in Afghanistan is volatile. There is an ongoing and high threat of terrorist attacks throughout Afghanistan, including around airports. Travel throughout Afghanistan is extremely dangerous, and border crossings may not be open. Women have been banned from going to parks, gyms, and public bathing houses. They have been stopped from pursuing education beyond the sixth grade. Their ability to work outside of health and education is all but prohibited.

By restricting children's access to a well-rounded education, the Taliban's strategy of limiting education to religious teachings, similar to "madrassa-style" instruction, raises hazards. This approach, when combined with unemployment and poverty, has the potential to encourage radicalization, which in turn raises the likelihood of domestic terrorism and instability in the region.

Vietnam, Afghanistan, and Iraq, as well as the Global War on Terror, were the losses, of course; the Cold War being the solitary win that must now be counted as a loss because its promise was so quickly discarded. The United States was the leading nation in the rebuilding or reconstruction of Afghanistan.

CHAPTER 15

The Axis of Evil

A mixed media composition of the 9/11 tragedy in the US masterminded by Bin Laden

Two Days after the assassination of Massoud, a series of devastating bombing attacks occurred in the United States on September 11, 2001, leading to the North Atlantic Treaty Organization (NATO), an alliance of countries from Europe and North America, invading Afghanistan and allying with Massoud's forces.

The September 11 attacks, often referred to as 9/11, were a series of four coordinated terrorist attacks by the Wahhabi Islamist terrorist group al-Qaeda against the United States on the morning of Tuesday, September 11, 2001. Four California-bound commercial flights were hijacked by 19 terrorists who planned to crash the plane into important American edifices. They managed to bring down the World Trade Center 110-floor Twin Towers complex in Lower Manhattan, in the heart of New York City. New York City is the most populous city in the U.S. The Twin Towers were, at that time, two of the tallest buildings in the world. The death toll was estimated to be over 10,000, as confirmed. A third flight crashed into the west side of the Pentagon (the headquarters of the American military) in Arlington County, Virginia, causing a partial collapse of the building. The fourth flight crashed in a field near Shanksville, Pennsylvania, after passengers forced their way into the cockpit and fought the hijackers over the controls. Investigators determined that Flight 93's target was either the White House or the Capitol Building.

Picture: Operation Neptune Spear

An initial bombing of the World Trade Center in New York City occurred during the Clinton Administration on February 26, 1993. The terrorists wanted the bomb to topple one tower, with the collapsing debris knocking down the second. This attack turned out to be something of a deadly dress rehearsal for 9/11, as noted in a statement obtained from Osama Bin Laden:

> *"We calculated in advance the number of casualties from the enemy who would be killed based on the position of the tower. We calculated that the floors that would be hit would be three or four floors. I was the most optimistic of them all due to my experience in this field. I knew that the fire from the gas in the plane would melt the iron structure of the building and collapse the area where the plane hit and all the floors above it. This is all that we had hoped for."*

The United States responded by launching the War on Terror and invading Afghanistan to depose the Taliban, which had not complied with U.S. demands to expel al-Qaeda from Afghanistan and extradite their leader, Osama bin Laden. In August 1996 and February 1998, respectively, Bin Laden issued two fatwas in which he declared holy war on the United States. The 1998 US Embassy attacks in East Africa were planned by him. After that, he was added to the FBI's lists of the most wanted terrorists and wanted fugitives. He was the mastermind of the September 11 attacks, which claimed almost 3,000 lives. As a result, the US invasion of Afghanistan started the war on terror. Bin Laden became the focus of an international manhunt that lasted over ten years. He fled to neighboring Pakistan after hiding in several hilly areas of Afghanistan during this time. U.S. special operations soldiers killed him on May 2, 2011, at his

Abbottabad compound in Pakistan. His body was interred in the Arabian Sea.

Osama bin Laden- Taken Down 2011

CHAPTER 16

The Al-Qaeda and Taliban Nexus

President George W. Bush and his inner circle, photographed in the Cabinet Room of the White House in December 2001. From left: Secretary of State Colin Powell, Vice President Dick Cheney, the President, National-Security Adviser Condoleezza Rice, White House chief of staff Andrew Card, C.I.A. director George Tenet (seated), and Secretary of Defense Donald Rumsfeld

Unlike the Taliban, which is mainly concerned with pushing out Western allies and exercising theocratic totalitarianism in Afghanistan, Al-Qaeda attacks the West everywhere. The United Nations Security Council adopted Resolution 1267 on October 15, 1999, creating the al-Qaeda and Taliban Sanctions Committee, linking the two groups as terrorist entities, and imposing sanctions on their funding, travel, and arms shipments. The U.N. identified Osama bin Laden, who guided the terror group from Afghanistan and Peshawar, Pakistan, in the late 1980s, to Sudan in 1991, and back to

Afghanistan in the mid-1990s. The Taliban, which rose from the ashes of Afghanistan's post-Soviet civil war, provides al-Qaeda sanctuary for operations.

> *"A war against all those who seek to export terror, and a war against those governments that support or shelter them."-President George W. Bush, 10/11/01.*

The world has responded with an unprecedented coalition against international terrorism. In the first 100 days of the war, President George W. Bush increased America's homeland security and built a worldwide coalition to destroy al-Qaeda's grip on Afghanistan by driving the Taliban from power. The agenda includes disrupting al- Qaeda's global operations, terrorist financing networks, and terrorist training camps. As well as help the innocent people of Afghanistan recover from the Taliban's reign of terror. Helped Afghans put aside long-standing differences to form a new interim government that represents all Afghans, including women.

196 countries supported the financial war on terror; 142 countries acted to freeze terrorist assets immediately; in the U.S. alone, 153 known terrorists, terrorist organizations, and terrorist financial centers were frozen; and major terrorist financial networks were shut down. The Office of Homeland Security and the Homeland Security Council were created to strengthen intelligence, and new air travel security measures were implemented.

"9/11" changed the world. However, the world thought the change was a worthy sacrifice. However, hastily passing the

Patriot Act in the name of national security was the first of many changes to surveillance laws that made it easier for the government to spy on ordinary Americans by expanding the authority to monitor phone and email communications, collect bank and credit reporting records, and track the activity of innocent Americans. While most Americans think it was created to catch terrorists, the Patriot Act turns regular citizens into suspects. There is also evidence that the Bush administration consciously deceived the world in his 2003 presentation, making a case for war with Iraq and Afghanistan. During the Bush administration, Collin Powell, Secretary, fabricated "evidence" and ignored repeated warnings that what he was saying was false and unverified statements in his presentation when making a case for war with Iraq at the United Nations on February 5, 2003.

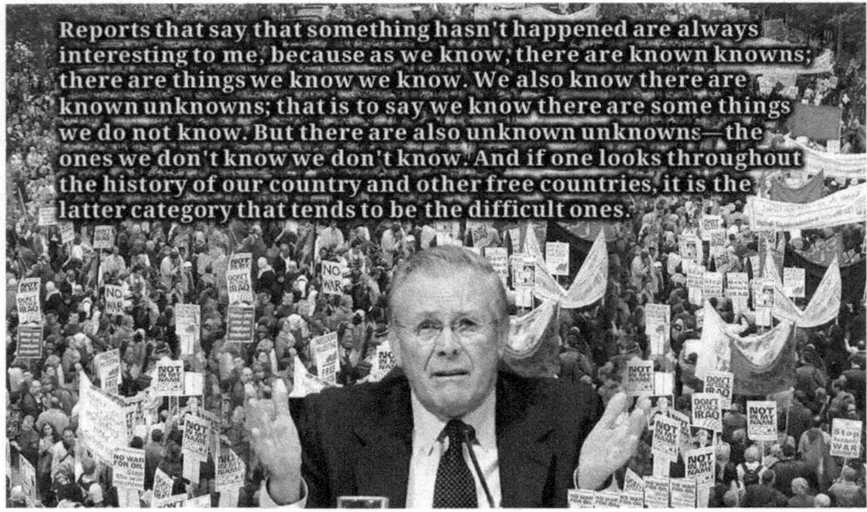

Secretary of Defense Donald Rumsfeld's famous quote amidst US protest the War.

Donald Rumsfeld (the 13th and 21st United States Secretary of Defense) was credited as the architect of the invasions of

Iraq and Afghanistan. As Secretary of Defense, Rumsfeld played a leading role in the invasion of Afghanistan and Iraq. Before and during the Iraq War, he claimed that Iraq had an active weapons-of-mass destruction program, yet no stockpiles were ever found.

"There are known knowns" is a phrase from a response United States Secretary of Defense Donald Rumsfeld gave to a question at a U.S. Department of Defense (DoD) news briefing on February 12, 2002, about the lack of evidence linking the government of Iraq with the supply of weapons of mass destruction to terrorist groups.

Rumsfeld's statement became a viral public discussion, which led to a 2013 documentary film, The Unknown Known, directed by Errol Morris.

A Pentagon Inspector General report found that Rumsfeld's top policy adviser "developed, produced, and then disseminated alternative intelligence assessments on the Iraq and al-Qaida relationship, which included some conclusions that were inconsistent with the consensus of the Intelligence Community, to senior decision-makers." Rumsfeld's tenure was controversial for its torture and the Abu Ghraib torture and prisoner abuse scandal. Rumsfeld gradually lost political support and resigned in late 2006.

In his retirement years, he published an autobiography, Known and Unknown, and Rumsfeld's Rules: Leadership Lessons in Business, Politics, War, and Life. He died on June 29, 2021, at the age of 88.

CHAPTER 17

Democracy in Afghanistan

On October 9, 2004, voters turned out in high numbers despite threats of violence and intimidation for the first democratic presidential election in the history of Afghanistan. Hamid Karzai won with 55 percent of the vote, while his closest rival, former education minister Younis Qanooni, polled 16 percent. Karzai's election victory was marred by accusations of fraud by his opponents and the kidnapping of three foreign U.N. election workers by a militant group. Afghans had not gone to the polls since 1969, during the reign of King Mohammed Zahir Shah, for parliamentary elections.

In 2005, more than six million Afghans voted for the Wolesi Jirga (Council of People), the Meshrano Jirga (Council of Elders), and local councils. Considered the most democratic elections ever in Afghanistan, almost half those casting ballots are women, viewed as a sign of political progress in a highly patriarchal and conservative society. Sixty-eight out of 249 seats are set aside for female members of Afghanistan's lower house of parliament, and 23 out of 102 are reserved in the upper house. However, gains in democracy also brought a quintuple wave of suicide attacks, while remotely detonated bombings more than doubled and increased exponentially.

With violence against nongovernmental aid workers increasing, U.S. Secretary of Defense Robert Gates criticized NATO countries in late 2007 for not sending more soldiers. "Our progress in Afghanistan is real, but it is fragile," Gates says. "At this time, many allies are unwilling to share the risks, commit the resources, and follow through on collective commitments to this mission and each other.

As a result, we risk allowing what has been achieved in Afghanistan to slip away." With reconciliation in mind, the U.N. Security Council split a sanctions list between al-Qaeda and the Taliban members days earlier, making it easier to add and remove people and entities. The Obama administration planned to train and equip the political and military institutions to assume responsibility for their affairs.

Polls show that an increasing number of Americans do not support the war, and Obama faces pressure from lawmakers, particularly Democrats, to reduce U.S. forces in Afghanistan. Obama confirms that the U.S. is holding preliminary peace talks with the Taliban leadership. By

2013, when NATO handed over control of the remaining security responsibilities nationwide to the Afghan forces, the U.S.-led coalition's focus shifted to military training and operations-driven counterterrorism. When President Barack Obama announced his plan to remain after the combat mission concludes at the end of 2014, limited to training Afghan forces and conducting operations against "the remnants of al-Qaeda," he received sharp criticism from former vice president Dick Cheney and Liz Cheney (daughter) in an op-ed in the Wall Street Times:

> "Rarely has a U.S. president been so wrong about so much at the expense of so many. Too many times to count, Mr. Obama has told us he is "ending" the wars in Iraq and Afghanistan—as though wishing made it so. His rhetoric has now come crashing into reality. Watching the black-clad ISIS jihadists take territory once secured by American blood is conclusive proof, if any were needed, that America's enemies are not "decimated. "They are emboldened and on the march."

Dick Cheney's criticism of Barack Obama as a "weak president" after Obama announced his plans to pull forces out of Afghanistan was met with criticism from members of the press, namely Megan Kelly of Fox News, who said it was Cheney that got it wrong so often, at the cost of so many. Meanwhile, Ashraf Ghani, the newly elected president, had just signed a power-sharing agreement with his chief opponent, Abdullah, who had mobilized thousands of protestors to challenge the voting results at a time when the Taliban are making gains in the countryside.

President Barack Obama sent seventeen thousand more troops to the war zone. Obama reaffirmed campaign statements that Afghanistan is the more critical U.S. front against terrorist forces. He said the United States would stick to a timetable to draw down most combat forces from Iraq by the end of 2011. As of January 2009, the Pentagon has 37 thousand troops in Afghanistan, divided between U.S. and NATO commands. Reinforcements focus on countering a "resurgent" Taliban and stemming the flow of foreign fighters over the Afghan- Pakistan border in the south. Speaking on the troop increase, Secretary of Defense Robert Gates describes the original mission in Afghanistan as "too broad" and calls for establishing limited goals such as preventing and limiting terrorist safe havens.

Obama said in a televised address that the additional U.S. troops would "help create the conditions for the United States to transfer responsibility to the Afghans." But later, aides said Obama felt jammed by military commanders pushing for a counterinsurgency strategy. By August 2010, U.S. forces in Afghanistan had reached 100,000. But it was in a different country, Pakistan, where U.S. intelligence tracked down bin Laden, who was killed during a Navy SEAL raid in May 2011. Shortly afterward, Obama announced he would begin bringing U.S. troops home to hand off security responsibilities to the Afghans by 2014.

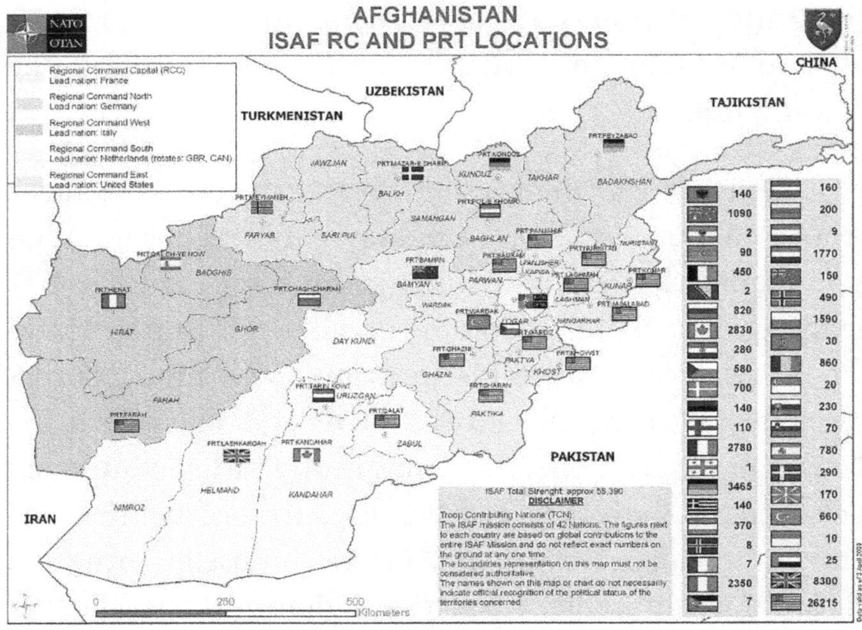

Over the following years, troop levels declined steadily as the U.S. engaged in fraught diplomacy with Afghanistan's leaders. By the start of his second term, Obama had adopted a view toward the country summed up by members of his team as "Afghan good enough"—a recognition that attempts to cultivate a western-style democracy were hopeless primarily and that taking out terrorists and keeping the Taliban in check amounted to the limits of the United States' role.

Terrorism remains an impediment to good governance. It is impossible to govern when terror looms. The Taliban do not want democracy and have chosen violence, often terrorism, to express that point.

CHAPTER 18

Mixed Signals for a Prolonged War

Picture: Moab and analysis

President Donald Trump's Afghanistan policy changed from his "original instinct, which was to pull out," to press ahead with an open- ended military commitment to preventing the emergence of "a vacuum for terrorists." Differentiating from Obama's policy, Trump's decisions about withdrawal would be based on "conditions on the ground" rather than arbitrary timelines. He asked India to play a more significant role in rebuilding Afghanistan while castigating Pakistan for harboring insurgents.

Trump ordered the United States to drop its most powerful non- nuclear bomb on suspected self-proclaimed Islamic State militants at a cave complex in eastern Nangarhar Province. The weapon, known colloquially as "the mother of all bombs," With newly elected President Donald Trump, decision-making authorities were delegated to commanders, including the possibility of adding several thousand U.S. troops to the 9,000 already deployed there. (There are about as many U.S. private contractors as well.) The bombing cast a spotlight on the emergence of the new Islamic Emirate in Afghanistan.

At the same time, the Taliban was formidable, and the U.S. military describes the war as a stalemate. The U.S. aggression was met by suicide bombings on a scale never seen before in Kabul, and the Taliban had gained control or were contesting more than a third of the country. The Trump administration also cut off security assistance worth billions of dollars to Pakistan for what President Trump called its "lies and deceit" in harboring Taliban militants.

President Trump abruptly broke off peace talks a week after top U.S. negotiator Khalilzad announced an agreement "in principle" with Taliban leaders. In a tweet, Trump says he canceled a secret meeting with the Taliban and Afghan President Ghani at Camp David after a U.S. soldier was killed in a Taliban attack. The Taliban says it is "committed to continuing negotiations" but warns that the cancellation would cause an increase in the number of deaths.

The decision to withdraw from Afghanistan was first made under the Obama administration. However, as part of the Doha Agreement, the Trump administration consented to a initial reduction of U.S. forces from 13,000 to 8,600 troops by July 2020, with a full withdrawal following on May 1,

2021. This was contingent on whether the Taliban kept its commitments. At the start of the Biden administration, there were 2,500 US soldiers left in Afghanistan.

Trump's former ambassador to the United Nations, Nikki Haley, took to Twitter after the final U.S. withdrawal to criticize the Biden administration for its improvised negotiations with the Taliban, meant to ensure the safety of U.S. evacuation operations in Kabul. But she unwittingly incriminated her boss, Mr. Trump, and Mr. Pompeo by saying, "Negotiating with the Taliban is like dealing with the devil." This statement caused a political uproar and further strained diplomatic relations. It also raised questions about her loyalty and judgment.

CHAPTER 19

The US Agreement for Peace to Afghanistan

Signing the Agreement for Bringing Peace to Afghanistan

The Doha Agreement, also known as the Agreement for Bringing Peace to Afghanistan, is a peace agreement signed by the United States and the Taliban on February 29, 2020, to bring the Afghanistan War to an end. This agreement was negotiated by Zalmay Khalilzad, United States Ambassador to the United Nations under President George W. Bush, and, briefly, President Barack Obama. The agreement, however controversial, is the most critical peace agreement in Afghanistan to date. So, whose idea was it to include the Taliban in the peace deal, and what is the peace deal anyway?

The real question is, what is peace in Afghanistan?

To the Taliban, peace was a free, independent Islamic state in their power. For many other warlords, peace is access to power. To some farmers, peace is the freedom to grow poppy seeds and trade without hindrance.

Taliban discussing together at the meeting in Doha.

To the clerics, peace is the power to enforce Sharia and issue fatwas at will. To the Afghan youth, peace is job availability and education. For Afghan women, most importantly, peace means ending all kinds of abuse, violence, and repression of women. To the educated middle class, peace is civilization, benign growth, prosperity, and order in society.

Afghan leaders praying for peace.

Here is a summary of the Joint Declaration between the Islamic Republic of Afghanistan and the United States of America for Bringing Peace to Afghanistan: U.S. Demands:

US Government Demand:

Afghanistan cannot harbor or be used as an incubator for terrorists and terrorism worldwide.

Afghan Government Demands

1. Unconditional withdrawal of all U.S. and Coalition forces from Afghanistan,
2. Political settlement negotiations must be used to resolve differences rather than violence
3. A permanent and comprehensive ceasefire.
4. The United States must continue to fulfill its commitment to provide funds yearly that support the training, equipping, advising, and sustaining

of Afghan security forces, so that Afghanistan can independently secure and defend itself against internal and external threats. Taliban Demand

5. Orthodox Islamic rule must be enforced in Afghanistan
6. Release war prisoners
7. Start diplomatic engagement with the UN Security Council to remove the Taliban from the sanctions list
8. The legitimization of Taliban authority must be achieved by May 29, 2020, and in any case, no later than 30 days after finalizing a framework agreement and a permanent and comprehensive ceasefire.

These are the conditions outlined in the Doha treaty.

Joint Declaration between the Islamic Republic of Afghanistan and the United States of America for Bringing Peace to Afghanistan

The Islamic Republic of Afghanistan, a member of the United Nations and recognized by the United States and the international community as a sovereign state under international law, and the United States of America are committed to working together to reach a comprehensive and sustainable peace agreement that ends the war in Afghanistan for the benefit of all Afghans and contributes to regional stability and global security. A comprehensive and sustainable peace agreement will include four parts: 1) guarantees to prevent the use of Afghan soil by any international terrorist groups or individuals against the security of the United States and its allies, 2) a timeline for the withdrawal of all U.S. and Coalition forces from Afghanistan, 3) a political settlement resulting from intra-Afghan dialogue and negotiations between the Taliban and an inclusive negotiating team of the Islamic Republic of Afghanistan, and 4) a permanent and comprehensive ceasefire. These four parts are interrelated and interdependent. Pursuit of peace after long years of fighting reflects the goal of all parties who seek a sovereign, unified Afghanistan at peace with itself and its neighbors.

The Islamic Republic of Afghanistan and the United States have partnered closely since 2001 to respond to threats to international peace and security and help the Afghan people chart a secure, democratic and prosperous future. The two countries are committed to their longstanding relationship and their investments in building the Afghan institutions necessary to establish democratic norms, protect and preserve the unity of the country, and promote social and economic advancements and the rights of citizens. The commitments set out here are made possible by these shared achievements. Afghan and U.S. security forces share a special bond forged during many years of tremendous sacrifice and courage. The Islamic Republic of Afghanistan and the people of Afghanistan reaffirm their support for peace and their willingness to negotiate an end to this war.

The Islamic Republic of Afghanistan welcomes the Reduction in Violence period and takes note of the U.S.-Taliban agreement, an important step toward ending the war. The U.S-Taliban agreement paves the way for intra-Afghan negotiations on a political settlement and a permanent and comprehensive ceasefire. The Islamic Republic of Afghanistan reaffirms its readiness to participate in such negotiations and its readiness to conclude a ceasefire with the Taliban.

The Islamic Republic of Afghanistan furthermore reaffirms its ongoing commitment to prevent any international terrorist groups or individuals, including al-Qa'ida and ISIS-K, from using Afghan soil to threaten the security of the United States, its allies and other countries. To accelerate the pursuit of peace, the Islamic Republic of Afghanistan confirms its support for the phased withdrawal of U.S. and Coalition forces subject to the Taliban's fulfillment of its commitments under the U.S.-Taliban agreement and any agreement resulting from intra-Afghan negotiations.

Joint Declaration between the Islamic Republic of Afghanistan and the United States of America for Bringing Peace to Afghanistan (page 1)

The Islamic Republic of Afghanistan and the United States therefore have made the following commitments:

PART ONE

The Islamic Republic of Afghanistan and the United States recognize that al-Qa'ida, ISIS-K and other international terrorist groups or individuals continue to use Afghan soil to recruit members, raise funds, train adherents and plan and attempt to conduct attacks that threaten the security of the United States, its allies, and Afghanistan. To address this continuing terrorist threat, the Islamic Republic of Afghanistan and the United States will continue to take the following steps to defeat al-Qa'ida, its affiliates, and other international terrorist groups or individuals:

1. The Islamic Republic of Afghanistan reaffirms its continued commitment not to cooperate with or permit international terrorist groups or individuals to recruit, train, raise funds (including through the production or distribution of narcotics), transit Afghanistan or misuse its internationally-recognized travel documents, or conduct other support activities in Afghanistan, and will not host them.

2. The United States re-affirms its commitments regarding support for the Afghan security forces and other government institutions, including through ongoing efforts to enhance the ability of Afghan security forces to deter and respond to internal and external threats, consistent with its commitments under existing security agreements between the two governments. This commitment includes support to Afghan security forces to prevent al-Qa'ida, ISIS-K, and other international terrorist groups or individuals from using Afghan soil to threaten the United States and its allies.

3. The United States re-affirms its readiness to continue to conduct military operations in Afghanistan with the consent of the Islamic Republic of Afghanistan in order to disrupt and degrade efforts by al-Qa'ida, ISIS-K, and other international terrorist groups or individuals to carry out attacks against the United States or its allies, consistent with its commitments under existing security agreements between the two governments and with the existing understanding that U.S. counterterrorism operations are intended to complement and support Afghan security forces' counterterrorism operations, with full respect for Afghan sovereignty and full regard for the safety and security of the Afghan people and the protection of civilians.

4. The United States commits to facilitate discussions between Afghanistan and Pakistan to work out arrangements to ensure neither country's security is threatened by actions from the territory of the other side.

PART TWO

The Islamic Republic of Afghanistan and the United States have consulted extensively on U.S. and Coalition force levels and the military activities required to achieve the foregoing commitments including through support to Afghan security and defense forces. Subject to the Taliban's fulfillment of its commitments under the U.S.-Taliban agreement, the Islamic Republic of Afghanistan, the United States, and the Coalition jointly assess that the current levels of military forces are no longer necessary to achieve

Joint Declaration between the Islamic Republic of Afghanistan and the United States of America for Bringing Peace to Afghanistan (page 2)

security objectives; since 2014, Afghan security forces have been in the lead for providing security and have increased their effectiveness. As such, the parties commit to take the following measures:

1. The United States will reduce the number of U.S. military forces in Afghanistan to 8,600 and implement other commitments in the U.S.-Taliban agreement within 135 days of the announcement of this joint declaration and the U.S.-Taliban agreement, and will work with its allies and the Coalition to reduce proportionally the number of Coalition forces in Afghanistan over an equivalent period, subject to the Taliban's fulfillment of its commitments under the U.S.-Taliban agreement.

2. Consistent with the joint assessment and determination between the United States and the Islamic Republic of Afghanistan, the United States, its allies, and the Coalition will complete the withdrawal of their remaining forces from Afghanistan within 14 months following the announcement of this joint declaration and the U.S.-Taliban agreement, and will withdraw all their forces from remaining bases, subject to the Taliban's fulfillment of its commitments under the U.S.-Taliban agreement.

3. The United States re-affirms its commitment to seek funds on a yearly basis that support the training, equipping, advising and sustaining of Afghan security forces, so that Afghanistan can independently secure and defend itself against internal and external threats.

4. To create the conditions for reaching a political settlement and achieving a permanent, sustainable ceasefire, the Islamic Republic of Afghanistan will participate in a U.S.-facilitated discussion with Taliban representatives on confidence building measures, to include determining the feasibility of releasing significant numbers of prisoners on both sides. The United States and Islamic Republic of Afghanistan will seek the assistance of the ICRC to support this discussion.

5. With the start of intra-Afghan negotiations, the Islamic Republic of Afghanistan commits to start diplomatic engagement with members of the UN Security Council to remove members of the Taliban from the sanctions list with the aim of achieving this objective by May 29, 2020, and in any case no later than 30 days after finalizing a framework agreement and a permanent and comprehensive ceasefire.

PART THREE

1. The United States will request the recognition and endorsement of the UN Security Council for this agreement and related arrangements.

2. The United States and the Islamic Republic of Afghanistan are committed to continue positive relations, including economic cooperation for reconstruction.

3. The United States will refrain from the threat or the use of force against the territorial integrity or political independence of Afghanistan or intervening in its domestic affairs.

4. The United States will continue to work to build regional and international consensus to support the ongoing effort to achieve a political settlement to the principal conflict in Afghanistan.

Joint Declaration between the Islamic Republic of Afghanistan and the United States of America for Bringing Peace to Afghanistan (page 3)

Given the agreement in this treaty, the Taliban did not have to invade Afghanistan and take it by force. That should have been a breach of the agreement. The Doha Peace Treaty Agreement signed by the U.S. envoy Khalilzad and the Taliban's Baradar did not clarify but expected civil process, ethical judgment, and peaceful negotiation between the Taliban and the Afghan government. It should have included that the Taliban could organize a political party and participate in peaceful elections. Instead, it was a U.S. surrender to the Taliban's threat and acceptance of their wish list.

Picture: Doha treaty Mixed media to illustrate flaws in the agreement

The U.S. traded its trump card in Afghanistan for guarantees from the Taliban that the country would not be used for terrorist activities. In other words, the peace deal gives back the nation to the Taliban on the assumption that the government belonged to them in the first place, and they could have it back. Many Afghans took to social media to express how the U.S. had sold them out.

The NATO military presence had dwindled, and the peace agreement had ordered them to leave. Since this agreement was vague and broadly worded, with no ramification of a ceasefire, insurgents used the opportunity to attack and take over the Afghan army garrison and U.S. weapons across Afghanistan. They then stormed Kabul, the capital of Afghanistan. Almost all pundits and scholars predicted these consequences on the topic with precision. The same Taliban violated the international treaty by attacking the UN building in Kabul to kidnap the former Afghan president, Najibullah, who was murdered publicly in the most gruesome way in Kabul. The Taliban does not consider the emotional stress it imposes on Afghans and the rest of the world.

Picture: Mixed media of Taliban painting over the peace mural

The same Taliban could not be trusted. Same Taliban who harbored terrorists and encouraged terrorism. This same Taliban used suicide attacks to kill former presidents of Afghanistan and its political leaders. This same Taliban was invited to the poker game in Doha, and they sure brought their game. The U.S. had a trump card, and they, the Taliban, had all the aces up their sleeves. They tendered the jokers. When Representatives of the Taliban and the Afghan government and civil society met face-to-face for the first time in Doha, Qatar, after nearly twenty years of war on September 12, 2020, both sides expressed eagerness to bring peace to Afghanistan and establish a framework for Afghan society after U.S. troops withdraw.

The government pushes for a ceasefire, while the Taliban reiterates its call to govern the country through an Islamic system. Although this does not look like an agreement, why was the peace treaty signed?

Well, the U.S.-led war in Afghanistan had been an unpopular war from the start. Many Afghans wanted the United States military out of Afghanistan. The democratic governments of Karzai and Ghani have spoken several times about that interest. Even the children throw stones at the U.S. military patrol. They are hated for their paranoia and indiscriminate arrest and killing, as they also had to do policing jobs on patrol, for which they were not skilled or prepared. Looking for terrorists on the street is like looking for a needle in a haystack and a death wish.

Western countries, in particular, are considered in Afghanistan as corrupt, amoral, and detrimental to traditional Afghan or Muslim values. The peasantry blames the United States for their insecurity and depravity. The Taliban also understands that Western countries will never recognize them as Afghanistan's rulers. As a result, they want the Western soldiers to go.

However, what the Afghans hated more than the U.S./ NATO's presence was the Taliban government. To stop the Taliban advance and aggression, the U.S. would have had to send more troops. However, it did so marginally to ensure the safety of the evacuee. The new administration would have had to violate the peace deal for the required surge in military personnel needed to be deployed. The U.S. personnel had no sufficient intelligence about the Taliban encroachment. They had no intelligence about the Taliban's capabilities. President Biden thought the Afghan army was better trained and prepared than the Taliban. He thought the Taliban were holding their side of the bargain entailed in the treaty. The president was misinformed about the technicality of the actual situation. Every American political leader wanted to get out of Afghanistan, but none wanted to leave a mess for their successor. Those who inherit a mess from their predecessor have the duty and obligation to protect the dignity and integrity of the United States. Only an unscrupulous one could act on the contrary.

President Joe Biden inherited the Afghan Peace Deal and was bound by its statutes. He could not pull out. The peace deal does not entail enforcement of the treaty or a quasi-military base like Germany or South Korea, which could be necessary to keep the peace.

Acting U.S. Defense Secretary Christopher C. Miller announced plans to halve the number of troops in Afghanistan to 2,500 by mid-January, days before President-elect Joe Biden was inaugurated. Thousands of troops had already been pulled out following an agreement with the Taliban in February, moving closer to fulfilling President Trump's campaign promise to end the so-called forever wars. The announcement comes as negotiations between the Afghan government and the Taliban are deadlocked and the militant group continues to launch deadly attacks. NATO warned that withdrawing troops too early could allow Afghanistan to become a haven for terrorists and the Islamic State to rebuild its caliphate.

President Trump invited leaders of the Taliban, the group that harbored Osama bin Laden in Afghanistan as the founder of Al Qaeda plotted his strikes on America, to join peace negotiations at the Camp David presidential retreat in Maryland in 2019. The notion of meeting with the Taliban close to September 11 stunned many Republicans. Trump was eager to engage with the militant group, which the United States had been fighting for almost 20 years, as he pursued his goal of removing American troops from Afghanistan by the end of his term. Trump was determined to define his term in office by demolishing what his predecessor, President Obama, built. He canceled the trade deals, withdrew from the climate pact, reinstated the embargo and sanctions on Cuba, partially reversed them, launched a war to dismantle Obama's Affordable Care Act, embraced the Russian president who had meddled in the U.S. elections, and decided to lure the Taliban into a peace deal.

Picture: Mike Pompeo, the secretary of state, meeting with the Taliban's chief negotiator, Mullah Abdul Ghani Baradar, in November 2020 Mixed media.

Trump designated absolute authority over the Afghan wars to field commanders. He ordered the State Department to talk face-to-face with the Taliban to negotiate an American exit. One could argue that he wanted to take his cue from Ronald Reagan, who met with the Mujahideen at the White House, even though that was a quite different situation. Pundits argue that Trump's decision was a political move rather than a strategic solution. Trump had invited the Taliban to Camp David but revoked the invitation after an American soldier was killed in a bombing in Kabul, but the peace talks continued after the Taliban threatened that there would be more fatal consequences.

The Taliban are not the Mujahideen initially supported, encouraged, and trained by the U.S. They are a murderous

> *lot, but that is not a deterrent to participating in Afghanistan politics. And if this peace deal does not work, knowing the Trump administration, there will be finger-pointing or some lame excuses that can only be made in the sanctity of insanity. – Time Magazine, Brian Bennett September 10, 2019.*

During the Trump administration, the United States secretary of state, Mike Pompeo, and the Taliban leader, Mullah Abdul Ghani Baradar, attended the signing ceremony in Doha. Some former senior Trump officials called that agreement fatally flawed, saying it did little more than provide cover for a pullout that Mr. Trump was impatient to begin before his re-election bid. They also said it laid the groundwork for the chaos unfolding now in Kabul.

"Our secretary of state signed a surrender agreement with the Taliban," Mr. Trump's second national security adviser, H.R. McMaster, said of Mr. Pompeo during a podcast interview with the journalist Bari Weiss after the pullout in 2021. "This collapse goes back to the capitulation agreement of 2020. The Taliban did not defeat us. We defeated ourselves." And in an interview on CNN with the former Defense Secretary Mark T. Esper said that, while President Biden "owns" the ultimate outcome in Afghanistan, Mr. Trump had earlier "undermined" the agreement through his barely disguised impatience to exit the country with little apparent regard for the consequences. Trump moved thousands of troops out of Afghanistan during his last year in office. Biden inherited just 2,500 troops in the country. Mr. Biden has cited the U.S. commitment in Doha to remove all remaining forces by May of this year, a deadline he did not meet, as a critical factor in his decision to continue the withdrawal.

The Taliban have choices because they have real wishes. More than anything else, the Taliban wants legitimacy from both internal and international civil societies and authorities. This is wonderful because the only way out of this mess is a carrot stick. A diplomatic solution is the best strategy. So, the Taliban signing the deal is considered an agreement not to harbor terrorists and engage in their first direct negotiations with the Afghan government, and it was binding that the United States agreed to withdraw in return for Taliban promises. The United States signed off on a deal where a whole country and 40 million people's lives and livelihoods are on the line, which is challenging to comprehend and arguably irresponsible.

Picture: The New Taliban government

SIRAJUDDIN HAQQANI, 48
Interior Minister, head of Haqqani Network, carries $10 mn bounty

MAULAVI MUHAMMAD YAQOOB, 31
Defence Minister, son of founder leader Mullah Omar

MAULAVI AMIR KHAN MUTTAQI, 53
Foreign Minister, part of first Taliban govt, Doha group

MULLAH HIDAYATULLAH BADRI, AGE NOT KNOWN
Finance Minister, not much information

SHEIKH MAULAVI NOORULLAH MUNIR, AGE NOT KNOWN
Education Minister, no information

MULLAH KHAIRULLAH KHAIRKHWA, 58
I&B Minister, part of the Guantanamo Bay Five

ABDUL HAQ WASEEQ, 46
Intelligence chief, also part of the Taliban's Guantanamo Five

ZABIHULLAH MUJAHID, AGE NOT KNOWN
Deputy I&B Minister, for long the face of Taliban

REST OF THE CABINET

SHEIKH NOOR MUHAMMAD SAQIB
■ Minister for Hajj and Auqaf

MAULAVI ABDUL HAKIM
■ Minister for Law

MULLAH NOORULLAH NOORI
■ Minister for Borders & Tribal Affairs

MULLAH MUHAMMAD YOUNAS AKHUNDZADA
■ Minister for Development

SHEIKH MUHAMMAD KHALID
■ Minister for Dawat & Irshaad

MULLAH ABDUL MANNAN UMERI
■ Minister for Public Works

MULLAH MUHAMMAD ESSA AKHUND
■ Minister for Minerals & Petroleum

MULLAH ABDUL LATIF MANSOOR
■ Minister for Water & Power

HAMEEDULLAH AKHUNDZADA
■ Minister for Civil Aviation & Transport

ABDUL BAQI HAQQANI
■ Minister for Higher Education

NAJIBULLAH HAQQANI
■ Minister for Communications

KHALIL-UR-REHMAN HAQQANI
■ Minister for Refugees

HAJI MUHAMMAD IDREES
■ Incharge, Afghanistan Bank

MAULAVI AHMED JAN AHMEDI
■ Incharge, Administrative Affairs

MULLAH MUHAMMAD FAZIL MAZLOOM AKHUND
■ Deputy Defence Minister

MAULAVI NOOR JALAL
■ Deputy Interior Minister

MULLAH ABDUL HAQ
■ Special Assistant (Narcotics) to Interior Minister

MULLAH TAJ MIR JAWAD
■ First Deputy to Intelligence Chief

MULLAH REHMATULLAH NAJEEB
■ Administrative Deputy to Intelligence Chief

SHER MUHAMMAD ABBAS STANEKZAI
■ Deputy Foreign Minister, had the only officially acknowledged contact on behalf of Taliban with India

QARI DIN MUHAMMAD HANIF (TAJIK)
■ Minister for Economic Affairs

QARI FASEEHUDDIN (TAJIK)
■ Army Chief

Source: Agencies. Photos: The NYT, AP, Reuters, US Department of State. Illustrations: Suvajit Dey

Picture: The Taliban Cabinet

The negotiations in Doha are a smokescreen. It is designed to give false hope to the United States, NATO, and particularly the Afghan government that there will be a negotiated solution. The Taliban's position has been the same for—well, for two decades now. It has stated in English on Voice of Jihad, its website, numerous times, even seven days after signing the Doha agreement, that the only acceptable outcome of this war would be the re-establishment of the Islamic Emirate with Mawlawi Hibatullah Akhundzada, its emir, as the Leader of the Islamic Emirate of Afghanistan. The Taliban, the Doha group, and the Taliban's Doha group are merely providing that screen.

Hibatullah Akhundzada has been appointed as the Head of the Islamic Emirate of Afghanistan and the Third Supreme Leader of the Taliban. The Taliban calls him Amir al-Mu'minin (Commander of the Faithful), which was the title of his two predecessors. Akhundzada is well known for his fatwas on Taliban matters. He served as the head of the Sharia courts of the Islamic Emirate of Afghanistan. This man is the one to be convinced. This is the one whose heart must be changed and who must be enlightened. The fate of so many Afghan people is in his hands and on his interpretation of the Sharia. The treaty must be extended to include all necessary and applicable tenets of universal human rights and the Sustainable Development Goals to ensure a lasting, unified, and prosperous Islamic Republic of Afghanistan.

CHAPTER 20

U.S. Total Withdrawal from Afghanistan

Picture: mixed media showing the US bidding farewell and taking colleagues, family, and friends along

President Biden announced that the remaining U.S. troops in Afghanistan would be withdrawn by 9/11, regardless of whether progress is made in intra-Afghan peace talks or the Taliban reduces its attacks on Afghan security forces and citizens. He also stated that Washington would continue to assist Afghan security forces and support the peace process. President Biden said the U.S. military counterterrorism mission in Afghanistan is complete.

"We went there for two reasons, George. Two reasons," Biden said. "One, to get bin Laden, and two, to wipe out as best we could, and we did, the al Qaeda in Afghanistan. He also said that the Taliban were an unsophisticated guerrilla force that was in no position to defeat the well-trained and well-equipped 300,000 Afghan troops. He said nation-building never made any sense to him. He placed his bet on the resistance and resilience of the Afghan army.

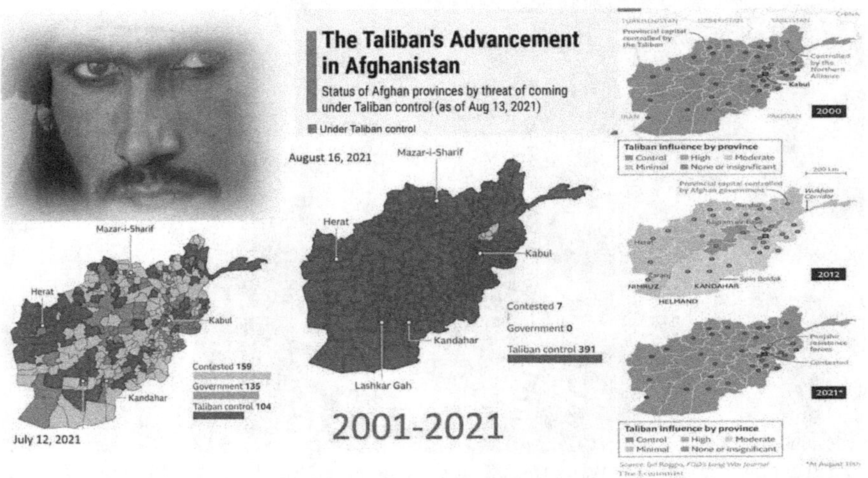

The Taliban advancement timeline. Mixed Media, African Views

As opposed to what the US press portrays, the Taliban army does not only consist of sluggish guerrilla forces. The Taliban has various units of world-class, well-trained forces. Badri 313 Battalion is one of the elite military units of the Taliban. The unit's name is associated with the Haqqani network, which is reportedly providing them with training. This unit was named after the Prophet Muhammad's army of 313 men at the Battle of Badr, an early Muslim military victory against the Quraysh on March 13, 624.

Elite Taliban units like the Badri 313 have been recognized as "critical in the takeover of Afghanistan. The Taliban's other elite unit is the Red Unit. These battalions are equipped with camouflage uniforms, combat helmets, body armor, night-vision goggles, M4 carbines, sidearms, and Humvees. It is unknown where they acquired the equipment or sourced it from Afghan military forces that surrendered around the country. The Taliban have acquired over $28 billion worth of sophisticated U.S. weapons.

According to experts, the equipment presented in the materials signals to the world that the Taliban were better prepared for war and even had the resources to conduct their raids than before. “But the Afghan Taliban has gone one step further.” They took weapons from the Americans, and the Afghan army says one of the Taliban is in the video. The Taliban are better prepared to take power this time around than in the past; they have the equipment, use social media, and have a prepared media strategy.

In 2003, Taliban officials proclaimed that they had regrouped themselves and were ready for war to expel U.S. forces from Afghanistan. In 2004, Mullah Omar announced an insurgency against America and its puppets to regain the sovereignty of our country. By 2009, a strong insurgency had coalesced, known as Operation Al Faath, the Arabic word for “victory” taken from the Koran, in the form of a guerrilla war.

In 2016, almost 20% of Afghanistan was under the control of the Taliban, with southernmost Helmand Province as their stronghold, as per Time Magazine. Towards the end of 2016, U.S. and International Resolute Support coalition commander General Nicholson stated that 10% of Afghanistan was in Taliban hands while another 26% was contested between the Afghan government and various insurgency groups.

In May 2020, reports emerged that Mullah Omar's son, Mullah Mohammad Yaqoob, became the leader of the Taliban after Quetta Shura members were infected with COVID-19. On May 1, 2021, the Taliban began a successful military offensive with allied militant groups against the Islamic Republic of Afghanistan. The offensive was concurrent with the withdrawal of U.S. and allied troops from the country, scheduled to be completed by September 11, 2021. It made significant advances during the first three months in the countryside and isolated urban centers and, on August 6, 2021, captured all provincial capitals of Afghanistan except Barak.

On August 15, 2021, Afghan President Ashraf Ghani fled Kabul before the Taliban entered the city, captured it, and took over the presidential palace. The nationwide militant victory happened in just 10 days. Just as swift as the US-led invasion that brought an end to Taliban rule in 2001. The Taliban faced little resistance as they overran Kabul's capital and took over the presidential palace hours after President Ghani fled the country.

Picture: The Taliban's 2nd coming

According to a former official, President Ghani, who had authored a book on how to fix a failed state, was astounded by how quickly the Taliban advanced on Kabul and managed to flee to the United Arab Emirates wearing only the clothes he was wearing. Ghani claimed in a video that he left the nation to avoid lynching by the Taliban. "If I had stayed in Afghanistan," he said, "the people of Afghanistan would have witnessed the president hanged once more." Ghani referred to the 1996 murder of former President Mohammad Najibullah, executed after the Taliban seized control of the country and took over Kabul. Mullah Omar and co-founder of the Taliban, Mullah Abdul Ghani Baradar, were reinstated. The country's name was changed to the "Islamic Emirate of Afghanistan," and the white flag with shahadah has been re-introduced.

The ousted president vowed to return to the country and denied allegations leveled by Mohammad Zahir Aghbar, the Afghan ambassador to Tajikistan, who said he stole $169 million from the country as he fled in exile. "Accusations were made in these days that money was transferred; these accusations are fully baseless," according to Ghani.

Photo: Ashraf Ghani, deposed

Picture: Mixed media composition, Ghani, and Karzai - future of Afghanistan

The U.S. Department of Defense identified the 13 members of the U.S. military who were among more than 100 people killed in a bombing attack near Kabul airport during the evacuation from Afghanistan on August 26, 2021. After the explosion, shooters opened fire into the crowd, and U.S. troops returned fire. The Islamic State of Iraq and the Levant—Khorasan Province (ISIL-KP) claimed responsibility for the attack.

ISIS-Khorasan, aka ISIS-K, is an affiliate of the Islamic State, or ISIS, which established a caliphate in Iraq and Syria, which was later destroyed by American forces. ISIS has geographical branches in Africa, the Middle East, and South Asia, and ISIS-K is its affiliate based in eastern Afghanistan near the Pakistan border.

Isis leader Abu Bakr al-Baghdadi: On 27 October 2019, Baghdadi killed himself and two children by detonating a suicide vest during the Barisha raid, conducted by the United States following approval from President Donald Trump, in Syria's northwestern Idlib Province

President Joe Biden met in solemn privacy with the families of the 13 U.S. troops killed in the attack as the remains of their loved ones returned to U.S. soil from Afghanistan. Biden and first lady Jill Biden also attended the "dignified transfer" of the fallen troops while at Dover Air Force Base, a military ritual of receiving the remains of those killed in foreign combat. President Biden vowed, "We will hunt you down and make you pay."

Memorial of Afghans civilian casualties

Thank you for the ultimate sacrifice. May peace be with relatives of the veterans.

On August 27, the United States launched an airstrike which the U.S. Central Command (CENTCOM) said was against three suspected ISIL- KP members in Nangarhar Province. On August 29, the U.S. conducted a second drone strike in Kabul, targeting a suspected vehicle carrying ISIL-KP members, but carrying an Afghan aid worker. Ten Afghans were killed in the drone strike, including seven children.

13 US Marines killed during US evacuation from Afghanistan.

List of the fallen 13 US Marines in Kabul on August 26:

1. Marine Corps Staff Sgt. Darin T. Hoover, 31, of Salt Lake City.
2. Marine Corps Sgt. Johanny Rosario Pichardo, 25, of Lawrence, Mass.
3. Marine Corps Sgt. Nicole L. Gee, 23, of Sacramento, Calif.
4. Marine Corps Cpl. Hunter Lopez, 22, of Indio, Calif.
5. Marine Corps Cpl. Daegan W. Page, 23, of Omaha.
6. Marine Corps Cpl. Humberto A. Sanchez, 22, of Logansport, Ind.
7. Marine Corps Lance Cpl. David L. Espinoza, 20, of Rio Bravo, Texas.
8. Marine Corps Lance Cpl. Jared M. Schmitz, 20, of St. Charles, Mo.
9. Marine Corps Lance Cpl. Rylee J. McCollum, 20, of Jackson, Wyo

10. Marine Corps Lance Cpl. Dylan Merola, 20, of Rancho Cucamonga, Ca
11. Marine Corps Lance Cpl. Kareem M. Nikoui, 20, of Norco, Calif.
12. Navy Hospital man Maxton W. Soviak, 22, of Berlin Heights, Ohio.
13. Army Staff Sgt. Ryan C. Knauss, 23, of Corryton, Tenn.

CHAPTER 21
Parallel Patterns

As the last plane carrying US expatriates was taking off from Kabul airport, Afghan civilians were desperate to get on board to escape the invading Taliban. The scene at the airport was chaotic, with people desperately waving their passports and pleading for a chance to escape. As the plane gained altitude, the heart-wrenching cries and desperate pleas of the Afghan civilians left behind echoed through the air. It was a stark reminder of the grim reality they now faced under Taliban rule, leaving many feeling a deep sense of despair and uncertainty for the future.

The U.S. combat mission in Afghanistan was America's longest war thus far. After two decades and the loss of tens of thousands of lives, many pundits view the legacy of the conflict as nothing more than an American foreign policy blunder. Several people worldwide had likened the evacuation of U.S. diplomats and military personnel when Taliban fighters entered the capital Kabul, Afghanistan, to Vietnam, when the U.S. Marines airlifted remaining Americans out of Saigon, Vietnam. Kabul fell to the Taliban forces on August 15, 2021, in Afghanistan, and Saigon fell to communist forces on April 30, 1975, in South Vietnam. The reactions of those who supported the U.S. in Vietnam were as disoriented and chaotic as they were in Afghanistan, even though the occurrences were almost 50 years apart. People still run Helter Skelter and react with panic in the same way when terror approaches. They feel abandoned.

Taliban fighters recreate famous Iwo Jima photographs to mock the US. This picture mockingly shows the Badri 313 Battalion, which has been deployed to patrol areas of Kabul, raising the white Taliban flag dressed in American tactical gear and camouflage, emulating the famous Iwo Jima photograph.

Mixed media US exit pattern

Picture: mixed media - Taliban Warlords takeover of presidential palace patterns (1994)

Picture: mixed media - Taliban Warlords takeover of presidential palace patterns (2021)

However, the outcomes of the conflicts and the messy exits are not the only similarities between the U.S. experiences in Afghanistan and Vietnam. The fundamental similarity to grasp is the fact that the conflict was between human rights and self-determination. It is American nature to promote human rights abroad. It does this under the premise of promoting democracy. Democracy is the right of people to govern themselves on their own terms and by their choice of leadership. Therefore, the U.S. promotes human rights to the detriment of the Taliban's wants and forms of self-determination.

The U.S. may continue to get it wrong if force is the only available option in its toolbox. The Taliban's violent method is also wrong. Here is the story of two wrongs, neither of which is right. The main problem is the acts of violence in war. Ironically, the Chinese philosopher Confucius puts it best: "It is only when mosquitoes land on your balls that you realize there is a way to solve problems without the use of force."

CHAPTER 22

The Price of Peace and the Cost of War

Private archive. Wale Idris at the United Nations: peace is underfunded, and war is overfunded. If peace is the goal, why not invest more in peace?

The cost of peace is complex and includes a range of initiative-taking and preventive actions intended to promote peaceful relations between countries and within populations. Nations frequently make significant investments in diplomacy to bring about peace, devoting a great deal of time and money to peacefully resolving disputes through negotiation. Another crucial factor is economic investment, as nations work to promote stability and prosperity in order to avert the circumstances that can spark conflict. Aid, trade agreements, and infrastructure initiatives that improve societies and lessen the chance of instability fall under this category.

Education and cultural exchange initiatives are also essential because they foster tolerance, understanding, and cross-border idea sharing, all of which help to keep miscommunication and mistrust from turning into hostilities. Furthermore, even peaceful countries need to commit a substantial amount of financial and human resources to maintain a certain degree of military readiness as a deterrent against future aggressors. To avoid internal strife and preserve social harmony, fair and just social policies must also be put in place.

Conversely, the consequences of conflict are profound and widespread. Human lives are lost at the highest and most painful cost; troops and civilians endure most of this. This loss has an impact on the families left behind as well as the communities that experience these human losses. Economically speaking, war depletes national coffers since it shatters important infrastructure, upends international markets, and takes funds away from necessities, all of which cause long-term problems for the economy and suffering for the populace.

Social displacement is a result of war; millions of people are frequently compelled to escape their homes, creating a refugee and internally displaced population. Social disintegration and chronic trauma brought on by this dislocation can linger for generations. Another major worry is the harm that war does to the environment since it can destroy ecosystems, deplete natural resources, and destroy entire landscapes. Finally, a war can have a significant effect on international relations by straining or severing diplomatic ties, which can have a long-term negative influence on trade and collaboration between nations. This can lead to economic decline and hinder global progress.

Rebuilding trust between nations and reaching full recovery might take decades or even generations. The costs of war are severe and long-lasting, but the price of peace necessitates ongoing attention and effort. Recognizing that the long-term effects of war outweigh the immediate costs of maintaining peace, it is crucial for nations and their leaders to carefully consider these factors when handling disputes. By doing so, they can make informed decisions that promote stability and prosperity for all involved parties.

Violence is a complex behavior that can be influenced by numerous factors, including, but not limited to, social, economic, political, and environmental conditions. It is shaped by individual experiences, education, cultural norms, the presence, or absence of the rule of law, and opportunities for peaceful conflict resolution. Afghanistan has a long history of conflict, which has undoubtedly affected its people. However, it is important to recognize that Afghan society, like any other, consists of a wide variety of individuals with differing personalities, beliefs, and behaviors. One must not make assumptions or generalize about the entire Afghan society based on the history of conflict alone. Few Afghans have been able to demonstrate that violence can be prevented and mitigated through comprehensive strategies that address its root causes through efforts to promote peacebuilding and conflict resolution. Mahatma Gandhi was able to use the principle of satyagraha, a policy of passive political resistance, to defeat colonial British rule in India. And, right next to him, as friend and ally practicing the same principle, was an Afghan by the name of Bacha Khan.

Mixed media: Abdul Ghaffār Khān and Mahatma Gandhi

Abdul Ghaffar Khān, who lived from February 6, 1890, to January 20, 1988, was a political and spiritual leader who was well-known for his peaceful resistance to British colonial control in India. He was also referred to as Bāchā Khān, or “King of Chiefs,” and was honorably addressed as Fakhr-e-Afghan, or “Pride of Afghans.” Bacha Khan had fought for decades for the growth of education and the rights of the people, collaborating with his great friend and fellow agitator, the Hindu Mohandas Gandhi. They collaborated to promote Hindu- Muslim harmony in the Indian subcontinent and held similar pacifist views. When the Indian National Congress accepted the partition plan in 1947 without consulting the Khudai Khidmatgar, a group called Ghaffār betrayed them, telling the Congress leaders, “You have thrown us to the wolves.”

Abdul Ghaffār Khān, Nehru, Mahatma Gandhi

Bacha Khan was one of the most incarcerated political pacifists, without charge. He was imprisoned several times between 1929 and 1988. In 1962, Bacha Khan was named the "Amnesty International Prisoner of the Year." Amnesty's statement about him said, "His example symbolizes the suffering of upward of a million people all over the world who are prisoners of conscience." He was nominated for the Nobel Peace Prize in 1984. His final major political challenge was against the Kalabagh dam project. Fearing that the project would damage the Peshawar valley, his hostility to it would eventually lead to the project being shelved after his death. He visited India and participated in the centennial celebrations of the Indian National Congress in 1985; he was awarded the Jawaharlal Nehru Award for International Understanding in 1967 and later the Bharat Ratna, India's highest civilian award, in 1987.

Bacha Khan died in Peshawar under house arrest in 1988 from complications of a stroke and was buried in his house in Jalalabad, Afghanistan. Over 200,000 mourners attended his funeral, including Afghan President Mohammad Najibullah. The then Indian Prime Minister Rajiv Gandhi went to Peshawar to pay his tributes to Bacha Khan, despite General Zia ul-Haq attempting to stall his attendance, citing security reasons. Additionally, the Indian government declared five days of mourning in his honor. His funeral procession was described as a caravan of peace, carrying a message of love from Pashtuns east of the Khyber to those on the west, marching through the historic Khyber Pass from Peshawar to Jalalabad. Bacha Khan planned this symbolic march to demonstrate his dream of Pashtun unification affirmatively and help that dream live on after his death. A cease-fire was announced in the Afghan Civil War to allow the funeral to take place.

Afghanistan has had several leaders who have been known for their efforts toward peace and stability at various points in its history. Here are a few more examples:

King Amanullah Khan (1919-1929): He was a reformist and a ruler who worked towards modernizing Afghanistan. After gaining independence from British influence, he attempted to implement social and educational reforms to bring peace and modernity to the country. His efforts, however, faced resistance from conservative factions, which eventually led to his abdication.

Ahmad Shah Massoud (1953-2001): Often referred to as the “Lion of Panjshir,” Massoud was a military leader renowned for his resistance against the Soviet invasion in the 1980s and later against the Taliban regime. He advocated for a political solution to Afghanistan's conflicts and worked towards a vision of a peaceful and united Afghanistan. Al-Qaeda assassinated Massoud just days before the September 11 attacks, and he is still celebrated for his leadership and vision for peace.

Hamid Karzai (2001-2014): As the first democratically elected president of Afghanistan following the fall of the Taliban, Karzai worked to bring various factions together and to promote national unity. His tenure included efforts to rebuild the country, establish democratic institutions, and improve relations with neighboring countries and the international community. Despite challenges and controversies during his presidency, his leadership focused on stabilization and reconstruction.

Abdul Sattar Sirat: An Afghan politician and Islamic scholar, Sirat has been involved in various peace processes, including the Bonn Agreement in 2001. He has held positions as Minister of Justice and has been a proponent of democratic principles and human rights in Afghanistan. These leaders, among others, have shown that there are individuals in Afghan history who have strived for peace and stability, often in the face of great adversity. It is essential to acknowledge the efforts of such leaders in working towards a peaceful future for Afghanistan.

The cost of war is too high for any nation to bear. Approximately 2,500 American service members have been killed in Afghanistan, according to Linda Bilmes of Harvard University's Kennedy School and the Brown University Costs of War project, as reported by the Associated Press. An additional 4,000 U.S. contractors also lost their lives. More than 20,000 soldiers were wounded in the conflict, many of whom now live with permanent disabilities. These figures did not compare to the 66,000 Afghan national military lives lost or the 50,000 Afghan civilians.

A further 52,000 Taliban and other opposition fighters were also reported to have been killed. Washington has spent approximately $2.3 trillion on the war, according to public reports. The question is, why? Is this worth it? This question is important because the U.S. is not some random, disorderly country. There is always a legitimate reason behind its action; though not all may agree with it, the truth is worth knowing.

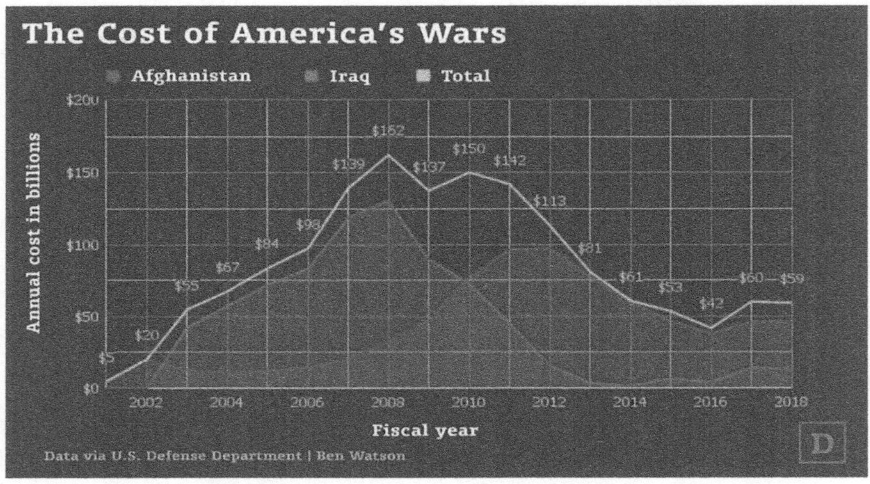

Chart: the cost of the American war in Iraq and Afghanistan

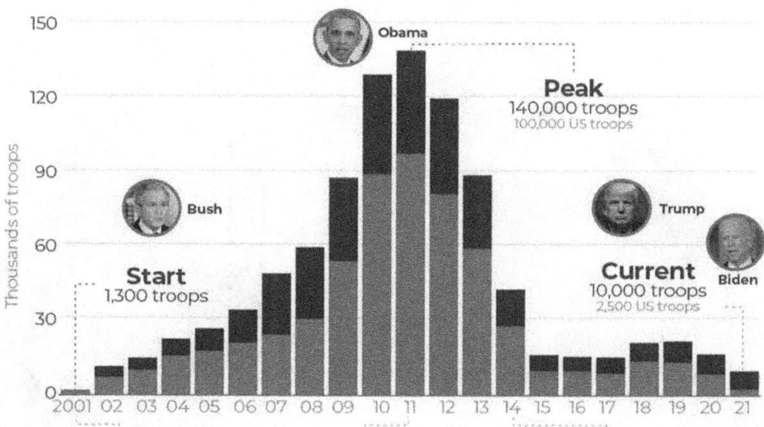

Chart: the cost of the Afghan US war under each president.

After 20 years and trillions of dollars gushing into the Afghanistan war and rebuilding effort, the private military contractors have profited significantly from the war. That is, on aggregate, an investment of $10,000 in America's top five defense contractors - stocks on September 18, 2001—the day President George W. Bush signed the Authorization for Military Force in response to the 9/11 terrorist attacks—and reinvested all dividends would now be worth $97,295. That is, defense stocks outperformed the stock market overall by 58 percent during the Afghanistan War.

Cost of the Afghan war to the US

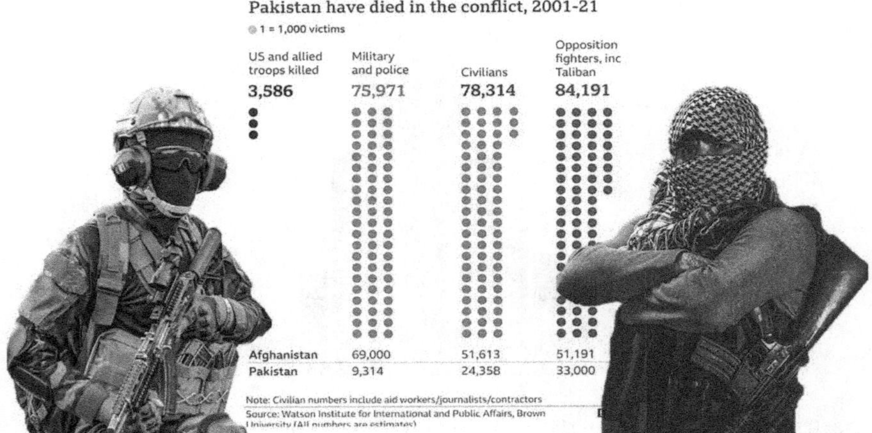

Casualties of the Afghan war distributed across countries: on the left, the Afghan army in US weaponry, and the Taliban on the right. All the US-funded weaponry is now in the hands of the Taliban. It would not matter now who had funded the Taliban war in the first place. The Taliban are further emboldened.

Afghanistan is a swamp for interventionists, according to the Taliban during an interview with CGTN.

A word is enough for the wise: Canada's former Chief of the Defence Staff, Rick Hillier, under whom Fraser served, recalled that a Taliban commander had assessed the massive firepower the West had assembled in Afghanistan, and even as he saw his forces lose battle after battle, he remained unmoved. "You have the watches," the Taliban commander told Hillier, "but we have the time." It haunts. The Taliban were prepared to wait out the West and take the losses. It was prophetic.

The potential for convincing the Taliban to improve the treatment of women in Afghanistan is a complex issue that hinges on a combination of international pressure, internal advocacy, and the potential for reinterpretation of religious texts. The international community can leverage diplomatic and economic tools, such as sanctions and conditional aid, to push for adherence to international human rights norms. Simultaneously, the courage of Afghan women and civil society groups advocating for equality from within the country is critical to effecting change. Influential Islamic scholars may also play a role in promoting progressive interpretations of Islamic law that support women's rights. The Taliban's desire for political legitimacy and the benefits that come with it, such as international recognition and aid, could provide incentives for them to alter their stance on women's issues. Moreover, educational initiatives and cultural exchanges could gradually shift perspectives. However, achieving such change is incredibly challenging given the Taliban's strict and conservative ideology, which historically has led to significant restrictions on women. While the international community continues its vigilance and advocacy, the success of these efforts remains uncertain and reliant on the Taliban's willingness to engage in meaningful reform.

The human cost of war

At the first high-level conference on Afghanistan since the Taliban re- took power, Western governments, big traditional donors, and others pledged more than $1.2 billion in emergency funds that the United Nations sought to cover costs through the end of the year to protect Afghans from a looming humanitarian disaster.

Chapter 23

The TAPI Pipeline project

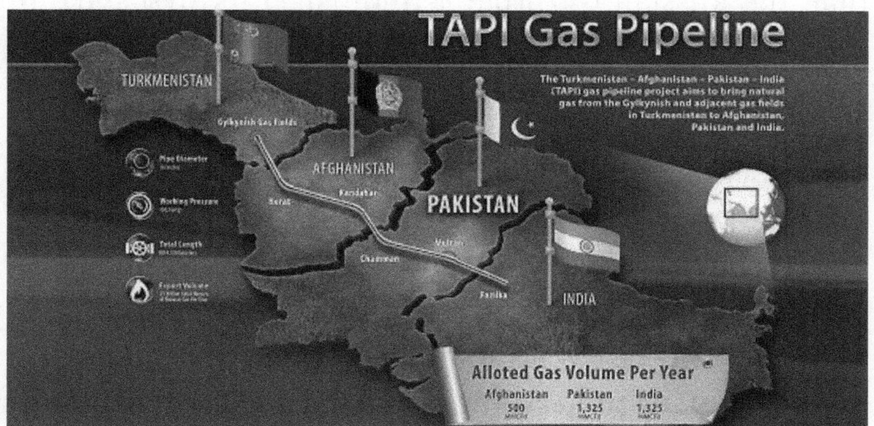

TAPI Pipeline project illustration

There are theories that the actual motive for the United States-led Western invasion of Afghanistan in 2001 was Afghanistan's importance as a conduit for oil pipelines to its neighboring countries and the Taliban's hindrance. The leading theory was based on the assessment that the Turkmenistan pipeline's purpose was to bypass Russian and Iranian territories and break the Russian and Iranian collective monopoly on regional energy supplies. The pipeline project started in 1995 between the governments of Turkmenistan and Pakistan, involving the U.S. company Unocal in conjunction with the Saudi oil company Delta, forming the Central Asia Gas Pipeline, Ltd. (CentGas) consortium for the construction in 1997, outbidding Argentinian competitor Bridas Corporation. The U.S. ambassador to Pakistan, Robert Oakley, left his post and was hired by CentGas in 1997. Since the pipeline was to pass through Afghanistan, it was inevitable to work with the Taliban. In January 1998, the Taliban authorized the CentGas project to proceed in Afghanistan. Shortly after that, the Russian Gazprom relinquished its 10% stake in the project. There are speculations on why Gazprom was divested, but the U.S. Unocal withdrawal was unequivocal.

The attack caused the California-based Unocal Corporation to withdraw from the consortium on December 8, 1998. Unocal had the largest share in the CentGas consortium, at 54 percent. In 1997, the American company even arranged travel to Texas for a senior Taliban delegation for negotiations, but the pipeline project was dismissed due to this political and security instability in 2001. By 2012, Turkmenistan's gas export ambitions and advocacy for expanded regional connectivity, trade, and development aided by the Afghan peace agreement to help sustain peace had progressed. The same year, Turkmenistan, Afghanistan, Pakistan, and India (TAPI) formally agreed to develop the transnational pipeline that supplies approximately 30 billion cubic meters per year of Turkmen natural gas to India.

Turkmengaz (Turkmenistan), Afghan Gas Enterprise (Afghanistan), Interstate Gas Service (Pakistan), and GAIL (India) established the particular purpose consortium company, TPCL, in November 2014 to develop the $7.5 billion project. The Taliban were never deterred from the project, as they could see that it would contribute to the prosperity and development of Afghanistan and pledge support across Afghanistan, providing reassurance for the viability of the project. Afghanistan would earn a total of $400 million per year from a "transit" fee. This new arrangement of the pipeline project provided the alternative argument that the theoretical pipeline was not a significant reason for the invasion. Instead, it suggested that the invasion's motivation was a desire to overthrow the Taliban regime and end the threat they posed to international security. The pipeline, though a beneficial addition, was merely a byproduct of the larger objective. As the project progressed, it became evident that the international community was more focused on stabilizing Afghanistan and empowering its people than solely exploiting its resources. This realization further diminished the notion that the pipeline was the primary motivation behind the invasion.

The Taliban have been very keen on the TAPI project. It is one of the key bases for the peace agreement.

China participates in the TAPI (Turkmenistan, Afghanistan, Pakistan, and India). The project is funded by the Asian Development Bank and the Islamic Development Bank. Traditionally, the natural gas exports from Turkmenistan have been to China. China is a beneficiary of ending the war in Afghanistan. America's withdrawal has opened a new opportunity for China to increase its influence in Afghanistan. China has assumed an increased responsibility in maintaining regional stability, preventing terrorism and violent extremism from destabilizing the region.

CHAPTER 24
Escalation of Terror

US Embassy Bombing in East Africa 1998

In hindsight, It would appear that the attack on the U.S. embassies in the two largest East African towns of Dar es Salaam, Tanzania, and INairobi, Kenya, on August 7, 1998, provides the answers. Eight years to the day after U.S. soldiers were dispatched to Saudi Arabia in the wake of Iraq's invasion of Kuwait, those countries were targeted in bomber assaults. According to Islamic law, Osama bin Laden, the leader of Al Qaeda, considered the presence of US military in Saudi Arabia, home to the holy cities of Mecca and Medina, to be haram, or forbidden. The symbolic retribution gesture predicted an older type of terrorism. In an effort to spread democracy and counteract the spread of communism, the United States government has a lengthy history of invading native cultures and developing nations. Because of this background, a new form of terrorism, state-sponsored terrorism, emerged. State-sponsored terrorism, a product of this background, has since further destabilized countries and perpetuated vicious cycles of violence.

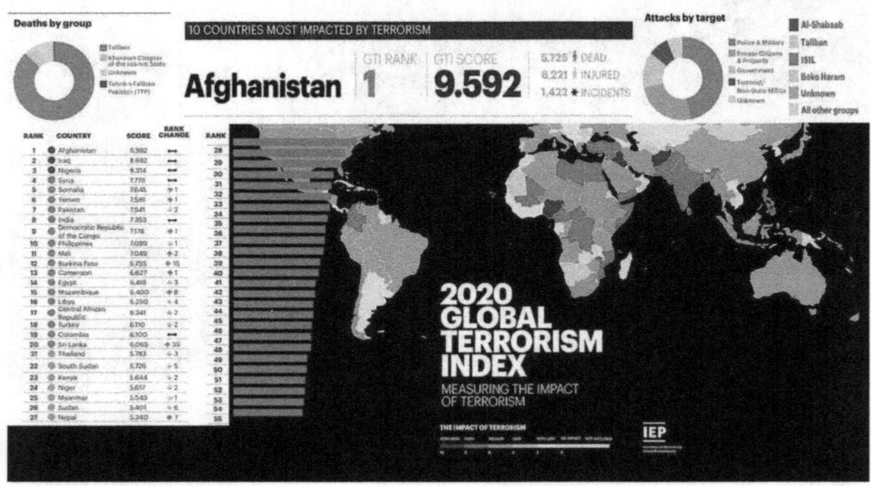

Global terrorism index

It was previously plane hijacking, taking hostages, kidnappings, car bombings, and assassinations, but never mass destruction or government building attacks. Then they moved to flight explosions, and in 1993, the first jihadist attack was carried out on February 26, 1993, at the World Trade Center in New York City. A group of terrorists planned the attack with ties to al-Qaeda. Terrorism is not only among religious fanatics. It can also come from political fanatics and homegrown ideological conspirators who strongly believe in vengeance or retribution to justify the authority's perceived hypocrisy or wrongdoings.

Oklahoma City bombing that killed 168 in 1995.

Timothy James McVeigh (April 23, 1968 – June 11, 2001) was an American domestic terrorist responsible for the 1995 Oklahoma City bombing that killed 168 people, 19 of whom were children, injured more than 680 others, and destroyed one-third of the Alfred P. Murrah Federal Building. The bombing was the deadliest act of terrorism in the United States before the September 11 attacks. It remains one of the deadliest acts of domestic terrorism in U.S. history. McVeigh sought revenge against the federal government for the 1993 Waco siege that ended in the deaths of 76 members of Christian Religious Branch Davidians, including 25 children, two pregnant women, and David Koresh, the leader of the group, and for the 1992 Ruby Ridge incident and American foreign policy. He hoped to inspire a revolution against the federal government and defended the bombing as a legitimate tactic against what he saw as a tyrannical government. 10 years before the Alfred P. Murrah Federal Building bombing, the Philadelphia Police Department bombed several housing blocks on the evening of May 13, 1985.

Waco siege that ended in the deaths of 76 members of Christian Religious Branch Davidians, including 25 children

The 1985 Philadelphia bombing by the police changed the city forever.

A dozen people were killed, including five children and the founder of the organization. Sixty-one homes were destroyed, and more than 250 citizens were left homeless. Before the Philadelphia incident, there had been several massacres of native Americans and African Americans in the United States when the U.S. government had played an integral or primary role. This includes U.S. direct or indirect involvement in countries such as Yemen, Libya, DRC, Haiti, Colombia, Nicaragua, Grenada, Cuba, Panama, Somalia, Angola, and others. In 1997, Osama bin Laden accused the United States of hypocrisy for not labeling the bombing of Hiroshima as terrorism. This challenge remains the primary reason for distrust of the American government.

CHAPTER 25

Trials & Terror

Most of the operatives on the most wanted list were apprehended during the Obama regime

The U.S. government segregates terrorism cases into two categories: domestic and international. However, questions remain: "Is the war a war against al-Qaida and the Taliban in Afghanistan? Or is it a war against terrorism broadly? Is it a war against al-Qaida and anything that shares al-Qaida's ideology, any organization that splits off from al-Qaida?" One of the fraught questions of the past 20 years has been whether the war on terrorism extends beyond the borders of Afghanistan. Since the 9/11 attacks, the entire U.S. Department of Justice has prosecuted 1,000 terrorist cases. More than 600 defendants have pleaded guilty to charges, while the courts found about 200 guilty at trial. Only a handful of detainees have been acquitted or seen their cases dropped or dismissed within a single-digit range. Guantánamo Bay detention camp, also called Gitmo, is the U.S. detention facility on the Guantánamo Bay Naval Base in Cuba, set up to hold enemy combatants' captives from Afghanistan, Iraq, and elsewhere within the context of the War on Terror.

Human Rights Watch brought the news of human rights abuses and humiliation of detainees in the U.S. military prison in Abu Ghraib, Iraq, to the public in April 2004. Former Army Reserve soldier Lynndie England was convicted for posing with a hooded and sexually humiliated Iraqi prisoner. The Central Intelligence Agency allegedly took—and still has—naked photographs of detained terrorism suspects before sending them to foreign partners. The facility became the focus of worldwide controversy over alleged violations of the legal rights of detainees under the Geneva Conventions and accusations of torture or abusive treatment of detainees by U.S. authorities.

Human Rights abuses in the U.S. Prison facilities

The administration of Republican President George W. Bush maintained that it was neither obliged to grant basic constitutional protections to the prisoners since the base was outside U.S. territory nor required to observe the Geneva Conventions regarding the treatment of prisoners of war and civilians during wartime, as the conventions did not apply to "unlawful enemy combatants." In 2006, the U.S. Supreme Court declared that the military commission system that was to be used to try selected prisoners held at Guantánamo violated the Geneva Conventions and the Uniform Code of Military Justice. The Supreme Court ruling led to significant changes in the treatment and legal rights granted to detainees at Guantánamo.

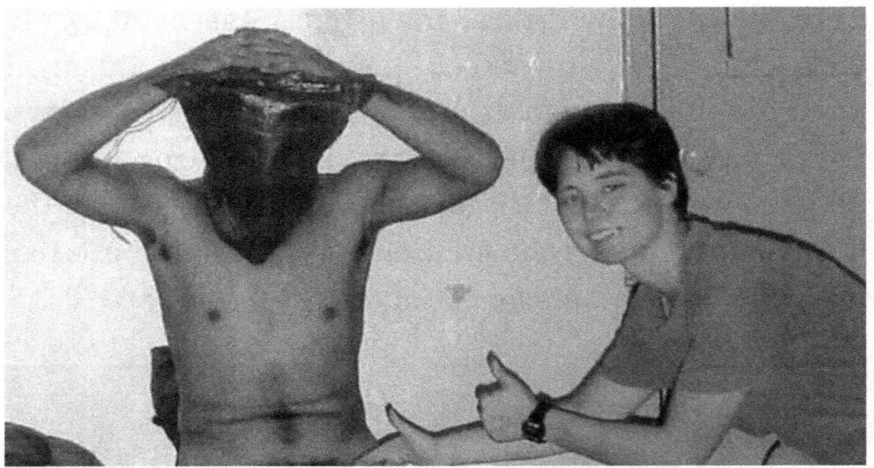

US prisoner abuses

The Military Commission Act, which also denied federal courts the authority to hear habeas corpus petitions on behalf of foreign detainees, restored the legality of the commissions in 2006. In 2008, however, the court overturned the latter provision of the law by ruling (in Boumediene v. Bush) that foreign detainees did have the right to challenge their detentions in the federal courts. Despite the court's decision, several prisoners who had been cleared for release in other countries or transferred to their home countries continued to be detained, either because no country would accept them or because their home countries were deemed too volatile to guarantee their secure imprisonment.

Experts have explained that the detainees are not considered regular prisoners of war. Instead, they are classified as unlawful combatants or alien, unprivileged enemy belligerents. "The reason they're unlawful combatants is that they don't follow the rules of combat under the international rule of war," Powers told Insider. "So, they're not entitled to the rights of prisoners of war." The term forever prisoners refer to detainees who have not been charged and are never expected to face trial but that the government deems too dangerous to release. A story of one of the detainees' sagas inspired a book and a movie titled The Mauritanian, which explores the torture and abuse of former prisoners at Guantanamo Bay.

Picture below: Scene from the Mauritanian

The camp was repeatedly condemned by international human rights and humanitarian organizations—including Amnesty International, Human Rights Watch, and the International Committee of the Red Cross—as well as by the European Union and the Organization of American States (OAS) for alleged human rights violations, including the use of various forms of torture during interrogations. In response to such criticism, the Bush administration insisted that detainees were well cared for and that none of the "enhanced interrogation techniques" employed on some prisoners were torturous. They argued that these techniques were necessary for national security.

Family members at the US embassy bombing victim memorial.

The U.S. Supreme Court rules that victims of the bombings and their family members are entitled to $4.3 billion in punitive damages, of a total of $10.2 billion in damages previously awarded against Sudan, for assisting the al Qaeda operatives. The United States has received the $335 million settlement from Sudan to be paid out to victims and families of individuals impacted by the 1998 bombings at the U.S. embassies in Tanzania and Kenya, the 2000 attack on the USS Cole, and the murder of a USAID employee in Khartoum. Timothy McVeigh was executed by lethal injection on June 11, 2001, at the Federal Correctional Complex in Terre Haute, Indiana.

In 2011, a video surfaced showing US Marines peeing on the bodies of deceased Taliban insurgents in Afghanistan. This act prompted outrage and condemnation from a variety of sources, both domestically and globally. The act was strongly condemned for its disrespect for the deceased, violation of war laws, and potential harm to the reputation of the United States military. The incident was investigated by the US Department of Defense, and the individuals implicated were disciplined. The episode damaged relations between the United States and Afghanistan and heightened regional tensions.

Such actions harmed the prestige of the United States military and its mission in Afghanistan. Such incidents can damage efforts to capture the hearts and minds of the local populace as well as contribute to an anti-American attitude. Furthermore, extreme groups utilized it as propaganda to recruit members and support their cause. It should be noted that the conduct of a few individuals does not represent the entire United States military or its mission in Afghanistan. The incident led to greater efforts within the military to enhance training on the laws of war, ethics, and cultural awareness in order to prevent similar incidents in the future.

Osama bin Laden consistently dwelt on the need for violent jihad to right what he believed were injustices against Muslims perpetrated by the United States and sometimes by other non-Muslim states. He also called for the elimination of Israel and called upon the United States to withdraw all its civilians and military personnel from the Middle East and every Islamic country. Bin Laden believed that killing Americans was justified because he claimed that Islamic law allows believers to attack invaders even when the enemy uses human shields. He also believed that since the United States is a democracy, all citizens bear responsibility for its government's actions, and civilians are fair targets. All these sentiments uncovered and brought to American attention resulted in the United States Federal Bureau of Investigation placing bin Laden on its top Ten Most Wanted list. After 9/11, Mullah Omar, the Taliban's leader, announced that bin Laden would be provided a haven in Afghanistan with the Taliban's support. After the invasion, the campaign to rid the Taliban of power and exterminate AlQaeda leaders, including Osama bin Laden, has been successful.

CHAPTER 26
The Unwinnable War

President Joe Biden urges calm and defends his decision to withdraw the US troops in Afghanistan.

After the U.S. withdrawal from Afghanistan, the Biden administration addressed critics and framed ending the conflict as a decision Biden made after concluding it was an "unwinnable war" and one that "does not have a military solution." President Biden also said, "How many more? How many more thousands of American daughters and sons are you willing to risk?" Biden added, "To those calling for the United States to extend the military operation, I will not send another generation of Americans to war in Afghanistan with no reasonable expectation of achieving a different outcome."

Afghanistan is a beautiful country. Afghans cherish their heritage, which gives them an extremely healthy sense of pride. The Afghans would die for their land, which could be why the Taliban are so tenacious and al-Qaeda can efficiently recruit. The people have sacrificed so much blood in the name of Islam. The Taliban has insisted on Sharia and has imposed strict laws at the expense of women's rights. Since women's rights are human rights, this is one of the critical issues that make this war so complicated and reveals a side of the United States that is, indeed, noble. The U.S. pullout was strategic, timely, decisive, and efficient, regardless of the circumstances. However, the U.S. and its allies knew that it would have had to take down Pakistan, Syria, Iraq, Tajikistan, Uzbekistan, and Turkmenistan to destroy the Taliban and other Islamic jihadist groups. There is a reckoning that violence or force is not tenable. Causalities would be devastating and unending. The war would still not be decisive. Violence cannot win the war against terrorists. Therefore, Biden's decision was not dictatorial or unilateral.

Americans are fatigued from the war in Afghanistan. Biden had to make a competent bet. The U.S. pullout was, therefore, a relief.

CHAPTER 27

The Taliban's Ploy

Return of the Taliban

The Taliban moved quickly to avoid a power vacuum as the withdrawal of American forces urgently became a mission to ensure a safe evacuation. Nevertheless, the Taliban rule, it seems, is back in Afghanistan after 20 years. For the Taliban, the goal of self- determination has been achieved. With the withdrawal of the American army from Kabul, the Taliban quickly acquired administrative districts and provincial hubs, took the Afghan capital, Kabul, and took the country's reins of power that they had lost 20 years before. The government quickly folded, with President Ashraf Ghani and other vital officials fleeing for safety abroad.

In 1996, when the Taliban captured power in Afghanistan, except for Saudi Arabia, the UAE, and Pakistan, no country had recognized them. Today, major powers are willing to establish relations with the Taliban. Arab countries, organizations, and personalities have expressed a mixture of reactions over the takeover of the Central Asian country, with some sending congratulatory messages and others making calls for maintaining stability and security in the country.

Peace talk Meeting with Taliban in Moscow: The Russians, the Chinese, the American, the Afghan Government, and the Taliban met on several occasions.

Qatar's Foreign Minister, Mohammed bin Abdul Rahman Al Thani, told a press conference during his visit to Jordan that Doha seeks a peaceful transfer of power in Afghanistan that paves the way for a comprehensive political solution. The Saudi Foreign Ministry said that it stands with the Afghan people and the choices they made on their own without interference. Jordan's Foreign Minister, Ayman Safadi, called on the Taliban to prioritize security and stability to avert further chaos. The Kuwaiti Foreign Ministry said it was concerned by the developments in Afghanistan and urged all Afghan parties to exercise "utmost restraint to prevent bloodshed" and ensure "full protection of civilians and the safe exit of stranded diplomats and foreign nationals." Calls for stability and security in Afghanistan were also reiterated by the United Arab Emirates (UAE), with the country's foreign ministry expressing hope that all Afghan parties will "urgently" make concerted efforts towards that end.

Arab reactions vary on Taliban takeover in Afghanistan at the meeting in Doha.

The Grand Mufti of Oman, Sheikh Ahmed bin Hamad Al-Khalili, congratulated the Afghan people for what he considered a "clear conquest and victory over the aggressor invaders" and urged all Afghans to unite and ensure "that tolerance and harmony prevail among them." The Palestinian Presidency said the events in Afghanistan prove that external protection "does not bring security to any country" and called on Israel to "absorb the lesson." Hamas political chief Ismail Haniyeh made a phone call with Mullah Abdul- Ghani Baradar, head of the Taliban's political bureau, to congratulate him on "the end of the American occupation of Afghanistan," saying their demise in Afghanistan is a 'prelude to the demise of the Israeli occupation of Palestine." Hezbollah leader Hassan Nasrallah said the scene of the US troop withdrawal from Afghanistan was "very big," in which Washington failed and was "defeated and humiliated." For his part, Muhammad al-Hamdaoui, the head of external relations for the Justice and Development Party, Morocco's largest party, said his party was following developments in Afghanistan and supporting "the Afghan people's independence from all foreign interference." He urged the Afghans to enter their new phase by ensuring respect for rights and freedoms and establishing a just state without violence, exclusion, or discrimination. Pakistan's Prime Minister Imran Khan said Afghans had "broken the shackles of slavery" while describing the Taliban's conquest of Kabul. Anwar Gargash, the diplomatic adviser to UAE President Sheikh Khalifa bin Zayed Al Nahyan, said that recent announcements by the Taliban had been "encouraging" regarding the general amnesty offered by the group's assurances of welcoming the role of women. America's withdrawal is also well received as a new opportunity to reestablish a political system based on Sharia, which will further legitimize their Islamic republic.

The al-Qaeda-linked news agency, the Global Islamic Media Front, released a statement of congratulations that said:

"May Allah grant the mujahideen in Somalia, the African Sahel, Yemen, Syria, Pakistan, the Indian subcontinent, and everywhere the same victory." Hay'at Tahrir al-Sham, the dominant faction in the insurgent-held regions of Syria's Idlib province, was also impressed, describing the Taliban's victory as an example of steadfastness in the face of foreign occupation. The Islamic State was not so positive. The Americans have struck a deal with the Taliban, and it has been agreed upon that the terrorists of yesteryears would not harm US interests. It is one of the reasons that the more militant organization, ISIS, is angry and feeling betrayed. ISIS is convinced that the Taliban has captured power with the connivance of the Americans. The recent suicide attack by the IS Khorasan at the Kabul airport in which more than a hundred have been killed indicated that discord between the two.

Representatives of Russia, China, the United States, and Pakistan announced opposition to restoring the Islamic Emirate in Afghanistan and urged the Taliban not to announce their Spring Offensive in March 2020. This was revealed in a joint statement issued after a regular meeting of the extended "Troika." The extended "Troika" comprises Russia, China, the USA, and Pakistan, focused on progressing the intra-Afghan process to reach a negotiated settlement and permanent and comprehensive ceasefire. The event was attended by representatives of the Afghan government, Afghanistan's High Council for National Reconciliation, prominent Afghan political figures, and representatives of the Taliban movement. Qatar and Turkey attended the event as guests of honor, according to the Russian Foreign Ministry.

Taliban holding its first press conference in Kabul.

UN Geneva

The four states participating in the extended 'Troika' have agreed on a 10-point joint statement that acknowledges the widespread and sincere demand of the Afghan people for lasting and just peace and an end to the war. The extended Troika also agreed that sustainable peace could only be achieved through a negotiated political settlement.

> *"As stated in UNSC Resolution 2513 (2020), we do not support the restoration of the Islamic Emirate, and we call on the Government of the Islamic Republic and the High Council for National Reconciliation to engage openly with their Taliban counterparts regarding a negotiated settlement,"-according to the joint statement.*

They strongly advocated a durable and just political resolution that would result in the formation of an independent, sovereign, unified, peaceful, democratic, and self-sufficient Afghanistan, free of terrorism and an illicit drug industry, which contributes to the creation of pull factors for the voluntary, sustainable, and expeditious return of Afghan refugees, stability, and global security.

They also called on all Afghans, including the government of the Islamic Republic and the Taliban, to ensure that terrorist groups and individuals do not use Afghan soil to threaten the security of any other country. "We reaffirm that any peace agreement must include protections for the rights of all Afghans, including women, men, children, victims of war, and minorities, and should respond to the strong desire of all Afghans for economic, social, and political development, including the rule of law," according to the statement. The four countries encouraged all concerned countries to support the Afghan people and contribute to lasting peace in the interest of all. "We reaffirm our commitment to mobilize international political and economic support for a post-political settlement in Afghanistan."

However, Taliban leader Mullah Baradar reaffirmed that the Taliban could only declare a ceasefire after implementing the Islamic system. He said the Taliban are committed to the Doha agreement, adding that if everything had been done in the way agreed upon in the Doha agreement, the internal issue of Afghanistan would have been resolved. Adding that durable peace would have been achieved, Afghans would have started an everyday life if the country had established the Islamic system. Shaheen said they aim to achieve an "Islamic government" that represents all Afghans.

Taliban supporters hold mock U.S. funeral as troops leave Afghanistan.

The Taliban invaded Kabul and toppled the Afghan government despite all the rhetoric and promises of peace. They could not prevent the terrorist attack that killed 100 people at the airport during the evacuation. The Taliban are preparing for international cooperation. Zabihullah

Mujahid, the Taliban's spokesperson, mentioned during a press conference held on August 17, 2021, that" we are going to allow women to work and study under the limits of Islam." "As for women, Islam dictates." The Taliban promised no harm would come to Afghans who worked with allied forces. They would not interrogate the Afghans; "they are free and guaranteed complete amnesty; they are our assets." The Taliban urged Muslim clergy to tell their congregants to remain in the country and counter "negative propaganda" on Thursday and urged Afghans to go back to work. The U.N. human rights chief, Michelle Bachelet, warned of a "new and perilous phase" for Afghanistan as she upbraided the Taliban for a disconnect between their words and actions.

Bachelet cited multiple allegations of Taliban forces conducting house-to-house searches looking for specific officials in the previous government and people who cooperated with U.S. forces and companies. She said that women had been progressively excluded from the public, contradicting Taliban assertions to respect women's rights. Primary among the Taliban's objectives must be to discipline their fighters, many of whom had only known about wars and had no idea about civility. International recognition is secondary, and they could get that at the United Nations with a majority vote at the UNGA, giving the probable backings of Muslim countries and others who resent foreign occupation. In any case, there would be individual countries that could abstain or hold out on recognizing the Taliban.

Afghans women judges took their oath of office in the presence of Afghan President Mohammad Ashraf Ghani: Great achievement.

The Taliban of today are a lot smarter. They pulled off a lousy agreement against the U.S. and the Afghan government. The Taliban do not respect the opinions of the international community. They just want their money, and they think they can get it without obeying the rules. They won on the technicality of self-determination. However, it was clear that they forced themselves on Afghanistan and its people, and they remain a terror to the Afghan people. The Afghan people have offered the Taliban to form a legitimate political party and run for election. In fact, the former president Ghani even offered to help the Taliban establish political office, but they refused the offer.

Only the Afghan people can justly prosecute the Taliban. Their Achilles heel is the women. The current condition makes both repression and resistance inevitable, and it is not clear if the Taliban are up to the task given the level of sophisticated intelligence and tradeoff required to manage this challenge.

CHAPTER 28

The Intersectionality of Culture, Politics, Religion, and Gender in Afghanistan

Sharia: the scale of justice and mercy under the Taliban

Islamic law and sharia law are sometimes used interchangeably, they are conceptually distinct. Sharia denotes the ideal of God's law and as such is considered perfect, while Islamic law involves different human constructs of God's law and so may be fallible. Islamic law was considered the supreme law of the Islamic Republic of Afghanistan while Sharia is the legal code of the current Islamic Emirate of Afghanistan. It is impossible to govern Afghanistan without Islam. Whether or not to govern by Islam has never been the issue with Afghanistan. The constitution of Afghanistan stated that "no law shall contravene the tenets and provisions of the holy religion of Islam in Afghanistan. Islam is a beautiful religion with 1.6

billion followers (23%), trailing Christians with 2.2 billion followers (31.5%) worldwide.

Regardless of their ethnic background, most Afghans adhere to Islam. Islam is the common denominator that serves as a unifying force amongst the diverse ethnic groups. Some Afghans lean towards a more orthodox form of Islam, embracing traditional religious practices, while others advocate for a more secular approach, emphasizing the separation of religion and state. Gender and religion discourse is a complicated and significant subject that calls for careful consideration, in-depth knowledge, and careful analysis.

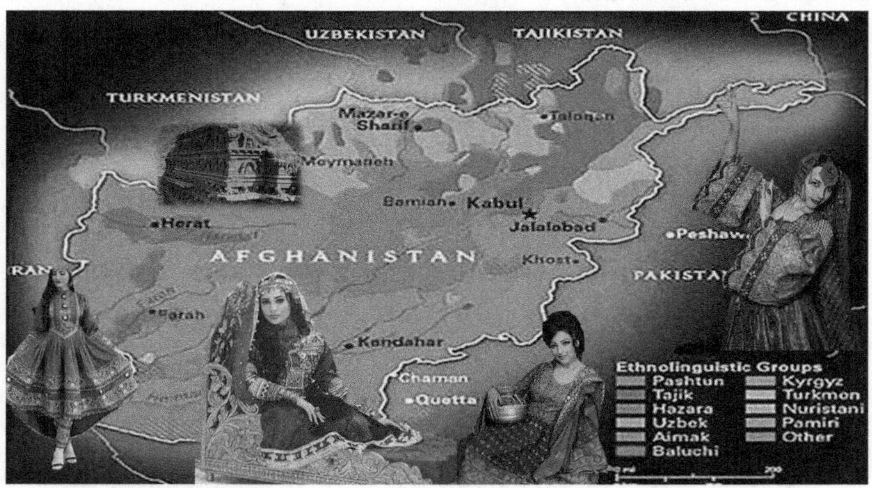

14 nationally recognized ethnic groups in Afghanistan Pashtuns (40%), Tajiks (30%), Hazaras (15%), Uzbeks (8%), Turkmen (2%), Aimaq (2%), Baloch (1%), Nuristani (1%), and Pashaye (1%).

Babus garden founder of the Mughal Empire, Babur, is buried in the garden that he built to celebrate the beloved, cosmopolitan city of Babur.

The founder of the nation came from the Pashtun ethnic group, which makes up 42% of the Afghan population. Since they make up about half of Afghanistan's population, they have always dominated politics and other developed industries. while other ethnic groups (especially the Uzbeks) dominate in the underdeveloped sectors. The Tajiks, an anti-Pashtun ethnic coalition, dominated the Republic of Afghanistan National Army (ANA). The Pashtuns dominate the Taliban Islamic Emirate of Afghanistan Army. Other groups have also formed a web of shifting alliances to challenge Pashtun dominance. This created a civil war-like situation in Afghanistan.

Pashtunwali is the culture and principles of the Pashtuns. It is considered to be the personal responsibility of every Pashtun to discover and rediscover Pashtunwali's essence and meaning. One Afghan intellectual says that Pashtun has the most complex simplicity. Ahmad Shah Abdali (1722-1773), the Father of Afghanistan, advises their nation, "Don't be a slave and don't make other people slaves." In short, they are brave and do not bow

before oppressors. loyal to their country, people, and ideology. A Pashtun cultural code, known as melmasty, shows hospitality and profound respect to all visitors, regardless of race, religion, national affiliation, or economic status, and does so without any hope of remuneration or favor in return. This cultural code is deeply ingrained in Pashtun society and is seen as a fundamental aspect of their identity and way of life.

Winston Churchill wrote: The Pashtun tribes are always engaged in private or public war. Every man is a warrior, a politician, and a theologian. Every large house is a real feudal fortress. Every family cultivates its vendetta, and every clan cultivates its feud. Nothing is ever forgotten, and very few debts are left unpaid. (My Early Life, Chapter 11: "The Mahmund Valley").

The Amir is the highest authority in the Islamic Emirate of Afghanistan, and the Ulamas are a group of Muslim academics with specialized knowledge of Islamic holy law and theology who promulgate Islamic law. The Ulamas are highly influential in the development and interpretation of Islamic law. The 1931 Constitution made Hanafi Shariah the state religion, while the 1964 Constitution prescribed that the state conducts its religious ritual according to the Hanafi school. The 1977 Constitution declared Islam the religion of Afghanistan but made no mention that the state ritual should be Hanafi. The Penal Code of 1976 and the Civil Code of 1977 cover the entire social justice field. The courts, for instance, were to consider cases according to secular law and only resort to Shariah in areas secular law did not cover. By 1978, the People's Democratic Party of Afghanistan (PDPA) government had announced its separation from religious establishments. This led the Islamist Movement to become a national revolt.

Afghanistan constitution commemorative stamp

Signatories of Afghanistan's 1964 constitution

The Islamist Movement started in 1958 at Kabul University, particularly in the Faculty of Islamic Law, founded in 1952, to raise the quality of religious teaching to accommodate modern science and technology. The founders were professors influenced by the Egyptian Muslim Brotherhood, a party formed in the 1930s dedicated to Islamic revivalism and social, economic, and political equity. Their objective was to develop a parallel political ideology with modernity based on Islamic virtues.

The liberalization of government attitudes following the passage of the 1964 Constitution ushered in a period of intense activism among students at Kabul University. Professors and their students set up the Muslim Youth Organization (Sazmani Jawanani Musulman) in the mid-1960s while the leftists were forming many parties. Initially, communist students outnumbered Muslim students, but by 1970, the Muslim Youths had gained a majority in students' elections. Members were from university faculties and secondary schools in several cities, such as Mazari Sharif and Herat. Some of these professors and students became the leaders of the Mujahideen rebels in the 1980s.

Afghanistan is composed of a multi-ethnic and multilingual society, reflecting its location astride historic trade and invasion routes between Central Asia, South Asia, and Western Asia. The population of Afghanistan is around 41 million as of 2023. Afghans are ambivalent towards foreign intervention. Although they are a diverse society, they are homogeneous in principles and beliefs. The colonial influence, specifically by Britain, has much to do with the controversy, conflicts, and confusion of the unrest amongst the people of Afghanistan.

The Afghans and the Brits had three significant wars. The Brits lost except for the 2nd war in 1891. Mortimer Durand, a secretary of the British Indian government, coerced King Abdur Rahman Khan (1844– 1901) of Afghanistan (1880–1901) into an agreement signed on November 12, 1893, to draw the Durand Line. The Durand Line, named after Mortimer Durand, is the controversial and contested line that separates Afghanistan and Pakistan. The Durand line was drawn while Pakistan was still a part of India. The United Kingdom ruled India from 1858 until India's independence in 1947, when Pakistan became a separate nation. Durand also set the boundary between northeastern Afghanistan and the Russian possessions, responsible for defining the size of Afghanistan and placing territory on the map.

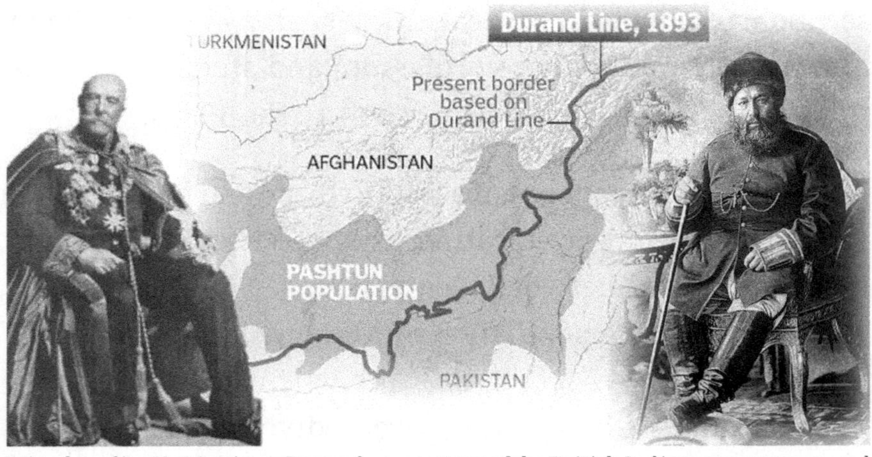

Mixed media: Sir Mortimer Durand, a secretary of the British Indian government, and Abdur Rahman Khan, the emir, or ruler, of Afghanistan. The Durand line agreement was signed on November 12, 1893.

The Punjabis and Pashtuns are the two main ethnic groups that the Durand Line affects. At the time, the Pashtuns were fighting to prevent the Punjabis from expanding farther into the mountains of southeastern Afghanistan. Punjabis are the largest ethnic group in Pakistan. Most Punjabis and Pashtuns are Sunni Muslims. Pashtuns are the largest ethnic group in Afghanistan. The Durand line split the Pashtuns into two countries, typical of the colonialists' divide and rule strategy. During this time, the Pashtuns sought the creation of an independent Pashtunistan that was separate from Afghanistan. They proposed a state along the Durand Line, the border between Pakistan and Afghanistan, and united Pashtuns living in both states. Political groups in Afghanistan were often formed along ethnic lines. For example, Pashtun nationalists banded together to form the Afghan Millat, a political party that fought to create Pashtunistan. The party's leadership describes it as social democratic. The party's current leader is Stanagul Sherzad, who became the new leader after the 6th party congress on October 3, 2012.

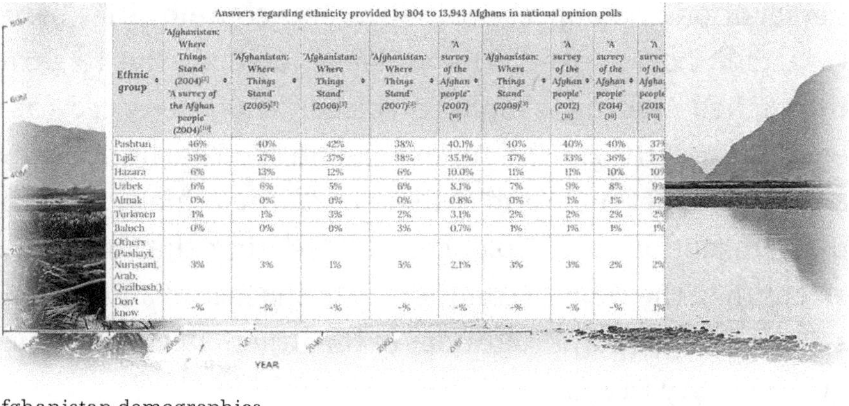

Answers regarding ethnicity provided by 804 to 13,943 Afghans in national opinion polls

Ethnic group	"Afghanistan: Where Things Stand" (2004)[1] "A survey of the Afghan people" (2004)[10]	"Afghanistan: Where Things Stand" (2005)[2]	"Afghanistan: Where Things Stand" (2006)[3]	"Afghanistan: Where Things Stand" (2007)[4]	"A survey of the Afghan people" (2007)[10]	"Afghanistan: Where Things Stand" (2009)[3]	"A survey of the Afghan people" (2012)[10]	"A survey of the Afghan people" (2014)[10]	"A survey of the Afghan people" (2018)[10]
Pashtun	46%	40%	42%	38%	40.1%	40%	40%	40%	37%
Tajik	39%	37%	37%	38%	35.1%	37%	33%	36%	37%
Hazara	6%	13%	12%	6%	10.0%	11%	11%	10%	10%
Uzbek	6%	6%	5%	6%	8.1%	7%	9%	8%	9%
Aimak	0%	0%	0%	0%	0.8%	0%	1%	1%	1%
Turkmen	1%	1%	3%	2%	3.1%	2%	2%	2%	2%
Baloch	0%	0%	0%	3%	0.7%	1%	1%	1%	1%
Others (Pashayi, Nuristani, Arab, Qizilbash)	3%	3%	1%	5%	2.1%	3%	3%	2%	2%
Don't know	-%	-%	-%	-%	-%	-%	-%	-%	1%

Afghanistan demographics

Afghans are ambivalent towards foreign intervention. Although they are a diverse society, they are homogeneous in principles and beliefs. The colonial influence, specifically by Britain, has much to do with the controversy, conflicts, and confusion of the unrest amongst the people of Afghanistan. The Khudai Khidmatgar leaders demanded that the Pashtuns should be able to choose between an independent state of Pashtunistan, which was to comprise all the Pashtun territories of British India, and not be included (as almost all other Muslim-majority provinces were) within the state of Pakistan, but the British government openly refused.

At the same time, King Abdul Rahman Khan was fighting to remove the Hazaras from Afghanistan. During this time, the Hazaras were set apart from Afghanistan's other ethnic groups due to their status as Shia rather than Sunni Muslims. Being a Sunni Muslim and a member of the Pashtun majority, King Abdul Rahman Kahn encouraged violence against the Hazaras with propaganda that Allah would reward them if they participated in this violence towards the Hazaras. As a result, the Hazaras faced widespread persecution and oppression, with their communities being targeted and attacked. The violence towards the Hazaras intensified, leading to forced displacements, massacres, and even mass killings. The funeral mentioned earlier became a symbol of defiance and resistance against this systematic discrimination and violence, representing the unity and strength of the Hazara community in the face of adversity. It served as a poignant reminder of the urgent need for justice and equality in Afghanistan.

King Abdul Rahman Khan and his cabinet

Sixty percent of Hazaras in Afghanistan were slaughtered or forced to escape to neighboring countries during this time of conflict. Afghans of other ethnicities, particularly the Pashtuns, enslaved and mistreated the surviving Hazara population. When Abdul Khaliq, a high school senior, assassinated King Nadir Shah on November 8, 1933, during a graduation ceremony, the authorities brutally put an end to the boy's life as well as the lives of sixteen members of his immediate family. This was a sign that Islamic faith was fostered with vindictive or harsh ideals in Afghanistan. In 1995, the Taliban murdered Hazara leader Abdul Ali Mazari, and in 2021, they vandalized his statue days after seizing power in Afghanistan.

King Nadir Khan promoted a constitution with an emphasis on Islamic orthodox denominational principles. His son, Mohammed Zahir Shah (October 1914–July 23, 2007), the last King of Afghanistan, was given the royal title "He who puts his trust in God, a follower of the firm religion of Islam."

At least five Afghan little Pul coins during his reign bore the Arabic title: المتوكل على الله محمد ظاهر شاه, “AlMutawakkil ‘ala Allah Muhammad Zahir Shah,” which means “The leaner on Allah, Muhammad Zahir Shah.” The title “AlMutawakkil ‘ala Allah,” “The leaner on Allah,” is taken from the Quran, Sura 8, verse 61. Nevertheless, Zahir Shah adopted a liberal approach to Islamic rule and faced opposition from numerous rebellions.

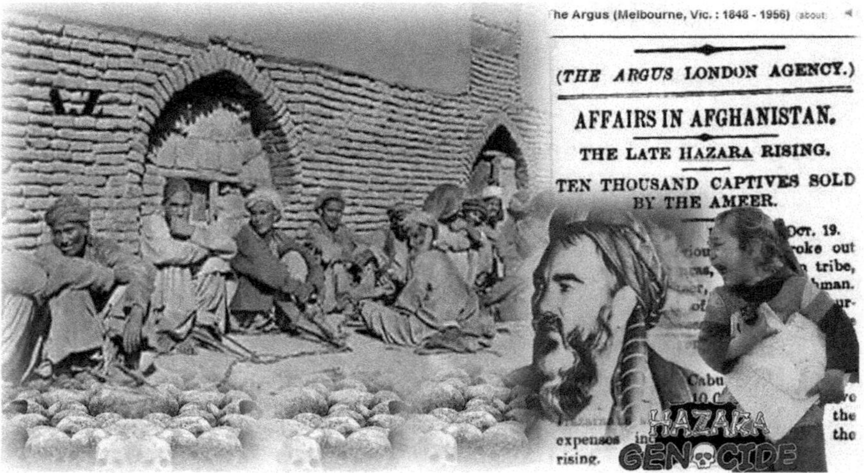

Mohammad Karim Khalili, former chairman of the Afghan Supreme Peace Council, said the Hazaras were highly vulnerable to killing and genocide.

Most of King Abdur Rahman Khan’s successors continued the momentum of secularization. Islam remained central to interactions, but the religious establishment remained non-political, functioning as a moral rather than a political influence. Nonetheless, Islam asserted itself in times of national crisis. Moreover, when the religious leadership considered themselves severely threatened, charismatic religious personalities periodically employed Islam to rally disparate groups in opposition to the state. They rose on several occasions against King Amanullah Shah (1919–1929). For example, during protest reforms, they believed western intrusions were inimical to Islam. Therefore, subsequent rulers were mindful of traditional attitudes antithetical to secularization and were stupendous to underline the compatibility of Islam with modernization. Even so, and despite its pivotal position within society, which continued to avoid distinction between religion and state, the role of religion in state affairs continued to decline. Even the Mujahideen were on the trajectory of modernism with the development of Afghanistan until the Taliban arrived.

Once in control, the Taliban began to demonstrate intolerance in the name of Islam and harsh rules, and the ethnic conflicts increased dramatically, especially with Hazaras and Uzbeks. The Northern Alliance was formed in opposition to the Taliban and was composed of Hazaras, Tajiks, and Uzbeks.

Some countries supported the Northern Alliance for several reasons, such as the United States, Iran, Russia, and India, due to their geopolitical interests in the region. The United States saw the Northern Alliance as a potential ally in their fight against terrorism, particularly after the 9/11 attacks. Iran, on the other hand, supported the Northern Alliance as a means to counter the influence of the Taliban, who had long been hostile towards Iran's Shiite population. Russia also had its own interests in supporting the Northern Alliance, as it sought to maintain a foothold in the region and prevent the spread of radical Islamic groups. India, too, had concerns about the Taliban's close ties with Pakistan, its rival, and supported the Northern Alliance to safeguard its own security interests. Many atrocities were committed in the name of Islam, which makes secularism a necessary step for foreign interventions. What needs to be well understood is not so much the role of Islam in Afghanistan as the critical role of Afghanistan in Islam.

Islam was introduced to Afghanistan in the 7th century. After conquering the Sassanian Persians in Nihawand in the 7th century, the Arabs of the Rashidun Caliphate moved into the area that is now Afghanistan. After this devastating disaster, Yazdegerd III, the last Sassanid monarch, escaped to the far east, deep within Central Asia. Arabs stationed a substantial portion of their force at Herat, northeastern Iran, and then advanced toward northern Afghanistan in pursuit of Yazdegerd. Hisham ibn Abd al-Malik and Umar ibn Abdul-Aziz were the Umayyad caliphs who were instrumental in converting many of the locals in northern Afghanistan to Islam. Abdur Rahman bin Samara launched attacks on the Zunbil-ruled territory of Zabulistan in the south.

The Friday Mosque in Herat dates back to the 12th century, making it one of the oldest mosques in the country and the Islamic world. During this time, often known as the Islamic Golden Age, Afghanistan surpassed Baghdad as the Muslim world's second-most important academic center. All Afghans share the desire for Afghanistan to continue to be a center of Islamic scholarship and an Islamic empire. With an estimated 99.7 percent of the population identifying as Muslim, Islam continues to be the state religion of Afghanistan. Approximately 90% are Sunni Muslims, while 10% are Shia. The Twelver sect of Shiism has the largest membership, whereas the Ismaili sect has a far smaller following. The Kandahar province of Afghanistan is still a hotspot for fighting between Shia Safavids and Sunni Mughals. Violence and instability have risen as a result of the feud between these two factions.

The name "Mazar-e Sharif" means "Noble Shrine," a blue-tiled sanctuary and mosque in the Shrine of Hazrat Ali or the Blue Mosque.

Sharia is Islam's legal system. It is derived from the Quran, Islam's holy book, and the Sunnah and Ḥadīth, the deeds, and sayings of the Prophet Muhammad. Sharia acts as a code of living that all Muslims should adhere to, including prayers, fasting, hygiene, diet, behavior, ethical standards, mores, and altruism. Additionally, Sharia encompasses laws regarding family, economics, and criminal justice.

Image composition of the Sharia law

In Arabic, Sharia means "the clear, well-trodden path to the water." It aims to help Muslims understand how they should lead every aspect of their lives according to God's wishes. All religious texts are sacred and central to the teachings of the given religion. They are significant as these texts convey spiritual truth, connect with the divine, foster communal identity, and promote mystical experiences and spiritual practices. Ḥadīths contain the sayings of the Prophet Muhammad and his followers. These are authoritative texts in Islam. Like any legal system, Sharia is complex, and its practice relies entirely on the quality and training of experts. Where an answer cannot be derived directly from these, religious scholars may give rulings as guidance on a particular topic or question. Islamic jurists issue guidance and rulings. The guidance that is considered a formal legal ruling is called a fatwa. Sunnis founded several schools of Islamic law (the Sharia), which became the foundation of Sunnism. Scholars belonging to these schools interpreted the Koran and Sunnah, which Sunnis believe are the only true sources of Islamic law. The theory of Twelver Shia jurisprudence parallels that of Sunni schools with some differences, such as recognition of reason ('aql) as a source of law in place of qiyas and extension of the notion of sunnah to include traditions of the imams.

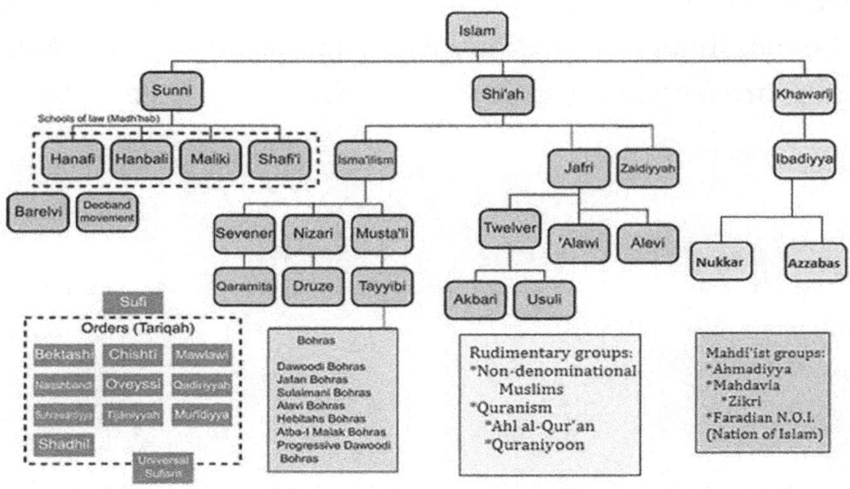

Identity of the branches of Islam and Schools of Thoughts: Qadl or Sadl

Sunni Muslims and Shia Muslims (also known as Shiites) comprise the two main branches of Islam. Sunni and Shia identities first formed soon after the death of the Prophet Muhammad in 632 C.E., centering on a dispute over leadership succession. Over time, however, the political divide between the two groups broadened to include theological distinctions and differences in religious practices as well. While the two groups are similar in many ways, they differ over conceptions of religious authority and interpretation as well as the role of the Prophet Muhammad's descendants, among other issues.

The modern-day changes in Islamic legal institutions have had a significant impact on the madhhab system. The position conferred on the madhhabs within national legal systems determines the extent to which they exert influence beyond personal ritual practice in most of the Muslim world. The principles of takhayyur (the selection of decisions without regard to individual madhhabs) and talfiq (the combination of sections of multiple rulings on the same topic) are frequently used in the codification of state law.

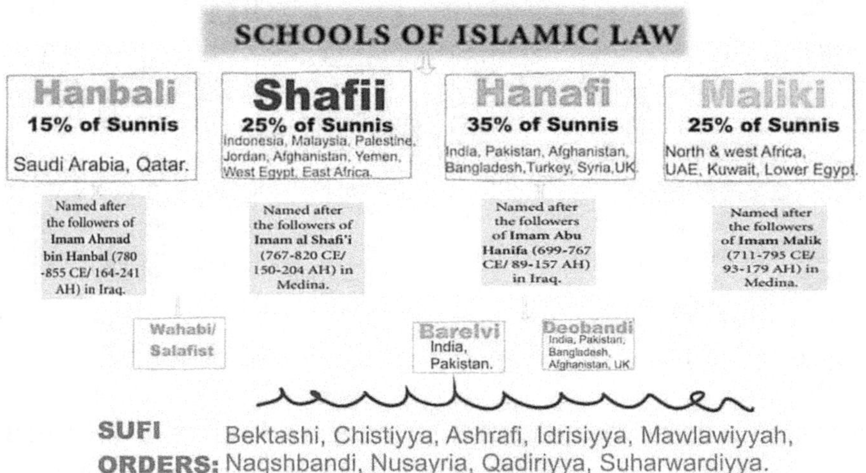

Schools of Islamic thoughts (Sunni)

In most places, modern law school graduates have replaced traditional ulemas as legal experts. There have been periods of time in Islamic history when worldwide movements have drawn from a variety of madhhabs and placed more emphasis on scriptural sources than classical law. The conservative currents of direct biblical interpretation held by the Salafi and Wahhabi movements can trace their roots back to the Hanbali school and its strict commitment to the Quran and ḥadīth. Many Islamic jurists in the 20th century broke away from more conservative schools of thought. The latter strategy is exemplified by groups of Indonesian ulema and other Islamic intellectuals who have advocated liberal interpretations of Islamic law and who now reside in nations with a Muslim minority.

Many of the changes in the madhhab system have taken place in Islamic legal institutions in the modern age. The position conferred on the madhhabs within national legal systems determines the extent to which they exert influence beyond personal ritual practice in most of the Muslim world.

The Madhhabs and the Jihadist

A madhhab is a school of thought within fiqh. Fiqh is the field of Islamic law that deals with how people understand and follow the Sharia, which is the Islamic divine law that is revealed in the Quran and the Sunnah.

The major Sunni madhhabs are Hanafi, Maliki, Shafi'i, and Hanbali. They subsisted from the ninth and tenth centuries CE and by the twelfth century to exclude dogmatic theologians, government officials, and non-Sunni sects from religious discourse. Almost all jurists aligned themselves with a particular madhhab. Sunnis prefer the madhhab specific to their region, with the expectation that qualified contemporary scholars must exercise ijtihad. Ijtihad is an Islamic legal term referring to independent reasoning or the thorough exertion of a jurist's mental faculty in finding a solution to a legal question. It is in contrast with Taqlīd. Most madhhabs rely on the Taqlīd, which is in Islamic law basically the unquestioning acceptance of the legal decisions without knowing the basis of those decisions. There is a wide range of opinions about Taqlīd among separate groups or schools of Muslims. Experts and scholars of fiqh follow the usul (principles) of their native madhhab, but they also study the usul, evidence, and opinions of other madhhabs.

During the era of Islamic gunpowder, the Ottoman Empire reaffirmed the official status of these four schools as a reaction to Shi'ite Persia. Some are of the view that Sunni jurisprudence falls into two groups: Ahl al-Ra'i ("people of opinions," emphasizing informed judgment and reason) and Ahl al-Ḥadīth ("people of traditions," emphasizing strict interpretation of scripture). Sunni schools of jurisprudence are each named after the classical jurist who taught them.

The four primary Sunni schools are the Hanafi, Shafi'i, Maliki, and Hanbali rites. The Zahiri school remains outside the mainstream, while the Jariri, Laythi, Awza'i, Thawri, and Qurtubi have become extinct. Abu Hanifa an-Nu'man founded the Hanafi school, which is commonly observed by Muslims in the Levant, Central Asia, Afghanistan, Pakistan, India, Bangladesh, Northern Egypt, Iraq, Turkey, the Balkans, and most of Russia's Muslim community. There are movements within this school, such as Barelvis and Deobandi, concentrated in South Asia. The Maliki school, founded by Malik ibn Anas, is commonly observed by Muslims in North Africa, West Africa, the United Arab Emirates, Kuwait, Saudi Arabia, and Upper Egypt.

Ian Dallas, a Scottish-born playwright, and actor who converted to Islam in 1967, founded the Murabitun World Movement, which is another organization that supports the school. The Murabitun World Movement was founded in the 1980s. After converting to Islam, Abdalqadir as-Sufi (born Ian Dallas; 1930–August 1, 2021) authored numerous books on Islam, Sufism, and political theory. The Maliki School was also followed in parts of Europe under Islamic rule, particularly in Islamic Spain and the Emirate of Sicily. The Shafi'i school founded by Muhammad ibn Idris ash-Shafi'I is commonly observed by Muslims in the Hejaz region of Saudi Arabia, Eastern Lower Egypt, Ethiopia, Eritrea, Indonesia, Malaysia, Jordan, Palestine, the Philippines, Singapore, Somalia, Thailand, Yemen, Kurdistan, and the

Mappilas of Kerala and Konkani Muslims of India. It is the official school, followed by the governments of Brunei and Malaysia. The Shafi'i schools are also common in Iraq and Syria. Muslims in Qatar commonly observe the Hanbali school founded by Ahmad ibn Hanbal, most Saudi Arabia, and minority communities in Syria and Iraq.

The majority of the Salafis attend this school. Minority communities in Morocco and Pakistan commonly observe the Zahiri school founded by Dawud al-Zahiri. Most Muslims followed it in Mesopotamia, Portugal, the Balearic Islands, North Africa, and Spain. In the hierarchical structure of Shia Islam, the Shi'ite Imams are flexible in that every jurist has considerable power to alter a decision according to his reasoning. The Jafari school uses intellect instead of analogy when establishing Islamic laws instead of common Sunni practice. The Usulis form the overwhelming majority within the Twelver Shia denomination. They follow a Marja-i Taqlīd about Taqlīd and fiqh. They are concentrated in Iran, Pakistan, Azerbaijan, India, Iraq, and Lebanon. Akhbari's are concentrated in Bahrain and like Usulis; however, they reject ijtihad in favor of ḥadīth.

Shaykhism, founded by Shaykh Ahmad in the early 19th century Qajar dynasty in Iran, has a minority following in Iran and Iraq. It began with a combination of Sufi, Shia, and Akhbari doctrines. In the mid- 19th century, many Shaykhis converted to the Bábí and Bahá'í religions, which regard Shaykh Ahmad highly. Alevism, sometimes categorized as part of Twelver Shia Islam and sometimes as its religious tradition, has a different philosophy, customs, and rituals. They have many Tasawwufī characteristics and express belief in the Qur'an and the Twelve Imams, but reject polygamy and accept religious traditions predating Islam, like Turkish shamanism. They are significant in east-central Turkey. They are sometimes considered a Sufi sect and have an untraditional form of religious leadership that is not scholarship-oriented like other Sunni and Shia groups. They number around 24 million worldwide, of which 17 million are in Turkey, with the rest in the Balkans, Albania, Azerbaijan, Iran, and Syria. Bektashism is a Sufi order overlapping Alevism. They are concentrated in Albania. Ismaili Muslims who adhere to the Shi'a Ismaili Fatimid fiqh through the contested successor of Jafar al Sadiq, Isma'il ibn Ja'far, follow the Daim al-Islam, a book on the rulings of Islam. It describes manners and etiquette, including Ibadat, considering the guidance provided by the Ismaili Imams. The book emphasizes the importance Islam has given to manners and etiquette along with the worship of God, citing the traditions of the first four Imams of the Shi'a Ismaili Fatimid school of thought.

Nizari, the most prominent branch (95%) of Ismā'īlī, is the only Shia group to have an absolute temporal leader in the rank of Imamate, which is invested in the Aga Khan. Nizārī Ismā'īlīs believe that the successor-Imām to the Fatimid caliph Ma'ad al-Mustansir Billah was his elder son al-Nizār. While Nizārī belongs to the Ja'fari jurisprudence, they adhere to the supremacy of "Kalam" in the interpretation of scripture and believe in the temporal relativism of understanding, as opposed to fiqh (traditional legalism), which adheres to an absolutism approach to revelation. State law codification commonly utilizes the methods of takhayyur (selection of rulings without restriction to a particular madhhab) and talfiq (combining parts of different rulings on the same question). Legal professionals trained in modern law schools have replaced traditional ulema as interpreters of the resulting laws. With its stringent adherence to the Quran and ḥadīth, the Hanbali school has inspired conservative currents of direct scriptural interpretation by the Salafi and Wahhabi movements.

Wahhabist heritage (the Duranni dynasty in Afghanistan)

Wahhabism is an Islamic movement based on the 18th-century reformer Mohamed ibn Abdul Wahhab principles (1703–June 22, 1792). The movement gained credibility by sacking Mecca, Saudi Arabia. Practitioners are sometimes referred to as Salafi, denoting orthodoxy about the salaf, the earliest generation of faith as handed down from the time of the Prophet Muhammad. The movement was associated with violence from the beginning. Wahhab himself was expelled from his hometown for his attempts at puritanical reform and for attacking the tombs of early Muslims; jihad was declared against Muslims who refused to adopt the ways of the salaf. After Wahhab's death, his followers became more violent, murdering their way across the land and, in 1803, forcing Mecca to surrender. In 2013, Strasbourg's European Parliament declared Salafism/ Wahhabism to be the primary source of global terrorism, with a report linking it to the Benghazi attacks and the war in Syria, among other atrocities. According to the New Statesman, Wahhabism has also been blamed for forming the root of the Islamic State's ideology, which is why it has become such a headache for Western and Islamic leaders alike. Wahhabism was revived in the 20th century when Abdulaziz ibn Saudi, an Arab tribal leader and statesman who founded Saudi Arabia, the third Saudi state, was King of Saudi Arabia between September 23, 1932, and his death in 1953.

In 1979, the Saudi Royal family saw its tactical use as part of an anti- Soviet campaign in Afghanistan and encouraged young Muslim men to travel there to fight a jihad against the Russians. The Saudis began spending heavily on mosques, propaganda, and teaching to spread the creed. If only these battles could be limited to the ideological realm in the institutes of learning rather than destabilizing the world's peace with terrorism in the name of Islam and creating havoc the world over. Al Qaeda and other groups used terror to express their Wahhabism with the expectation that it would bring back the old glory of Islam to the Muslim world.

Instead, they brought shame, hate, blood, and fear with the terror they continued to unleash.

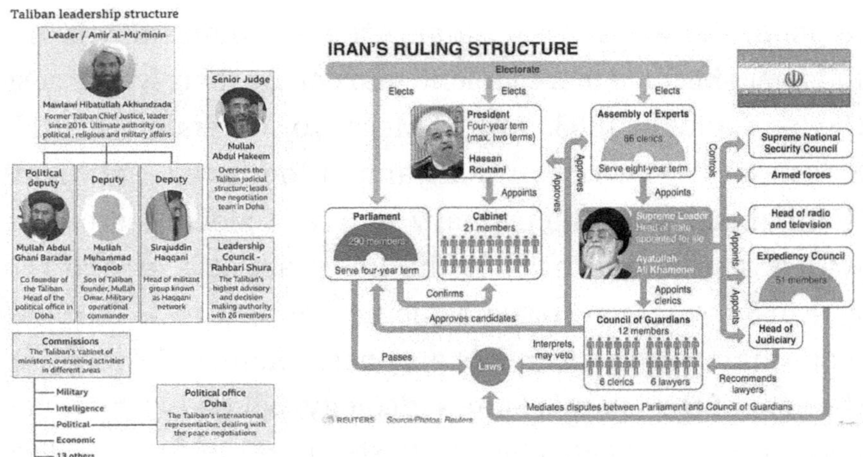

Comparison of Sunni and Shiite political system (Iran and Afghanistan)

There is an imminent threat to all four known freedoms from any form of autocratic theocracy. The Taliban has been a suicidal, trigger- happy, warring guerrilla group that epitomized religious fanaticism, anti-modernity, and anti-progress. The Taliban in power is equivalent to Boko Haram taking over the Nigerian government. Such a situation of governing an already willful society on a trajectory of modernism brings the fear of going back to dark ages where barbarism and a lack of moral virtues ruled. The Taliban was about a creed of Islam that was antagonistic to whatever was suitable within Islam. They are looked upon as bloodthirsty wolves who want to devour modern civilization and its citizens with their barbaric mentality. The Afghans are terrified, and many are fleeing their homelands to other countries. People who cannot leave are in despair. Women are in danger. They are afraid of the total annihilation of their newly regained rights, choices, and liberty. The Taliban has promised amnesty and a fair justice system with the dictate of Sharia, but people remember the version of the Taliban's guerrilla judgment at the whims of an illiterate mullah.

The Taliban government declares "Sharia" as its legal system. It will have to write a new constitution if it expects people to believe that it can rule with mercy and justice. The Taliban's new plea for peace must be unequivocal. To judge the Taliban, one must begin with a good understanding of what the Sharia entails.

Afghan communities trust and respect religious leaders. They also know that interpretations of religious doctrine about inferiority are rigged with ignorance and ambition and promote fanaticism and violence. This makes patriarchal systems and structures that hinder women's full participation in society an acceptable norm. Thus, religious leaders must play a role in addressing injustices that inhibit women and girls from developing and contributing to society.

USAID (United States Agency for International Development) led the initiative in Afghanistan for the literacy project based on Sharia principles. The Asia Foundation's programs also assisted conservative leaders in changing their attitudes toward community women. Women's rights organizations also encouraged mullahs to go beyond rights-awareness programs to push for rights. The programs outlined in Afghan law and sharia, including a need for women's consent for marriage, protection of women's inheritance, land rights, and other Women's rights under Afghan law were discussed by citing analogous laws in Islamic law and illustrating themes with Quran and Sunnah quotes. Following extensive debate, religious leaders recognized that communities flagrantly violate women's human rights based on interpretations of religious law.

Legal-aid providers educate and employ mullahs and religious scholars about the Universal Declaration of Human Rights and its sequels, which provide a normative framework that recognizes the inherent dignity of the individual and outlines the rights and responsibilities of a peaceful society.

Grand Mufti Sheikh Abdulaziz al-Sheikh and King and Prime Minister of Saudi Arabia, Fahd bin Abdulaziz Al Saud

In 2014, Sheikh Abdulaziz al-Sheikh, the Grand Mufti of Saudi Arabia and the country's highest member of the

Permanent Committee for Islamic Research and Issuing Fatwas, declared a fatwa, a religious edict, saying: "The ideas of extremism, radicalism, and terrorism do not belong to Islam in any way, but are the first enemies of Islam and Muslims." They pose a threat to the peaceful teachings and principles of the religion.

CHAPTER 29

The Role of Women in Islam

Art Exhibition at Newark Museum: a woman of the fiqh by Lalla Essaydi

Islamic teachings promote the equitable treatment, respect, and dignity of women, and the Quran and Ḥadīth (the sayings and deeds of the Prophet Muhammad) highlight the significance of women in society. It is crucial to remember that there are various interpretations and behaviors among Muslims and that the position and role of women in Islam can vary greatly based on cultural, societal, and regional circumstances. Furthermore, regional laws and practices may have an impact on Muslim women's rights and experiences, which may not always be consistent with Islam's central tenets.

From the early 7th century, when Islam was founded, until the present, women have played a crucial role in the development of the faith. However, certain male fundamentalists continue to suppress the enormous contributions that women have made alongside men throughout history.

It is important to distinguish between cultural traditions and Islamic precepts while addressing the complicated and varied topic of women's abuse in some Islamic nations, such as Afghanistan. The following are some of the elements that make this issue worse: When it comes to the mistreatment of women, cultural customs and long- standing tribal traditions frequently take precedence over Islamic teachings. Because they are so ingrained in the community, these customs may have existed before Islam was introduced to the area. Some people or organizations may misunderstand or utilize certain passages of Islamic literature to support the oppression and maltreatment of women. This is frequently the outcome of either purposeful manipulation of religious teachings to uphold power systems or a lack of adequate religious education and knowledge.

It is crucial to remember that these kinds of maltreatment occur throughout the world in many cultures and religions, not just in Islamic nations. A multipronged strategy is needed to combat women's abuse, including legal reform, education, economic empowerment, and the questioning of detrimental cultural norms. Many Muslims and Islamic groups actively support women's rights and fight against abuses, highlighting the differences between cultural customs and the genuine teachings of Islam, which demand that women be treated fairly and with respect.

The biographies of the Muslim prophet Muhammad's wives serve as examples of the role that women played in the development of Islamic history. The first Muslim woman in history was Khadija, Muhammad's first wife. She became the "mother of believers" in the Islamic faith when she accepted the concept of a single deity and the message of the revelations found in the Qur'an in 610 CE, long before Muhammad realized he was a prophet of God. Khadija is regarded as the most venerated lady in Islamic history due to her role model status as a perfect wife, mother, and friend. Furthermore, 'A'isha and Umm Salama, two of Muhammad's wives who lived after his death in 632 CE, had a significant role in the transmission of ḥadīth, or the Prophet's traditions. The Qur'an and the ḥadīth are the two most authoritative sources for Muslims looking for solutions to common queries. Following his passing, Muhammad's friends—including his wives, who were still alive—compiled accounts of his sayings and deeds to help Muslims learn how to live devout lives by following the Prophet's example. Muhammad's wives had exclusive access to him, which made them significant players in the ḥadīth transmission process and cemented their historical influence on Islamic law.

Early in the history of Islam, women like Khadija, 'A'isha, and Muhammad's daughter Fatima rose to prominence in society. Nonetheless, patriarchal social structures and beliefs persisted in considering women inferior to men in many spheres of public life within the framework of Arabian culture. For instance, the Fitna, or crisis of Muslims battling Muslims in battle, which resulted from 'A'isha's challenge to 'Ali, the fourth Caliph, might have set the precedence for prohibiting women from participating in politics in some Islamic schools of thought.

Image of the battle of the camel between Ali (flame on white horse) and Aicha (on camel back) in 656 near Bassora, Indian or Pakistani miniature from "Hamla-i haydari" by Bazil, 19th century

The Battle of the Camel, sometimes referred to as the Battle of Jamal or the Battle of Bassorah, took place in Basra, Iraq, on November 7, 656. Regarded as the fourth Rashidun Caliph of the Sunnis and the first Imam of the Shias, Ali ibn Abi Talib was the son-in-law and cousin of the late Prophet Muhammad. Leading the attack against Ali were Zubayr, A'isha, and Muhammad's wife, Talhah, and the latter two claimed they were seeking revenge from those who had assassinated Uthman, the third caliph, who had just been killed in a rebellion. The fight was a component of the wider struggle known as the First Fitna, a civil war that broke out following the death of Uthman ibn Affan, the third caliph. Talha ibn Ubaidullah and Zubair ibn al-Awwam, two of the Prophet's friends, and Aisha organized an army to challenge Ali ibn Abi Talib, the fourth caliph, since they believed he had not done enough to stop Uthman's murder.

The pivotal conflict "First Muslim Civil War" ended with Ali's decisive victory bringing the battle to a close in the second chapter of the First Fitna. The dispute "fueled the fire" for the major division in the Muslim world known as the "Shia-Sunni" split. Some Muslim feminists hail this episode as an example of female political engagement, arguing that the ill-fated war proves why women should not be permitted to lead. Following this occurrence, prophetic traditions emerged that are used to discourage or hinder women from taking leadership roles.

Scholars who said that the idea that a woman could lead or advise an army was discredited after the Battle of the Camel, even though women continued to play important leadership roles. A notable account was an Arab Muslim warrior in the service of the Rashidun Caliphate, Khawla bint al-Azwar (died 639), who played a major role in the Muslim conquest of the Levant and fought alongside her brother Dhiraar. She has been described as one of the greatest female soldiers in history. Yet, Aisha's role in the battle of the camel illustrates that women in early Islamic history were active participants in political affairs. Her role demonstrates that women were not excluded from public life or political engagement from the onset. The event underscores the fact that women, including the Prophet's wives, played various roles in society. They were not confined to domestic spheres but could also be influential in political and social matters. The Quran and Ḥadīth are the primary sources for Islamic teachings on gender relations, and they advocate for the fair and respectful treatment of women. The interpretations and applications of these teachings can vary across different Islamic societies and cultures, and the historical event of the Battle of the Camel is generally not used as a basis for the contemporary treatment of women in Islam.

The subjugation of women can be found in many other religions as well. In Christianity, the story of Eve in the book of Genesis has had a more profoundly negative impact on women throughout history than any other biblical story. Early Christian writers depicted Eve as subordinate and inferior to Adam—because she was considered weak, seductive, and evil, the cause of Adam's disobedience and held up as the paradigm for the evil inherent in all women. An example can be found in 1 Timothy 2:11-14 Let a woman learn quietly with all submissiveness. I do not permit a woman to teach or to exercise authority over a man; rather, she is to remain quiet.

Throughout several Islamic historical periods, women's roles seemed to be much inferior to men's. Women, for example, vanished from public documents and events throughout the Abbasid era as the idea of isolating women grew in popularity among men who wished to project their dominance. Political elites adopted concubinage and large harems as standard practices, and many of them believed that women had less social value than men. Notwithstanding the Qur'anic affirmation that men and women were equal in God's eyes and the female Companions' role in passing down the ḥadīth, women were usually kept out of positions of religious authority. Patriarchal ideals were ingrained more and more in Muslim women's daily lives and the sharia, or Islamic law. Nevertheless, as time passed, women remained essential to political life in a number of Islamic dynasties. In the 13th century, for example, regal Ayyubid ladies in Egypt and the Levant were well-known as prominent public personalities who used their money and status to establish hospitals, schools, and other philanthropic organizations. Furthermore, Shajarat al-Durr, the wife of Ayyubid emperor Salah al-Din, confounded the Mamluk dynasty, despite having a brief reign as an independent queen. Ottoman ladies in the Sultan of Istanbul's harem were renowned for their political activism. The women of the Ottoman harem chose the sultan's spouse and future children even from within their own walls, preserving the monarchy for almost 700 years.

In the Sufi movement, one of Islam's mystical movements, women also rose to prominence. Rabi'a al-'Adawiyya was, in fact, one of the most influential founders of Sufi thinking. Most people agree that this Basra woman from the eighth century was the first to articulate the now-common Sufi doctrine of holy love. She is regarded as one of the most revered Sufis in history because of her poems, which are devoted to a mystical union with God, and her role model, a saint. Many women in Islamic history, like al-'Adawiyya, have looked to Sufism for spiritual strength as well as for the religious community and authority. Women began to value their pilgrimages to Sufi shrines, especially those who could not afford to travel to Mecca.

According to the Quran, men and women have the same moral agency and will be rewarded equally in the hereafter. Islam segregates social functions because it emphasizes the complementarity of the feminine and masculine polarities. A woman's domain is her home, where she holds a dominant role, while a man's domain is the outer world. In many facets of domestic life, women are held in great regard. They are commended for their expertise in ceremonial work, healing, childrearing, and arranging marriages within their community. The historical background of the Muslim world at the time these interpretations were published influenced both their application and interpretation. Islam prescribes modesty, or Haya, as a religious duty. The Quran forbids both men and women from showing off their bodies or their clothing, and Muḥammad said that Islam places a high value on modesty. Islamic clothing for women covers the body from the ankles to the neck, whereas traditional Muslim clothing for men usually covers the head and the region between the waist and the knees. Additionally, some Muslim women hide their faces. The Quran mentions shielding women's "ornaments" from strangers outside the household in the context of women (24:31). Both Islamic scholars and the general Muslim public frequently view this kind of action as indicative of a state of spiritual ignorance (al-Jhiliyyah). Every traditional school of Sharia law mandates that one covers one's body when out in public, especially the neck, ankles, and area below the elbow. Only the wives of Muhammad are required to wear veils; none of the other old legal systems really make this requirement (33:59).

Various parts of the Islamic world developed different styles of dress based on the commandment to be modest, but some styles were remnants of earlier, pre-Islamic Near Eastern societies; for example, women were expected to cover their hair in earlier communities of Jews and Christians. The Virgin Mary is always depicted in Christian art with her hair covered; both Georgian and Armenian Christians, as well as Oriental Jewish women, continued this tradition into the modern era. Catholic women did not start wearing head coverings to church until well into the twentieth century. Women have always considered covering one's hair to be a symbol of modesty and, more importantly, of deference to God.

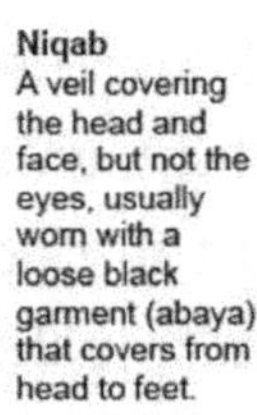

Explained: the differences between the burka, niqab, hijab, chador and dupatta. *(ABC News: Lucy Fahey)*
Images of Islamic traditional dress codes.

Muslim women's fashion choices still vary in the twenty-first century, in part due to the Islamic world's extreme geographic and cultural diversity. In the same way that the end of communism in Albania and the Yugoslav republics also meant an end to highly restrictive secular apparel legislation, laws requiring women to wear "modern," Western-style clothing were relaxed in recent years in states (such as laïcist Turkey and Tunisia) that had campaigns of Secularism in the 20th century. The 1928 amendment to the 1924 Constitution removed the provision declaring that the "Religion of the State is Islam," and Mustafa Kemal Atatürk's reforms set the administrative and political requirements to create a modern, democratic, secular state, which ended the Ottoman Empire, eliminated Islam as the state religion, and established secularism in Turkey. Despite secularism, the Turkish government banned headscarves for women in the public sector. Lifting the restrictions required lengthy legal battles. Turkish Prime Minister Recep Tayyip Erdogan, a moderate Islamist, openly pushed Islamization, causing political and social tensions with secularists. Despite its harsh implementation, secularism in Turkey has been credited with giving women more opportunities in education, employment, wealth, political, social, and cultural freedoms, and modernization than countries with a greater religious influence.

Consequently, women in these nations are now permitted to wear clothing that suggests a (post-)modern Islamic identity in public, such as the headscarf, also known as the ḥijāb. Muslim women wear various styles of head coverings, most notably the khimar, hijab, chador, niqab, paranja, yashmak, tudong, shayla, safseri, carşaf, haik, dupatta, boshiya, and burqa, in countries where the practice varies from mandatory to optional or restricted. In conservative countries such as Iran and Afghanistan, wearing the hijab is required. School officials in Gaza, State of Palestine, agreed to mandate young girls to wear hijab, despite the fact that the Palestinian Authority considers the hijab optional and has punished those who have attempted to enforce it. Some Muslim-majority nations (such as Morocco and Tunisia) have reported limitations or discrimination against women who wear hijab, which might be interpreted as an indication of Islamic fundamentalism. Tunisia (since 1981, partially lifted in 2011), Turkey (gradually and partially lifted), Kosovo (since 2009), Azerbaijan (since 2010), Kazakhstan, and Kyrgyzstan are four Muslim- majority nations that have outlawed the burqa and hijab in public schools, universities, or government buildings. Women in Tajikistan's Muslim-majority country have been jailed and harassed by authorities for wearing hijabs.

According to a 2018 survey by the Institute for Social Policy and Understanding, Muslim American women were "the most likely" to "wear a visible symbol that makes their faith identity known to others" when compared to other domestic religious communities. According to the ISPU survey, 46% of Muslim women say they always wear a visible symbol of their faith in public (including the hijab), compared to 19% who only do so occasionally and 35% who do not. Age or race did not significantly differ, according to the report.

Muslim American women respond in several ways to the issue of why Muslim women wear the hijab in the modern world, with the most common answers being "piety and to please God" (54%), "so others know they are Muslim" (21%), and "for modesty" (12%). Just 1% of respondents claimed to wear it "due to a spouse or family member's requirement." Islamic personal status regulations distinguish between the rights of men and women. While women are typically prohibited from having numerous husbands and marrying non- Muslim men, certain Islamic legal traditions permit men to practice polygamy and marry non-Muslim women. Furthermore, the inheritances of females are usually half those of their male siblings. Islamic criminal law also places a strong emphasis on witness testimony. In many cases, the testimony of women is insufficient to condemn a murderer; instead, the testimony of men is required to validate the case.

Mandatory veiling is perceived in certain regions as a means of dividing people into gender-based categories. The requirement to wear a veil is not based on any one universal Islamic law; rather, it developed due to various cultural factors. Mandatory veiling has been given as an example, including the dress restrictions enforced by the Taliban dictatorship in Afghanistan and the Islamic Republic of Iran, as well as Islamic schools that mandate headscarves for girls. These mandatory veiling laws have come under fire for being coercive tools of gender segregation that violate the autonomy and agency of women. However, oppositional arguments contend that forced veiling does not represent gender apartheid and that society has mistakenly appropriated the veil to stand for gender inequality. The Taliban government interpreted Sharia law in line with Mullah Omar's religious decrees and the Hanafi school of Islamic jurisprudence throughout the five years that the Islamic Emirate of Afghanistan existed. In addition to being prohibited from working and attending colleges or universities, women were also asked to practice purdah and be escorted outside of their homes by male relatives. Violators of these regulations faced punishment. Men had to wear turbans outside of their homes and were not allowed to shave their beards; instead, they had to allow them to grow and be kept long, as the Taliban desired. The Taliban prohibited, among other things, male and female participation in games like chess and football as well as leisure pursuits like kite flying. The Islamic fundamentalist worldview, according to Mahnaz Afkhami, "singles out women's status and her relations to society as the supreme test of the authenticity of the Islamic order." The practices of awrah (covering one's body with garments) and purdah (physical separation of the sexes) serve as symbols for this. Like many other parts of the world, organizations that suppressed women were losing ground until the end of the 20th century, when Islamic fundamentalism made a comeback. According to Walid Phares, "secular anticlericalism" in Turkey and Marxism in the Soviet Union and China compelled women to "integrate themselves into an antireligious society," which led to an Islamic fundamentalist backlash of "gender apartheid." He points out that "other religions have also witnessed comparable historical struggles." The Saudi Arabian Ministry of the Interior ordered a fatwa in 1990 that officially outlawed women drivers. This ban was exclusive to Saudi Arabia and gave rise to mockery on a global scale. Salman bin Abdulaziz Al Saud, the King and Prime Minister of Saudi Arabia, personally signed a royal decree on September 26, 2017, ordering the Ministry of the Interior to lift the prohibition. The edict stated that "the original Islamic ruling in regard to women driving is to allow it" and that those who disagreed with this viewpoint "used excuses that are baseless and have no predominance of thought.". 2018 was the planned month for the decree's complete implementation. Hala Al- Dosari, a Saudi scholar at Harvard University's Radcliffe Institute for Advanced Study, suggested in an interview with The Atlantic that the ban on women driving was political rather than religious or cultural. She also pointed out how ridiculous it was that women were allowed to ride camels during the time of Muḥammad (570–632) and that this was not a problem. The royal proclamation was "not some bold initiative to present a new religious interpretation of the issue," as author and scholar Haifaa Jawad emphasized. From a theological perspective, the prohibition was never warranted and is not supported by the Quran or Ḥadīth."

In addition, some commentators have asserted that the Public Investment Fund of the Kingdom of Saudi Arabia's US$3.5 billion investment in the ride-sharing app Uber, along with other anticipated economic advantages, made it possible to lift the ban on women driving.

The Quran, the writings of ḥadīth, and the sunnah—the oral or practical example ascribed to Muhammad—all support equal rights for men and women to pursue knowledge. The Quran encourages Muslims to study, ponder, reflect, and learn from the signs of God in nature; it commands all Muslims, regardless of their biological sex, to work hard in the quest for knowledge. Muhammad also advocated for education for both sexes, saying that it was a Muslim man's and woman's religious responsibility to pursue knowledge. Like their male counterparts, women have a moral and religious duty to pursue knowledge, grow intellectually, widen their perspectives, nurture their abilities, and employ their potential for the good of society and their own souls. Copyists stated in the ḥadīth literature that it is everyone's duty, male or female, to seek knowledge, making it clear that women were entitled to acquire an education just as much as any man. Some people hesitated to support these principles because they thought a well-educated, literate woman was harmful. This was an opportunity that many women in the Muslim world seized to further their education.

Islam places a specific emphasis on acquiring knowledge in subjects that are complementary to these societal duties, as it acknowledges that women are primarily spouses and mothers. According to James E. Lindsay, Islam promotes Muslim women's religious education. A number of nations with most Muslims have controversial rape laws. Some of these nations—Morocco, for example—have no basis in Islamic law or substantial influence from it; other nations—Pakistan, with its Hudood Ordinances—have codes that include components of Islamic law. Some academics contend that Islamic law, including verse 4:34 of the Quran, permits and condones domestic abuse of women when a husband suspects his wife of nushuz, or disobedience, treason, rebellion, or unruly behavior. Some academics argue that wife beating, for nashizah, is incompatible with contemporary interpretations of the Quran.

Numerous fatwas condemning domestic abuse have been issued. In recent years, several distinguished scholars belonging to the "orthodox Islam" tradition have issued fatwas, or legal decrees, denouncing domestic abuse. These include the Shī'ite scholar Mohammed Hussein Fadlallah, who issued a fatwa in 2007 on the occasion of the International Day for the Elimination of Violence Against Women, declaring that men are not allowed to use any form of violence against women in Islam; Shakyh Muhammad Hisham Kabbani, the Chairman of the Islamic Supreme Council of America, who co-wrote The Prohibition of Domestic Violence in Islam (2011) with Homayra Ziad; and Cemalnur Sargut, the president of the Turkish Women's Cultural Association (TÜRKKAD), who stated that men who commit acts of violence against women "in a sense commit polytheism (shirk)": "Such people never go on a diet to curb the desires of their ego... On the other hand, Rumi states in his Mathnawi that a woman might love another woman because she recognizes Allah reflected in herself. Tasawwuf says that a woman is the light of Allah's beauty shed on this earth. In the Mathnawi, Rumi said that a smart and kind-hearted guy who is attentive to women is empathetic and understanding of them and would never purposefully damage them. In reality, because of a respect for Sharia law, the legal theories of many Islamic nations have restricted the legal protections afforded to Muslim women by declining to consider or prosecute cases of domestic abuse. For example, in 2010, the United Arab Emirates' Federal Supreme Court affirmed a lower court's decision permitting a spouse to physically "chastise" his wife and children. The United Arab Emirates' penal law, Article 53, acknowledges the right of "chastisement by a husband to his wife and the chastisement of minor children," if the attack stays within Sharia-compliant bounds. In Lebanon, up to 75% of women have at some point suffered physical abuse at the hands of their husbands or other male family members. Over 85% of Afghan women say they have been victims of domestic abuse. Saudi Arabia, Yemen, Iran, Egypt, Pakistan, Syria, and Morocco are a few other nations with incredibly high rates of domestic violence and no legal safeguards. A Government of Turkey report states that in some Islamic countries, such as Turkey, where laws against domestic abuse have been passed, women who experience repeated acts of domestic violence from their husbands and other male family members are accepted by the victims without seeking legal assistance. The Council of Europe Convention on preventing and combating violence against women and domestic violence, also known as the Istanbul Convention, because it was first made available for signature in Turkey's largest city on May 11, 2011, was ratified by Turkey on March 14, 2012, making it the first nation in Europe to do so. The Istanbul Convention is a crucial international treaty that aims to protect women and domestic violence, and its ratification in Turkey was a significant step forward for gender harmony in the Islamic world.

Traditional Muslim writers created three conceptual lines that were believed to be in ascending hierarchical order: natural love, intellectual love, and heavenly love. The concept of 'Ish, or enthusiastic love, is ascribed to the Persian writer Ahmad Ghazali and is not mentioned in the Qur'an. Muhammad was birthed with a love for women because, according to Ibn 'Arab, who felt that the only way to see God is through experiencing Him in the human form as a woman, women mirror God. One could contend that she is not created because she is the Creator.

"A woman is not your beloved; she is the radiance of God."
– Rūmī

It is evident from another well-known ḥadīth that loving conduct toward one's spouse is commensurate with a great degree of religious understanding: "The most perfect in faith amongst believers is he who is best in manner and kindest to his wife."

Muslim-majority nations have different conditions for women and marriage rituals. Although it is rarely common, Islamic law permits polygamy, in which a Muslim man can be married to four wives simultaneously under certain restrictions. Since Sharia requires polygamous men to treat each of their wives equally, ancient Islamic scholars have said that it is best to abstain from polygamy entirely in order to minimize the possibility of engaging in the prohibited practice of treating one's wives unfairly. Polygamy is a legal but discouraged behavior. Certain nations, such as Morocco, with its Moudawwana family code, have implemented restrictions on polygamy. Beyond the four permitted marriages, Iran permits Shia men to enter into extra temporary unions, such as the custom of sigheh marriages and Nikah Mut'ah in Iraq. In contrast, polyandry— the practice of a woman having more than one husband—is forbidden. This includes temporary marriages that occur after a woman pays a certain amount of money to a guy or his family.

Endogamous and consanguineous arranged weddings make up over 65% of all marriages in Saudi Arabia and Pakistan; in Mauritania, Libya, Sudan, Iraq, Iran, Jordan, Syria, Yemen, Kuwait, the United Arab Emirates, and Oman, they make up over 40% of all marriages.

Muhammad purposefully discouraged cousin marriage as his sunnah, or the way to follow; of his thirteen brides, only one was a cousin, Zaynab bint Jahsh, a divorcee who historians claim was extraordinarily beautiful. The remaining spouses of the Prophet were of various socioeconomic and religious origins; Safiyya bint Huyayy and Rayhana bint Zayd were Jews.

First cousin marriages account for about one in three weddings in Saudi Arabia, Iran, and Pakistan,. Nevertheless, endogamy is widespread in certain nations, with a predominance of Muslims. Consanguineous marriages, in which the bride and groom share a biological grandmother or other close ancestor, account for the majority of endogamy that is seen. First-cousin marriages are the most frequently seen, followed by second-cousin marriages. Women in Muslim societies in the Middle East, North Africa, and Islamic Central Asia are most likely to be married in consanguineous endogamous unions.

Islamic law prohibits secret marriages because it values openness. Marriages must be public, a vow taken in front of the community. The European Council for Fatwa and Research says that a Muslim marriage meets the requirements for a religious marriage under sharia if two witnesses are present at the state registration of the marriage. This is because it shows (a) mutual consent and (b) a public declaration of commitment. Although child marriage was originally widely acceptable, it is now discouraged in most nations; however, it is still practiced in small areas of the Muslim world. Each country has a different Islamic marriage age for women. Islam has customarily allowed girls under the age of eighteen to get married since Sharia law bases Islamic law on the customs of Muhammad. 28% of Afghan girls are married before the age of 18 and 4% are married before their 15th birthday. 7% of Afghan boys are married before the age of 18.

Some Islamic scholars contend that a girl's biological age determines when she is eligible for marriage under Islamic law, not her chronological age. These Islamic scholars assert that a girl is considered marriageable in Islam when her closest male guardian certifies that she has reached sexual maturity. Depending on the girl, this age may be less than ten years old, twelve, or another number. In numerous Muslim communities across the globe, some clerics and traditionalist members of the community have maintained that it is their Islamic right to marry girls younger than fifteen. Saudi Arabia revised its laws in December 2019, bringing the marriage age up to 18. When a Muslim woman is on her period, in the postpartum phase, fasting, engaged in certain religious activities, incapacitated, or in iddah after divorce or widowhood, she is not allowed to have intercourse. Islam forbids women from getting married to men or from engaging in same-sex partnerships. IVF (in vitro fertilization) is allowed in Islam, although ovaries, sperm, and embryos cannot be donated. Forced marriage is common in Niger. Niger has the highest prevalence of child marriage in the world, and the highest total fertility rate. Girls who attempt to leave forced marriages are most often rejected by their families and are often forced to enter prostitution to survive.

Sharia law states that a Muslim woman cannot marry outside of her religion; however, it is permissible for a Muslim man to marry a Christian, Jewish, or lady of any other religion that has been revealed to the divine. Growing globalization has made it more typical for Muslim women to wed non-Muslim men who continue to practice their faith outside of Islam.

When a man dies without leaving children, his wife inherits 25% of the property, and the husband's blood relatives—parents, siblings, and so on—share the remaining 75%. His parents and any living children would receive the remaining share of the property, with an eighth going to each of his wives if he had offspring from any of them. The widow inherits some of her late husband's transportable things, but nothing from his immovable property, which includes farms, real estate, land, and other valuable items, is divided. The deferred mahr of the deceased widow and the outstanding debts of her late husband are settled before any inheritance is used. According to Sharia law, a widow must receive less than her daughters, a daughter must receive half as much as a boy, and the deceased's male family must be included in the bequest.

According to WHO, UNICEF, and UNFPA, female genital mutilation is any procedure that involves cutting or removing part or all a woman's external genitalia or hurting her genital organs in some other way for reasons that are not medical. The majority of FGM occurs in or close to Muslim populations. The prevalence percentages in different Muslim countries vary according to area and ethnicity. The term for this practice in Arabic is either khifaḍ or khafḍ. Male circumcision, or khitan can also refer to female genital mutilation. FGM is common in some Muslim nations, but some nearby Christian and animist communities also practice it. Most interpretations of Islam do not mandate the practice, and fatwas have been published endorsing, discouraging, or recommending against female genital mutilation while leaving the choice up to the parents. However, the advent of the Shafi'i school of Islamic law views the practice as mandatory. However, most Muslim scholars condemn female genital mutilation as a violation of human rights and argue for its complete abolition. Sayyid Sabiq, the author of Fiqh-us-Sunnah, asserts that there is no genuine ḥadīth about female circumcision.

FGM was thought to guarantee women's virginity and lessen female desire throughout history. Several observers argue that the practice originated in prehistoric societies seeking to regulate women's sexual conduct. FGM is a worldwide issue that is also practiced in Asia and Latin America, while being most common in Africa and the Middle East. Female genital mutilation is still practiced among immigrant populations in Western Europe, North America, Australia, and New Zealand. There are cases of female genital mutilation in Afghanistan, primarily along the country's southern border with Pakistan. Other nations where FGM is practiced include Pakistan, Yemen, Afghanistan, Kurdistan, Indonesia, Malaysia, Turkey, and South Thailand.

Prevalence of Female Genital Cutting

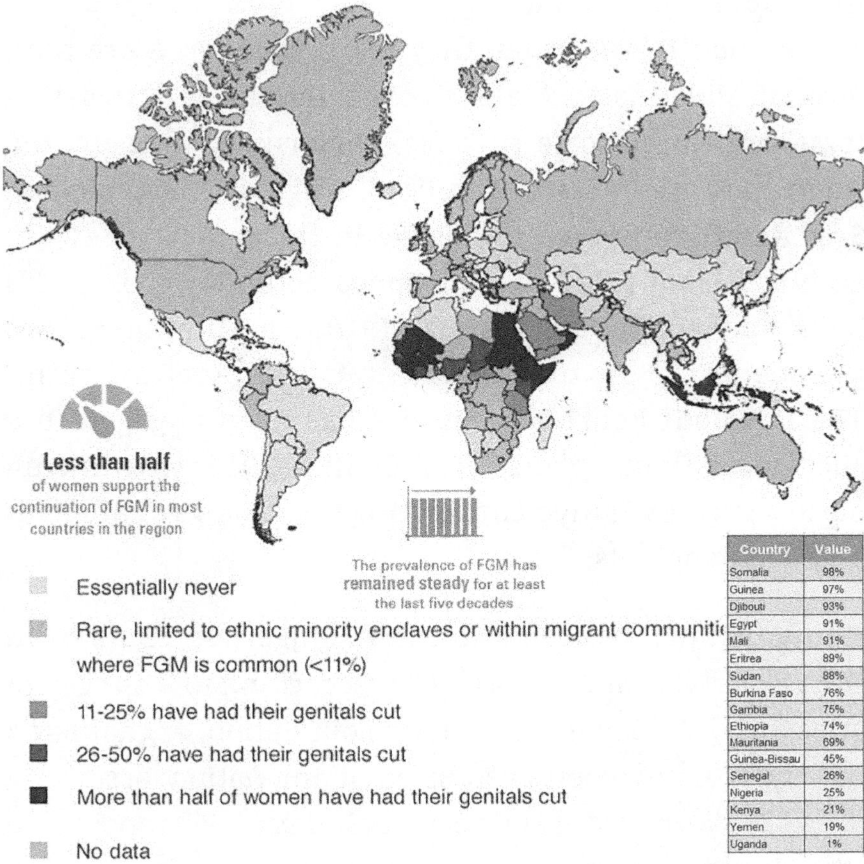

Country	Value
Somalia	98%
Guinea	97%
Djibouti	93%
Egypt	91%
Mali	91%
Eritrea	89%
Sudan	88%
Burkina Faso	76%
Gambia	75%
Ethiopia	74%
Mauritania	69%
Guinea-Bissau	45%
Senegal	26%
Nigeria	25%
Kenya	21%
Yemen	19%
Uganda	1%

In recent years, there has been increasing evidence supporting female genital mutilation in Iran. Numerous small-scale studies have been conducted, and one thorough study that discusses the various findings today makes it evident where FGM is most widespread in Iran. A significant frequency of FGM was discovered in a study conducted in Iran among Afghan refugee women.

According to a recent poll by Oxford, 18.2% of women in a Saudi obstetrics and gynecology clinic self-reported having had FGM/C when they were younger. More than 90% of Muslims in Malaysia and Indonesia, according to several large-scale surveys, perform FGM, including their diaspora in South Thailand, Singapore, Brunei, and Sri Lanka are known to engage in this activity. Several activists from the Dawoodi Bohra community in India have spoken out against FGM, and a filmmaker has included FGM in his documentary "A pinch of skin." The Dawoodi Bohra community has been engaged in a successful fight against FGM/C since 2015, with media outlets such as Sahiyo chronicling the group's challenges and achievements.

Afghanistan has been the most dangerous country in the world for women since 2011, according to a survey of experts by the Thomson Reuters Foundation. Afghanistan has the worst women's condition of any nation, according to a 2023 World Peace and Security Index (WPS) report. The WPS Index, which measures women's inclusion, justice, and security in 177 countries, is based on reliable data sources and is issued by the Institute for Women, Peace, and Security (GIWPS) at Georgetown University and the Centre on Gender, Peace, and Security at the Peace Research Institute Oslo. The WPS Index measures women's status using thirteen categories, which range from laws and organized violence to work and education. The fourth edition of the Index reveals that nations with prominent levels of female achievement are also more peaceful, democratic, affluent, and better equipped to deal with the effects of climate change.

Denmark tops the 2023 rankings as the greatest country for women to live in, with a score more than three times greater than Afghanistan, which has the lowest score. Yemen is ranked second from the bottom worldwide, and the Central African Republic is ranked third. This year, the US is ranked 37th, with scores in the second quintile that are comparable to those of Taiwan, Slovenia, and Bulgaria.

The national averages for women's inclusion, justice, and security tallied with the significance of geography and the ways it interacts with security, ethnicity, and forced migration to determine a woman's position. In the world's lowest-ranked nation, the COVID-19 outbreak, and the Taliban takeover made matters worse for women and girls.

FIGURE 1.4 Widest range of 2021 WPS Index scores in the Middle East and North Africa, the Fragile States group, and South Asia regions

Index score

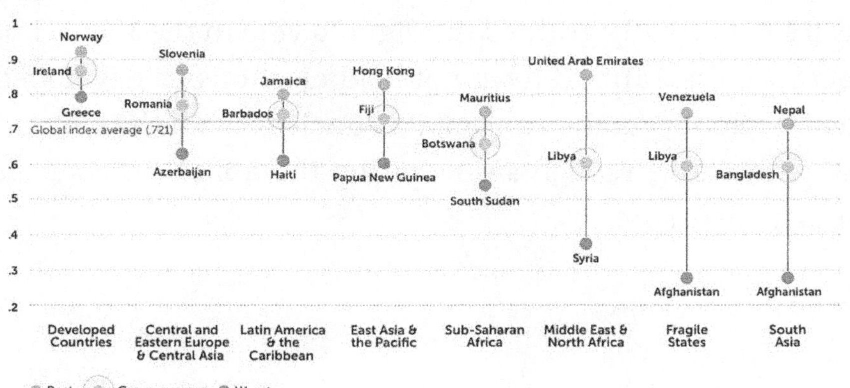

Note: Possible index scores range from a low of 0 to a high of 1. See statistical table 1 for data sources and scores. Countries in the Fragile States group are also included in their regional group.

Every morning, Afghan women find themselves without a job, an education, or any degree of personal liberty. The fact that every woman in Afghanistan is incarcerated should serve as a wake-up call to world leaders, according to Torunn L. Tryggestad, director of the Peace Research Institute Oslo's Center for Gender, Peace, and Security. The Taliban denies women in Afghanistan these fundamental rights, despite the Sharia granting them the ability to vote, own and sell property, operate enterprises, demand dowries at any time during a marriage, and actively participate in all aspects of life, including politics.

The Taliban government does not employ any women in leadership roles. Following their takeover of Afghanistan in August 2021, the Taliban established an interim administration entirely made up of men. Since then, there have been no formal declarations or actions suggesting the involvement of women in positions of authority. Under Taliban leadership, the situation regarding women's voting rights is complicated and unclear. Afghan women were historically granted the right to vote in the 1960s. But because the Taliban have not held elections or developed a clear policy on the subject, it is unclear what the current state of women's rights—including the ability to vote—is under their rule.

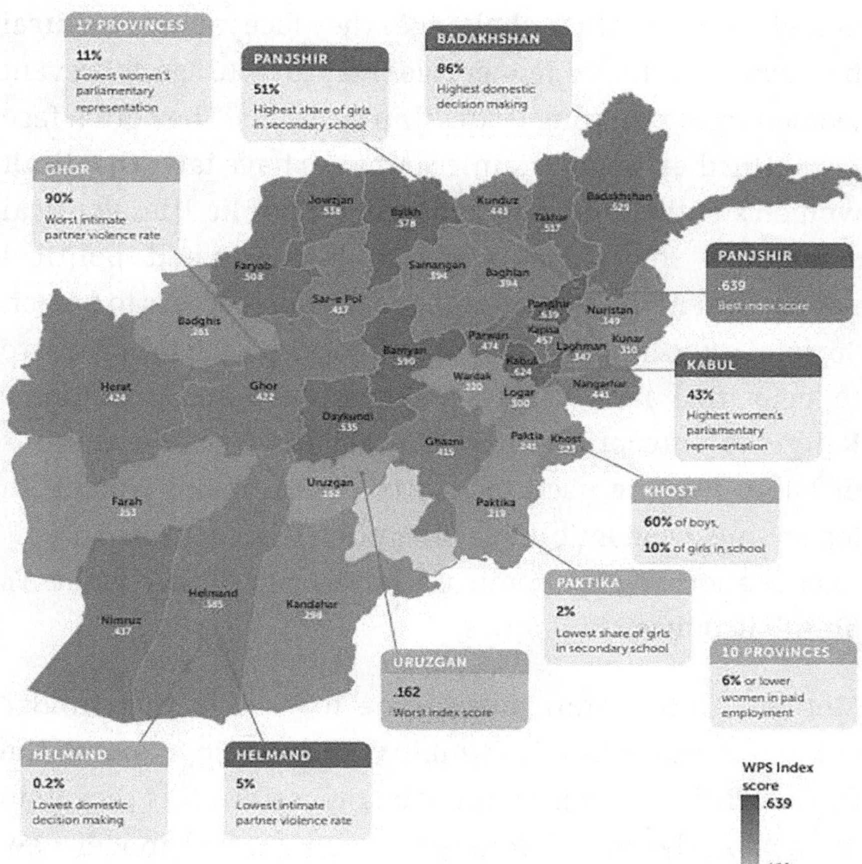

The Taliban has historically restricted women's rights and liberties, and there is widespread concern that women's rights—including their ability to participate in politics—are under attack. It is important to note that the situation in Afghanistan is devolving and dire. It is even more crucial today to closely monitor and support organizations that advocate for gender equality, as they play a vital role in protecting women's rights in the country. Women in Islamic countries often face significant challenges in rising to positions of national leadership like prime minister or president. Some of the challenges they face include cultural barriers. Traditional gender roles may discourage or prevent women from pursuing leadership positions. They often face Legal Hurdles. Some Islamic countries have laws that limit women's rights and participation in public life. Political structures sometimes make Male-dominated political parties and networks can impede women's access to power. Societal expectations: Women often face societal pressure to prioritize family roles over professional ambitions. Religious Interpretations: Conservative interpretations of Islam may be used to justify resistance to women in leadership. Economic disparities often lead to limited access to education and economic resources can hinder women's ability to engage in politics.

Men in Afghanistan must come to realize that, under current conditions of inequality, the development of the full potential of their country is impossible. It is they who must find the moral courage to convey and model new understandings of masculinity. Religious leaders must unhesitatingly raise their voices against the violation of human rights, against all forms of violence and fanaticism, and against the denial of equality perpetrated in the name of religion.

It is necessary to emphasize unequivocally that gender equality is a feature of human existence, not just a goal to be reached for the greater good. That which distinguishes humans—their intrinsic dignity and nobility—is neither male nor female. The quest for meaning, purpose, and community—the capacity to love, create, and persevere—knows no gender. This limitation does not only affect Afghanistan, adversely. It has far-reaching ramifications for the organization of all aspects of human society. Women have demonstrated the prowess of leadership across time, and some held significant political power in Muslim-majority countries. While there is only one woman currently ruling as prime minister in countries where Islam is the predominant religion, there have been more instances of women country leadership than in most majority Christian nations in history. Proving further that the Taliban is wrong.

Here are a few examples:

Sheikh Hasina She served as Prime Minister of Bangladesh three times: from 1996 to 2001, 2009 to 2014, and 2014 to today. Sheikh Hasina is the longest-serving prime minister in the history of Bangladesh.

Benazir Bhutto: She was the Prime Minister of Pakistan from 1988 to 1990 and again from 1993 to 1996, making history as the first woman to lead a Muslim-majority country in the modern era.

Tansu Çiller: She served as the Prime Minister of Turkey from 1993 to 1996.

Khaleda Zia served as the Prime Minister of Bangladesh from 1991 to 1996 and again from 2001 to 2006.

Megawati Sukarnoputri: She was the President of Indonesia from 2001 to 2004.

Mame Madior Boye: She was the Prime Minister of Senegal from 2001 to 2002.

Atifete Jahjaga: She served as the President of Kosovo from 2011 to 2016. Even though some nations do not recognize Kosovo as an independent state, the majority of the population is Muslim.

Cissé Mariam Kadama Sidibé: She served as the Prime Minister of Mali from 2011 to 2012.

Aminata Touré: She was the Prime Minister of Senegal from 2013 to 2014.

Roza Otunbayeva was sworn in as President of Kyrgystan in 2010 after acting as interim leader following the 2010 April revolution that deposed President Kurmanbek Bakiyev.

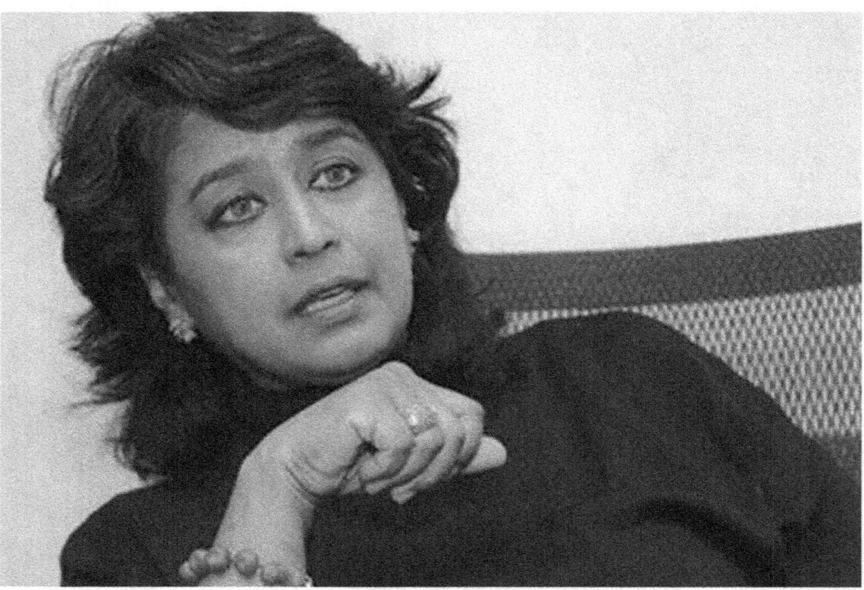

Ameenah Fakim: She is Mauritius' sixth President, and the first woman to ever run the Hindu-majority country. As well as her successes in politics, Fakim is a highly distinguished biodiversity scientist, having worked in the roles of Dean of Faculty and pro-Vice Chancellor at the University of Mauritius.

Maryam Rajavi is the President-elect of the National Council of Resistance of Iran (NCRI). Although, she is not yet the leader of the country. She is globally recognized.

CHAPTER 30

The Long Struggle of Women in Afghanistan

The dignity of women in Afghanistan is at risk once again in Afghanistan. Mixed media

The topic of women's condition under the Taliban is about life and death, not embracing western ideologies or modernity versus religious ethos. The Taliban is notorious for its misogyny and violence against women. The entire Taliban cabinet of the 33 members was made up of men, not a single woman in government. That is one of the indications that women's voices are once again silenced in Afghanistan. Women become commodities once again, owned and placed under the control of their men. They address their principles for women. This is hypocrisy at its dullest point. The sad part here is that while the Taliban cannot see it, the women of Afghanistan feel it, and the world cries with them. Instead of repressive chastising of women because their openness might seem suggestive or provocative, leading to temptation for me, why have they not found that eureka moment to utilize the same powerful message in the Quran to teach men those essential standard ethics, especially to resist temptation, and learn moral virtues that allow for peace and harmony that forbid such aggression to women and children, and cultivate cultural and gender harmony for the whole society?

Mixed media of madrassas, turmoil, Burka oppression of women, and ordinary youth life

The Taliban's ideology of repressing women based on Islamic grounds is both untrue and hypocritical. The idea that women exist solely to serve men and not to bother them is the apex of machismo. Women are only fit for the roles of housewife and mother so as not to pollute the morals of men who are conducting "Allah's work." It was unsettling then, and it is unsettling now that this kind of thinking can lead to a principle. This is the current situation for Afghan women. In a world that has progressed in unison thousands of years ahead, the effect of those husbands, dads, grandfathers, uncles, and nephews' actions on daughters, spouses, mothers, and sisters is heartbreaking and awful. If all things are considered, it becomes clear that the psychological damage done by the Taliban's rule, beyond the physical toll of women executed unjustly for any number of reasons. CNN reported in 2011 that Gulnaz, a shy and retiring Afghan woman, had become a media sensation thanks to a documentary she appeared in about the status of women in Afghanistan. A male relative raped and pregnant her when she was 16 years old. When she reported it, the police immediately arrested her, and she was sentenced to 12 years in prison for adultery. Her assailants were a married couple.

An international uproar occurred, and the president issued a pardon that led to Gulnaz's release. The young woman would essentially be moving from one prison to another. Gulnaz was raped and then forced to marry her attacker, who had a daughter with her. She became pregnant with his third child in 2015, and she and his first wife and their kids all lived together. Being at someone else's mercy is a terrible experience. Muttering, "I didn't want to ruin my daughter's life or leave myself helpless, so I agreed to marry him," Gulnaz explained why she had married the man. As a people, we like to stick to our roots. We would rather die than have to face the social stigma of a negative reputation.

In a culture where sex roles are heavily influenced by men, Gulnaz's experience is not unusual. Afghanistan is currently experiencing the same problem. Things like running away from an abusive situation, rape, and having sexual relations with someone outside of a marriage (Zina) are all considered "moral crimes." Human Rights Watch estimates that nearly all teenage females incarcerated in Afghanistan's juvenile detention institutions committed "moral crimes," while half of all women (non-juveniles) in prisons in that country were incarcerated for such offenses.

The facilities are overcrowded and unsanitary, exposing the female inmates to a wide range of health risks. It is common to hear that the staff beats the convicts. Also, many infants and toddlers have either been born in prison or have been brought there by their mothers after their imprisonment. Through the eyes of the inmates themselves, the video examines the ways in which "moral crimes" have a stranglehold on women in Afghanistan. The film demonstrates that women who escape violent husbands are given worse sentences than people who commit murder. The fact that most of these ladies are so young is also a concern. In rural, impoverished areas of Afghanistan, girls typically experience stunted growth because of poor nutrition, making their teenage bodies even less equipped for childbearing. According to Dr. Nafiza, Chief Surgeon at the Malalai Fistula Clinic, premature births frequently result in obstructed labor, a condition in which prolonged pressure on the pelvic bone prevents blood flow to the surrounding tissue. This tissue gradually dies and wastes away, leaving a gap between the birth canal and the bladder (or, less frequently, the rectum). A fistula is the medical term for this defect.

Mural in Kabul (Hope)

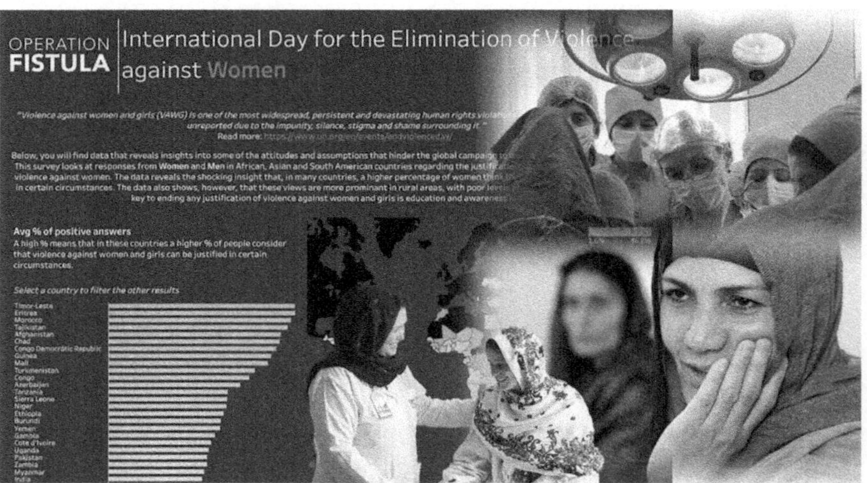

Fistula conditions in Afghanistan compared worldwide with Afghan ranking 4th, globally.

A fistulized woman has constant bladder leakage. Urine or feces pour from her vagina all the time, making it difficult for her to keep herself clean and compounding the problem for those who lack access to running water. The acid in the urine of certain people causes painful burns on their legs.

However, the emotional toll of a fistula is sometimes the hardest to bear. Because of the stench that comes from her incontinence, the woman is constantly humiliated.

The United Nations Population Fund (UNFPA) in Afghanistan is working to enhance maternity and reproductive health, and according to Dr. Bannet Ndyanabangi, the country director for UNFPA in Afghanistan, an estimated 3,000 women in Afghanistan have fistulas. Ndyanabangi cites maternal health as a metric. “When maternal mortality is high, then the prevalence of fistulas is high.” According to UNFPA 2021, the maternal death rate in Afghanistan is approximately 327 per 100,000 live births. It is down significantly from 2002’s rate of 1,600 per 100,000 live births, but it is still quite high. According to Ndyanabangi, “that means 12 women a day die in childbirth in Afghanistan.” “Fistula cases could be three or fivefold that.” Unfortunately, Farida was eventually shunned by her peers. Despite her recovery, the memory of the shame she felt at weddings still brings her to tears.

“I would wear my nicest clothes and [incontinence] pads,” she recalled softly. “I would sit among the other guests, and eventually, I would notice them holding their noses because of my smell.” Extreme stigma and humiliation are sometimes the result of a fundamental misunderstanding of what causes the harm. “I hear a lot from my patients that they believe [their fistula] is a punishment from God,” explains Nafiza. Communities and families tend to hold this common belief. Nafiza claims that husbands often accuse their wives with fistulas of adultery and other “sinful” actions. “Often their husbands divorce them, and they’re forced to go back to their parents," according to her. "Once, we had a patient at the hospital for two-and- a-half years, and she didn't have a visitor that entire time." Despite their decades of knowledge in medicine, many female doctors in Afghanistan left the country when the Taliban took power. Dr. Pashtun Kohestani was one of the few women authorized to serve at Malalai during the Taliban era in the maternity section. Fistulas are treatable. Because of the cost and level of competence required, fewer doctors can escape the Taliban because of this procedure.

The Taliban's gender apartheid and sexist limitations, which they justify by citing Islamic law, are baseless and arbitrary. Theft, adultery, and other crimes are all listed in Sharia, along with their respective punishments should the accusation be proven. As a moral and spiritual guide, it tells us when and how to pray, when and how to get married, and when and how to get a divorce. When the Taliban ruled Afghanistan from 1996 to 2001, they outlawed popular culture such as television and music. They have started holding regular press briefings and making regular TV appearances. Among the Taliban's many atrocities against women are the prohibition of education and employment, the marriage of minors, the slaughter of children, the destruction of cultural artifacts, and the practice of female genital mutilation. Women's lives under the Taliban's rule are untenable. Leaving the house without a male chaperone is forbidden, and most professions are off-limits to women. Women who did not follow the standards set down by the morality police, who patrolled in pickup trucks, were publicly lashed, and humiliated. According to Amnesty International and other organizations, in 1996, a woman in Kabul had the tip of her thumb cut off for wearing nail paint, and many more were executed on the spot for similar offenses.

Mixed media of Taliban destroying tv in 1992 and tv appearance in 2021

Promises of amnesty and counterterrorism efforts from the Taliban are not being taken seriously. Outside of Kabul, some Taliban have been implementing the old restrictions, such as telling women they cannot go anywhere without a male relative's permission or barring them from attending university. Some schools for girls and health centers for women have also been closed. Terrorist attacks persisted in Kabul after the United States pulled out. Heavy casualties were sustained as the suicide bombing proceeded. Afghanistan's former deputy minister for women's affairs, Hosna Jalil, expressed doubt to the German network Deutsche Welle that the Taliban will adopt a more liberal interpretation of Shariah in the future. She was afraid that under Shariah rule, they would have "literally nothing," including no access to education, limited access to health care, no access to justice, no safe place to live, no guaranteed source of food, and no reliable source of income.

After the fall of the Taliban government in 2001, an agreement was signed at the Bonn Conference to entrust the draft of a new constitution—the eight—for the country to the Afghan Constitutional Commission, which had 35 members. The draft stated, in its 22nd article, that Afghan citizens, both men and women, had equal rights and responsibilities under the law and intended to guarantee the rights of Afghan women, which had been baffled over and over by the Taliban regime, often banning them from getting access to basic health care and education.

Image: A collage of Afghan women protest against violence in 2021.

Mohammad Ashraf Rasoli, a Senior Adviser to the Afghan Minister of Justice, was a member of the commission at the time recalls the heated debate around this article during the Constitution's draft revision in Parliament. He said, it created a lot of controversy, because there are different interpretations of Islam in this regard. The debate lasted several days. Finally, it was decided that the citizens of Afghanistan, both men and women, have basic rights and duties before the law. Women should have equal rights under the law, because they are human beings, and they deserve to be treated with dignity and respect. They should not be discriminated against based on their gender.

Unfortunately, the Taliban discarded the 2001 constitution of Afghanistan, which protected women's rights, promoted women's advancement, and ensured equal legal treatment for men and women. However, Afghan women remained unambiguous in their demand for equality. Afghan women have changed from how they were 20 years ago. Women took to the streets to protest the extremity of the Taliban toward Afghan women. Some protest the new form of employment for women, but many more are staying home or, for reasons of anonymity, are burning their degrees. Most people agree that there is a new threat to Afghanistan and its women's future. Given that the Taliban is a totalitarian regime, what measures will be taken to address this issue? When will the Taliban address the growing resistance from women? In Islam, what function does love play? Why don't the Taliban preach love? How do the Taliban explain the teachings of a merciful and forgiving Allah? The current priority should be finding solutions to these issues.

Women's rights in Afghanistan have been varied throughout its history. Women in Afghanistan have experienced unprecedented abuse and gender violence. In 2015, the

World Health Organization reported that 90% of women in Afghanistan had experienced at least one form of domestic violence. Old customs and traditions of patriarchal rules that restricted women and girls from self-development, making personal choices in their pre-marriage and post-marriage relationships, or their ability to assert their economic and social independence prevail. Most married Afghan females are faced with the stark reality that they are forced to endure abuse. They are stigmatized, ostracized, excommunicated, persecuted, arrested, or killed if they resist or protest. This purpose of convenience of the status quo with the dictates of traditions is why the literacy of western education is frowned upon as a taboo among the population, compounding the already high illiteracy rate. This tradition is expected in the Islamic faith, especially among practitioners of Wahhabism. Reversing this general acceptance of abuse was one of the main reasons the Elimination of Violence Against Women (EVAW) was signed into law in 2009.

Fear of the Taliban

The EVAW was created by multiple organizations assisted by prominent women's rights activists in Kabul (UNIFEM, Rights & Democracy, Afghan Women's Network, the Women's Commission in the Parliament, and the Afghan Ministry of Women's Affairs). Women officially gained equality under the 1964 Constitution. However, these rights were taken away in the 1990s by different temporary rulers, such as the Taliban, during the civil war. Especially during the latter's rule, women had little to no freedom, specifically in terms of civil liberties. Ever since the Taliban regime was removed in late 2001, women's rights have gradually improved under the Islamic Republic of Afghanistan, and women are once again de jure equal to men under the 2004 constitution, which was primarily based on that from 1964. However, their rights are still complicated by a reactionary view of women held by certain classes of schools, particularly in rural areas, which continues to cause international concern. When the Taliban took control of most of Afghanistan in 2021, concern about the future for women in the country increased.

During the Durrani Empire (1747-1823) and the early Barakzai dynasty, Afghan women customarily lived in a state of purdah and gender segregation imposed by patriarchal customs. While this was the case in Afghanistan, the customs differed between areas and ethnic groups. Nomad women, for example, did not have to hide their faces and even showed some of their hair. Though Islam's rules of warfare offered protection to non-combatants such as women, monastics, and peasants in that they could not be slain, their property could still be looted or destroyed, but they could be abducted and enslaved.

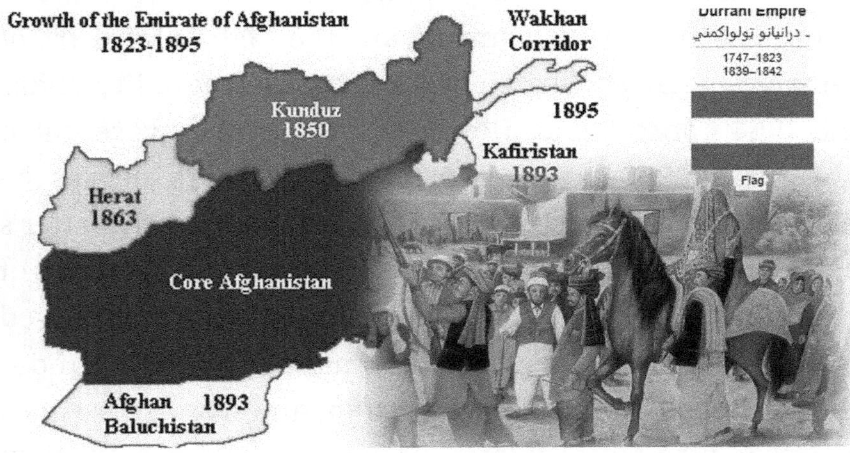

Durani empire and the evolution of Afghanistan

For the purposes of tribal marriage diplomacy and enslaved women held in the royal harem, Afghan kings were allowed to take as many as four official brides and many unofficial wives and concubines. There were no prominent roles for women in society. Some harem ladies, however, achieved notoriety as poets and authors thanks to the fact that these creative endeavors could be pursued amid the harem's isolation. Zarghona Anaa, Mirmon Ayesha, and Babo Jan are just a few examples of women who exerted political power from within the royal harem.

There have been attempts by certain Afghan rulers to expand women's rights. These efforts fell short of their goals. Some leaders, however, were able to implement lasting reforms. From 1919 till 1929, King Amanullah oversaw significant reforms that brought the country closer together and brought it into the modern era.

King Amanullah Khan and Queen Soraya in Europe

During his reign from 1919 to 1929, King Amanullah worked to reduce the influence of patriarchal families by advocating for greater freedom for women in public life. The education of girls was a priority for King Amanullah. He advocated for girls to go to school, but also for women to be unveiled and to dress more like women in the West. Polygamy was popular in Afghanistan at the time (1921), but he passed a law that outlawed it and other abusive marriage practices, such as forced marriage, child marriage, and bride pricing. Amanullah Khan instituted sweeping political and social reforms to model contemporary Afghanistan after the West. There was resistance to quick industrialization in the form of the Khost Rebellion, which was put down in 1925. In 1929, Habibullah Kalakani, leader of the "Saqqawists," led a new rebellion that toppled him. During his time in office, Amanullah introduced modern education to the region's youth and abolished centuries-old customs, such as the need for women to cover their hair and shoulders. With the help of his father-in-law, Foreign Minister Mahmud Tarzi, he advocated for a modernist constitution that included equal rights and individual freedoms. His approach to women was heavily influenced by his wife, Queen Soraya Tarzi.

Family picture: Mahmud Tarzi, sheikh Saleh el-mesudi, resmiya khanum, Soraya and moin-e saltanat khayria khanum, Prince Amanullah.

Mahmud Tarzi was a major inspiration and motivator for Amanullah. Tarzi's monogamous behavior served as an explicit example in the development and implementation of improvements for women. Queen Soraya Tarzi, his daughter, became the public face of these reforms. Tarzi also had another daughter, who married Amanullah's brother. Throughout Kabul and the countryside, King Amanullah Khan advocated for girls' education and opposed the veil and polygamy. In the middle of the twentieth century, Afghan King Amanullah addressed a crowd in his palace in Kabul to discuss the country's future. His remarks were deliberate:

"Islam does not require women to cover their bodies or wear any kind of veil." Religion does not mandate that women cover their hair or wear any style of veil. No one should be forced to conform to tribal norms without his or her consent.

The first wife of the Prophet Muhammad, Khadijah, was a wealthy businesswoman who financed his career before and after the establishment of Islam. King Amanullah Khan used this fact as an example of women's participation in battle while remaining covered. Queen Soraya Tarzi, the king's wife, was there as well; she was the equivalent of Khadijah to Amanullah. In his final remarks, he cited a passage from the Quran: "As for those who lead a righteous life, male or female, while believing, they enter Paradise, without the slightest injustice." Al-Qur'an, verse 4:124

As her husband finished his speech, the Queen smiled and looked at the King with pride and affection as she gently tore off her veil (hijab), and the wives of other officials present at the meeting followed suit. Many women from Amanullah's family publicly participated in organizations and became government officials later in life. Throughout her husband's reign, Queen Soraya sent shockwaves across the Afghan society. This well-choreographed scene was not recorded on film but passed on by word of mouth from one generation of Afghans to another. Many refer to it today as the country passes through yet another juncture in its long history, with the Taliban returning to power in Kabul.

Although her father, the poet Sardar Mahmud Tarzi, was sent into exile for his modernist leanings and liberal beliefs, Queen Soraya, born on November 24, 1899, in Damascus, Syria, became one of the most influential female campaigners in all of Afghanistan and the Muslim world. In 1913, Amanullah Khan married Soraya Tarzi. It was a customary practice at the time, even though she was only 14. As the first and only wife of a king, Queen Soraya demonstrated equality between the sexes by proving that a man could be happy with just one wife.

Mixed media Queen Soraya Tarzi carrying the original flag of Afghanistan.

Rora Asim Khan, a Swedish memoirist who married an Afghan in 1926 and later lived in Afghanistan, wrote glowingly of her time spent with Queen Soraya. A reporter for the French publication La Vie once stated: “Of all the many women and queens that I have interviewed, the Queen of Afghanistan, Soraya, is the smartest and the most talented, full of knowledge, who would lead her country to progress and bring the country in line with progressive countries in the world.”

A mixed media art Newark Museum: background artwork by Lalla Essaydi

In 1926, the Queen took on the important function of Minister of Education, proving that women could successfully lead in male- dominated fields. As Amanullah Khan was quoted as saying, “I am your king, but the minister of education

is my wife, your queen." She established both the Ershad-i-Niswan (Guidance for Women) journal and the Anjuman-i Himayat-i-Niswan organization for women in 1927. Masturat School and Ismat (Malalai) School, both for girls, were established during her tenure as minister of education. While her mother was editor of the women's periodical Ishadul Naswan (1922), she helped found the Masturat Hospital for Women the same year.

Social reforms championed by Queen Soraya and King Amanullah Khan led to widespread opposition and a revolt that led to their ouster. In 1929, the King abdicated and handed power to his brother, Inayatu'llah Khan, to avert a civil war. From January 17, 1929, to October 13, 1929, his successor, Habibullah Kalakani, "Bacha-ye Saqao," reintroduced the veil and resisted the reforms in women's rights, enforcing purdah.

In exile, King Amanullah and Queen Soraya spent the rest of their lives. On April 20, 1968, Soraya Tarzi passed away in Rome, Italy. The Italian military contingent escorted the coffin from Rome to the airport, and from there it was sent to Afghanistan for a state funeral. She joined her husband, the King, who had passed away eight years earlier on April

25, 1960 (at the age of 67) in Zürich, Switzerland, in the family mausoleum in Jalalabad.

The Afghan woman continues to carry Queen Soraya's legacy. She had inspired many women to fight for the equality that Islam guaranteed them, which religious authorities had no authority to revoke. The example she established for women in Afghanistan was revolutionary, and it has had far-reaching effects. She demonstrated the importance of women being strong and persistent in their pursuit of equality.

On August 19, 1926, the seventh anniversary of Afghanistan's Independence, Queen Soraya delivered an eloquent and inspiring speech:

> *"It (Independence) belongs to all of us, and that is why we celebrate it. Do you think, however, that our nation from the outset needs only men to serve it? Women should also take their part as women did in the early years of our nation and Islam. From their examples, we must learn that we must all contribute toward the development of*

our nation and that this cannot be done without being equipped with knowledge. So, we should all attempt to acquire as much knowledge as possible so that we may render our services to society in the manner of the women of early Islam."

Mohammed Nadir Shah was a pious Muslim who advocated for the gradual and modest advancement of women's rights. His son Mohammed Zahir Shah, who came to power after World War II, veered slightly from his father's policies by enacting a number of modernizations changes he saw as a necessity for the country, measures that ultimately led to the revival of the women's movement. Female students were first admitted to Kabul University in 1950–1951, and in 1946, the government-backed Women's Welfare Association (WWA) was established with Queen Humaira Begum as patron to provide girls' education and vocational training.

King Zahir Shah and Queen Humaira Shah in Germany

Women were admitted to parliament for the first time. Only four of the 216 members of parliament, for which Daoud Khan was elected Prime Minister in 1953, under the then-King were female, but the country's prospects for freedom and equality between the sexes were bright. King Zahir Shar's regime promoted societal reforms that gave women more opportunities to participate in public life. One of the king's goals was to end the Islamist habit of treating women as second- class citizens, which is common in more fundamentalist sects. He contributed to the progress of modernity during his lifetime.

On August 29, 1959, Queen Humaira Begum, Princess Bilqis, and Zamina Begum, the wife of the prime minister, attended a public military parade event on the second day of the Jeshyn festival without their veils. And a few Islamic religious leaders protested by writing a letter to the Prime Minister demanding that the laws of Sharia be observed.

Arbitrary proclamations by theologians persist.

The Prime minister answered by inviting them to the capital and presenting proof that the holy scripture demanded the chadri. When the clerics could not find such a passage, the Prime Minister declared that the female members of the Royal Family would no longer wear veils because the Islamic law did not demand it. While the chadri was never banned, the example of the Queen and the Prime Minister's wife was followed by the wives and daughters of government officials as well as by other urban women of the upper class and middle class, with Kubra Noorzai and Masuma Esmati-Wardak known as the first commoner pioneers.

Afghan women have had the right to vote and run for office since the country's constitution was ratified in 1964. In urban areas, women had more freedom and access to education, allowing them to participate fully in society and pursue careers in fields such as science, teaching, medicine, and public service.

Afghan women in traditional dress, May 1968

Women also began making appearances in the media and the arts. In the 1960s, Rukhshana rose to fame as one of the first female pop singers in Afghanistan. Afghan women gained the right to vote and run for office since the country's constitution was ratified in 1964. In urban areas, women had more freedom and access to education, allowing them to participate fully in society and pursue careers in fields such as science, teaching, medicine, and public service. Despite the WWA's best efforts, most women still were not able to take advantage of these advancements because the changes largely affected only the metropolitan elite and had little impact outside of the cities. Women in rural areas were mostly insulated from urbanization because of the region's deeply patriarchal, tribal culture. But everything changed ten years later when Mohammed Daoud Khan, the prime minister and cousin of King Zahir Shah, conducted a peaceful coup d'état. Although his was a bloodless coup de tat, it was followed by a bloodier coup called the Sowr revolution, also called the April Coup, conducted by the People's Democratic Party of Afghanistan in 1978 paving the way for the advent of the communist era.

In 1978, under Nur Muhammad Taraki's leadership, the government officially recognized women's equality. Women were granted legal parity with men in 1978, while Nur Muhammad Taraki was president. The complete prohibition of the purchase and sale of females was one of the first regulations issued by the Revolutionary Council. The law ensured that they could make their own decisions regarding marriage and professional pursuits. This went against the custom that allowed the brother of the deceased man to inherit the bride. The monarchy had limited women's rights to the urban elite, but the Communists tried to expand gender equality and women's rights to all segments of society, including those living in rural areas. The rural conservative populace reacted strongly negatively to the unveiling and implementation of compulsory education, which aided in the resistance against the Soviets and the Communist regime. Literacy efforts for rural women were one way the communist government tried to implement its ideology of female emancipation, but they were met with fierce resistance, especially in the Pashtun tribal areas. Due to the Communists' social modernization reforms, the rural conservative Islamic and anti-Communist resistance movement began labeling the urban population as degenerate. This was due to the Communists' enforcement of female emancipation, which allowed urban women to mix with men and participate in public life fully unveiled.

Huda Sha'arawi, an Egyptian feminist who famously removed her veil in 1923 and urged Muslim women to do the same, complemented Soraya's audacious act with a potent gesture. Huda Sha'arawi was a pioneering Egyptian feminist leader, suffragette, nationalist, and founder of the Egyptian Feminist Union. She was born on June 23, 1879, in Minya, Egypt, and died on December 12, 1947, in Cairo, Egypt. Thousands of women in the Islamic world took their cue from Shaarawi.

Huda and the Egyptian women' rights movement

Sha'arawi decided to stop wearing her religious veil and her headscarf after her husband's death in 1922. After returning from the International Woman Suffrage Alliance Congress in Rome, she removed her veil, a signal event in the history of Egyptian feminism. Women who came to greet her were shocked at first, then broke into applause, and some of them removed their veils. Within a decade of Huda's act of defiance, all Egyptian women stopped wearing the religious veil and religious headscarf for many decades until a retrograde movement occurred. Her decision to unveil herself as part of a more significant movement of women was influenced by a French-born Egyptian feminist named Eugénie Le Brun but contrasted with some feminist thinkers like Malak Hifni Nasif. In 1923, Sha'arawi founded and became the first president of the Egyptian Feminist Union.

> *"So, if the traditions and culture of the Eastern community are blindly compelled to hurt a woman's dignity, insult, and degrade her in the name of cultural unity, then I*

am ready to burn myself. If it means facing prosecution and rejection to highlight these difficult truths, I intend to vocalize my pain and start a revolution for the silent women who faced centuries of oppression."
- Huda Sha'arawi

Ladies and gentlemen, the Arab woman, equal to the man in duties and obligations, would not accept the distinctions between the sexes that the advanced countries have done away with within the twentieth century. The Arab woman would disagree with being chained to slavery and pay for the consequences of men's mistakes concerning her country's rights and her children's future. The woman also demands, with her loudest voice, that her political rights, granted to her by the Sharia and dictated to her by the demands of the present, be restored. The advanced nations have recognized that man and woman are to each other like the brain and heart are to the body; if the balance between these two organs is upset, the whole-body system would be upset. Likewise, if the relationship between the two sexes is not balanced, the nation will disintegrate and collapse. After careful examination into the matter, the advanced nations have believed in the equality of sexes in all rights, even though their religious and secular laws have not reached the level Islam has reached in terms of justice for women.

This movement ushered in an era when other Muslim nations, like Turkey, Iran, Afghanistan, and Egypt, were also on the path to civilization. During the communist regime, between 1978 and 1987, when communist ideology toppled Mohammed Daoud Khan's regime, women in Afghanistan enjoyed unparalleled levels of equality. The Democratic Women's Organization of Afghanistan (DOAW) and later the Afghan Women's Council (AWC) enthusiastically supported the government's women's emancipation policy and worked to see it implemented. Masuma Esmati-Wardak oversaw a team of eight women who ran the AWC until 1989. The AWC counted close to 150,000 members and maintained branches in every Canadian province.

Anahita Ratebzad communist party and female parliament in Afghanistan in the 80s

The AWC helped Afghan women by teaching them new skills in secretarial work, tailoring, hairstyling, and manufacturing, among other areas, as part of its fight against illiteracy. The governments of Afghanistan and the

Soviet Union both backed women's rights throughout the Communist era. The Afghan Women's Council (AWC) and its predecessor, the Democratic Women's Organization of Afghanistan (DOAW), advocated for and fought to realize the government's goal of women's liberation. Masuma Esmati-Wardak oversaw a group of eight women who led the AWC up until 1989. The AWC has about 150,000 members and branches in every province in Canada. As part of its campaign against illiteracy, the AWC educated Afghan women in fields such as secretarial work, tailoring, hairstyling, and manufacturing. During the Communist era, both the Afghan and Soviet governments supported women's rights.

Under the monarchy, women's rights were restricted to the urban elite, but the Communists tried to bring these protections to all parts of society, even the countryside. As a tool in the fight against the Soviets and the Communist state, compulsory education was met with considerable opposition from the rural conservative population. The communist government's attempts to educate rural women in the name of female emancipation were met with intense hostility, especially in the Pashtun tribal areas. Conservative Islamic anti- Communists in the countryside blamed the urban population's perceived degeneration on the Communists' social modernization measures. Urban women could now freely mingle with males and take part in public life without hiding their bodies because of the Communists' strict enforcement of female emancipation.

In February 1987, an Afghan student activist, Meena Keshwar Kamal, was assassinated for her political work. Meena Keshwar Kamal was responsible for founding the Revolutionary Association of the Women of Afghanistan (RAWA) in 1977. RAWA, a group that advocates for Afghan women's rights. In the Afghanistan-Pakistan region, RAWA promotes secular democracy and gender equality. RAWA is still active in the Afghanistan-Pakistan region, where it campaigns for gender equality and secular democracy. The assassination of Meena marked the beginning of the protests of the Afghan proletariat, which would later become the Mujahideen.

The Mujahideen were not a particular group but a coalition of various factions, each with its own set of beliefs and practices. Attitudes toward women varied among these factions, with some being more moderate and others more conservative. During the conflict with the Soviet Union, societal norms, including those affecting women, were often overshadowed by the immediate realities of war. In comparison to the Taliban, known for their strict and often extreme interpretations of Islamic law regarding women's rights. During their rule from 1996 to 2001, they imposed severe restrictions on women's education, employment, and visibility in public life. Unlike the Mujahideen, the Taliban enforced their policies uniformly across the areas they controlled, leaving little room for variation or dissent.

A Taliban leader announces new laws and rules to a crowd in Kabul 1996

Overall, while some Mujahideen groups may have held conservative views on women's roles, the Taliban were more uniformly and severely restrictive in their policies toward women. Most Taliban soldiers, like their leader Mullah Omar, were uneducated villagers from remote regions who had attended Wahhabi schools in neighboring Pakistan. Pashtuns from Pakistan joined them. The Taliban decreed that women could not leave their houses or hold jobs outside the home without a male guardian's permission. When they did venture out, they had to cover their entire bodies with a burqa. Women were forbidden to attend school and were instead expected to raise their families.

During the five years the Taliban ruled Afghanistan, women were effectively imprisoned at home and were compelled to cover their windows with paint to prevent outsiders from peering inside. Women who had previously held high jobs were demoted to beg for food while hiding their faces under burqas. Due to the UN's refusal to recognize the Taliban administration and the US's subsequent severe sanctions, the country's economy has collapsed. Most teachers were women prior to the Taliban dictatorship; therefore, the severe shortage of educators had a profound impact on the quality of education for both boys and girls. Women were not allowed to work in most professions, including teaching, but they were allowed to work in the medical industry since the Taliban mandated that only female doctors serve female patients. Many high-ranking members of the Taliban and Al Qaeda in Pakistan participated in kidnapping and selling women into prostitution and enslavement.

Afghan and Pakistani Taliban in their elements

In March 2012, the Ulema Council released a "code of conduct" that stated "women should not travel without a male guardian and should not mingle with strange men in places such as schools, markets, and offices." President Karzai backed this code of conduct because of the U.S. occupation. According to Karzai, the regulations were drafted with input from an Afghan women's group and are consistent with Islamic law. Human rights groups and women's activists have warned that Karzai's endorsement of this code of conduct threatens "hard- won progress in women's rights" made since the fall of the Taliban in 2001. Despite gains made under the American occupation and under the Afghan democratic government, notably in the country's larger cities, the situation for Afghan women in the countryside remained dire.

Sushmita Banerjee and Taliban movie

> *The Afghans, despite their backwardness, are a friendly lot, but the Taliban are as barbaric as the Huns from the past. - Sushmita Banerjee*

Indian writer Sushmita Banerjee, better known by her pen name Sushmita Bandopadhyay, settled in Afghanistan after marrying an Afghan businessman. She had already escaped the Taliban's execution squad twice in 1995 before making her way to India. Escape from the Taliban is a Bollywood adaptation of her narrative of the escape. In 2013, militants in the Paktika province assassinated the Indian author

Sushmita Banerjee for allegedly disobeying Taliban directives. Though they have been conjectured upon, the motives behind her murder remain unproven. Some claim that because she was Indian- born and vocal in her criticism, the Taliban singled her out. Some speculate that her efforts to educate local women or her employment as a health clinic manager may have contributed to her death. It is still unknown why she was killed, as the Taliban did not formally accept responsibility for it at the time. Nonetheless, a lot of people think that the Taliban targeted her because of her activism and attempts to empower women.

Violence against women practices is common in Afghanistan and occur not only during the Taliban regime. The United Nations reported in 2013 that domestic violence against women had increased by 20%, frequently because of conservative religious and cultural views. In February 2014, the Afghan parliament passed a bill restricting the government's power to compel some family members to be witnesses to domestic violence. Human Rights Watch said that the government's response to cases of violence against women is "poor," citing the 2009 Law on the Elimination of Violence Against Women as an example.

A group of Muslim extremists in Kabul brutally murdered Farkhunda Malikzada, a 27-year-old Afghan woman, in March 2015 after falsely accusing her of desecrating the Quran. Some high-profile public figures took to Facebook shortly after the murder to express their approval of the gruesome lynching. It turned out that she was framed and had not burned the Quran.

The former president of Afghanistan, Ashraf Ghani, signed a law allowing Afghan women to put their names on their children's birth certificates and identification cards. This law served as a significant victory for Afghan women's rights activists, including Laleh Osmany, who campaigned under the social media hashtag #WhereIsMyName for several years for both parents' names to be included.

Farkhunda Malikzada questioned some heterodox practices at the Sufi shrine of Shah-e Du Shamshira in Kabul. Zain-ul-Din, shrine's caretaker.

Fawzia Koofi

In 2018, Amnesty International reported that both state and non-state actors perpetrated violence against women. However, under the Taliban regime, Afghan women have once again been stripped of their right to put their names on their children's birth certificates and identification cards. This marks a devastating setback for the progress made by women's rights activists like Laleh Osmany, who tirelessly fought for gender equality and recognition of both parents' names. The repressive actions of the Taliban highlight the ongoing challenges faced by Afghan women in their pursuit of basic rights and freedoms.

On August 14, 2020, an assassination attempt on a member of Afghanistan's peace negotiating team, Fawzia Koofi, left her with injuries. On July 12, 2021, Taliban insurgents in Faryab Province beat to death a local woman and then set her house on fire. Taliban insurgents in Balkh Province executed an Afghan woman in August 2021 for not having a male relative with her and for dressing provocatively.

There is still a lot of risk in Afghanistan, especially for women. Random acts of terrorism, including targeted killings, roadside bombings, and attacks on universities, persisted at the hands of ISIS and Taliban dissidents. In recent months, the Taliban and groups associated with the Islamic State have murdered several prominent women, including journalists and doctors. There is still a high rate of both reported and unreported cases of abuse against women. A Georgetown Institute's research confirms Afghanistan's position as the world's worst nations for women.

Delbar Nazari Speech of H. E. Delbar Nazari, Minister of Women's Affairs, Government of Afghanistan

Since the Taliban regime was ousted by the United States in 2001, women in Afghanistan have been free to return to the workforce, and the years between then and 2021 have seen great progress in this area. Women in Afghanistan were guaranteed 20% of parliamentary seats. During the 2018 parliamentary elections, some women won more votes than men. There were 69 female representatives out of a total of 249, or 27.7 percent. There were 102 senator's total; the president appoints 34 of them. 50% of those seats are set aside for women.

According to the World Bank, this indicates that women in Uzbekistan make up 32% of the parliament, which is a much higher percentage than in any of the surrounding or even some developed countries (Iran: 6%, Pakistan: 20%, China: 25%, Tajikistan: 25%, Turkmenistan: 25%, and Uzbekistan: 32%). Women make up a slightly bigger percentage of the legislature in the former than they do in Afghanistan. This advancement has been rolled back since the restoration of the Taliban, which is a major setback for the inclusion of women in the Afghan Parliament.

Women's rights advocates spent two decades building a nationwide system of assistance, but it has disintegrated. Employees of protection and advisory organizations face danger and frequently must operate covertly. The Law on the Elimination of Violence Against Women (EVAW Law) has been used to prosecute 22 instances of abuse against women since 2009, but this law is now defunct. There is no longer a Ministry for Women's Affairs. When the Taliban took over in 2021, they immediately began releasing convicts around the country.

Many of these inmates had been incarcerated for perpetrating crimes of gender-based violence. There was cause for alarm when they began systematically releasing convicts, many of whom had previously been incarcerated for perpetrating acts of gender-based violence.

is a member of the negotiation team, former deputy chair of HPC and reformer during post-Taliban reconstruction in Afghanistan. In 2005, she was appointed as Governor of Bamyan which made her the first Afghan woman to become a governor of any province in the country. She previously served as Afghanistan's Minister of Women's Affairs. Sarabi has been instrumental in promoting women's rights and representation and environment issues.

#CrisisandOpportunity

As the first female governor of Afghanistan, Habiba Sarabi created history. When Azra Jafari was chosen to serve as the first female mayor of Daykundi Province's capital, Nili, history was created. Roya Rahmani became the first female ambassador of Afghanistan to the United States in 2018, making history. A few notable women who have made development in Afghanistan are Shukria Barakzai, Nilofar Ibrahimi, Fauzia Koofi, Fauzia Gailani, and Malalai Joya. The women who became ministers include Suhaila Seddiqi, Sima Samar, Husn Banu Ghazanfar, and Suraya Dalil, to name a few. Afghanistan became the first nation in history to be appointed to a seat on the United Nations Commission on the Status of Women in September 2020, despite its reputation for mistreating women. Since the Taliban took power, everything has altered once more. Although granting women a separate seat in Parliament is one of the most notable achievements for Afghan women in the past 20 years, some women's rights activists claim that there are still other barriers to achieving gender parity and effective representation. "Sadly, there are still problems with supporting female candidates," the Afghan Women's Network's Mari Akrami says. "And the fact that not many people vote for women has an impact on women's rights all over the country." Decades of progress in several areas could be at risk if the Taliban are defeated.

Anisa Rasooli, Judge. Since the release of the prisoners in Kabul, several women judges have fled, and few women judges have been murdered.

The Afghan National Security Forces (ANSF), especially the Afghan National Police, had many female members. One member of the Afghan National Army is Brigadier General Khatol Mohammadzai. The presence of female soldiers in Afghanistan is unique. Generals who are women are far less common. General Khatool Mohammadzai is the only female general serving in Afghanistan.

In 2012, Niloofar Rahmani became the first female pilot in the pilot training program to fly solo in a fixed-wing aircraft, after Colonel Latifa Nabizada became the first Afghan woman pilot to operate a military helicopter. Naghma, Aryana Sayeed, Seeta Qasemi, Yalda Hakim, Roya Mahboob, Aziza Siddiqui, Mary Akrami, Suraya Pakzad, Wazhma Frogh, Shukria Asil, Shafiqa Quraishi, Maria Bashir, Maryam Durani, Malalai Bahadur, and Nasrin Oryakhil are among the other well-known Afghan women on the list. According to a World Bank compilation of development statistics from reliable sources, by 2020, women would account for 26.2% of Afghan labor force participation.

In addition to being overrepresented in the media and medical industries, women are now entering the legal system. About half of all Afghan doctors were women, since women were actively urged to consult a female doctor whenever feasible. The professions of law, journalism, and medicine were attracting more women. That has now devolved due to the Taliban regime, resulting in limited opportunities and restrictions on women's participation in these professions.

Women in the Afghanistan Military

All types of Afghan women worked in the airway sector. According to the corporation, women accounted for 30 percent of Ariana Afghan Airlines' employment in 2020. A private airline called Kam Air also employed more than a hundred women. In February 2021, Kam Air operated its inaugural domestic trip from Kabul to Herat with a female pilot and all other staff members. This marked a significant advancement toward gender equity in the aviation sector. But things have changed now.

The international community issued a call to action, led by former first lady Laura Bush, emphasizing the value of funding girls' education as a way to improve the situation of Afghan women. Washington considered the education of girls to be the ultimate success of the foreign operations and a key element in winning over common Afghans. When forces backed by the United States toppled the Taliban in 2001, almost no girls were enrolled in schools in the country. Soon after the U.S. invasion, tens of thousands of females registered in schools across the nation, a clear indication of success. According to World Bank data, 65% of Afghan females enrolled in first grade in 2011, the second year of former President Barack Obama's troop surge.

Image: Laura Bush and Zenat Karzai talk with Afghanistan

School attendance in Afghanistan With and Without the Taliban

In Afghanistan, there were more than 9 million pupils enrolled in schools in 2021. There were about 300,000 students attending universities and colleges. Furthermore, 480,000 additional teachers were placed in Afghanistan's classrooms. The United States Agency for International Development (USAID) funded their study abroad initiatives. When given the chance, Afghan children do remarkably well in educational environments. It is very uncommon for a child in Afghanistan to drop out of school once they are enrolled. Approximately 85% of children who start primary school will go on to secondary school. Furthermore, 90% of girls and 94% of boys who enroll in secondary school graduate with a diploma. The majority of cities have a high degree of literacy. Afghanistan's rural areas still have poor literacy rates, despite increases in the country's urban districts. 34.7% of females in urban areas were literate. With a rate as high as 68%, men in urban areas are far more literate than those in rural areas.

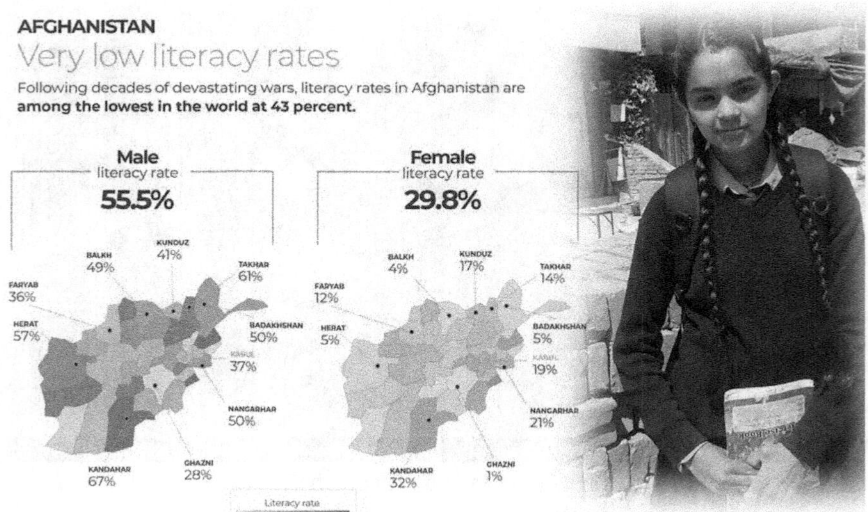

Image showing literacy rate in Afghanistan, and Afghan school girl without hijab before the Taliban return.

An initiative launched in October 2019 by Kazakhstan, the European Union, and the United Nations Development

Programme would see several dozen Afghan women attend Kazakh educational institutions in a succession of five years. Many Afghans fear that women's institutes and schools will be forced to close by the Taliban. Extremist propaganda implies that households with daughters in school are intolerant of heretics. There might be more opposition to women's rights in Afghanistan than merely the present restrictions on schooling. The world has made significant investments in Afghanistan's recent development, and if the modest gains made by women and girls in education are squandered, women's potential to shape the future of the country could be jeopardized. Hundreds of billions of dollars have been spent on the war in Afghanistan, and as a result, women have prospered in the media, administration, education, and civil society.

The way the Taliban treats women and girls is a yardstick for professionals. Beginning in early May 2021, terrorists in Kabul killed at least ninety students; the bulk of them were female students belonging to the Shi'ite Hazara minority, a group that has long been subjected to discrimination by the Taliban. Although they denied any involvement in the event, the Taliban placed the blame on the Islamic State. Girls are only permitted to attend school up to the seventh grade, or about the age of twelve, in nearly every area where the Taliban has political power. Locals and elders made a fruitless attempt to convince the Taliban to let girls finish school past the seventh grade. "Unfortunately, I'm not very optimistic that the Taliban will change," stated the former chair of Afghanistan's independent human rights commission. Here are Sima Samar's thoughts toward the Taliban. In the areas they controlled, there was little indication that the Taliban's views on women's rights had changed. It has not improved.

The Center on Armed Groups at the ODI has found that the Taliban's approach to schooling offers minimal guidance for female students. The radical group's instructional manual has 101 chapters, only two of which are devoted to women in society. In summary, the articles say that compulsory education is required for girls before puberty, but the situation is less clear for those who are old enough to attend secondary school, requiring the fulfillment of a number of "favorable" requirements before moving on to the areas of Islamic education and security. The Taliban, according to their spokesman Zabihullah Mujahid, wanted "separation between girls and boys, women and men, in universities, schools, or madrassas."

Peace for all Afghans.

The Taliban have not given many details about how they want to administer the 40 million people living in the country, despite the fact that it seems like a completely different country. They have stated that women can work, go to school, and participate in public life, but that these liberties are subject to "Islamic injunctions," a term that is ambiguous enough for various local commanders to interpret it differently.

Hijabs and burqas are simply a portion of the issue facing Afghan women, even though they are symbols of patriarchal dictatorship or, in other situations, just a way of life or habit that some women carry with them everywhere they go. The goal of the women's movement is to eradicate poverty on a national and personal level. The concept of a separate piece does not exist. Consequently, it is the responsibility of the entire system to ensure that every part operates to its highest potential. Feeling that we are a part of the country makes more sense than believing that it is ours.

CHAPTER 31

Gender Harmony in Afghanistan

Image: Mixed media illustration of the Parliament of Afghanistan with women and men 2001-2021

If men in Afghanistan show support for women, it might usher in a new era in which the country makes strides toward gender harmony. Support like this would be essential to increasing girls' and women's access to education, which may spark a boom in the number of women entering the workforce and, in turn, spur economic growth. Men standing with women could also be a sign that society is moving in the direction of defending women's rights and a decline in gender- based violence. Consequently, this would lead to a rise in women's political representation, guaranteeing a more equitable and comprehensive approach to government. Better healthcare results, especially in the areas of maternity and child health, as well as stronger, more stable family units, would result from this support. In addition, Afghanistan's reputation abroad might improve because countries that support gender equality might provide stronger backing. Finally, women's contributions to literature, the arts, and cultural practices would enrich Afghan culture and paint a picture of a society that recognizes and elevates the potential of all its members if they were given equal chances.

The Taliban have won the battle for Afghanistan, but they have not won peace. The country may be silent, but they are not at peace. The victory of Islam is to win peace. If the faith of Afghan women were in the dictates of Islam, as the Taliban says, it would be a good thing because Allah is the most merciful, most benevolent, most gracious, and most loving. This means saving the dignity of Afghan women for the sake of self-determination, faith, and country. A country, faith, and the dignity of women are the breath, scope of self-pride, blood, and soil of the country. In people's minds everywhere, especially in Afghanistan, the Taliban is synonymous with terror. The worst of all kinds of terror is the one that haunts. Women and children are frightened because they think they are prey to the extremists. This condition is not tenable. Most Afghans live in poverty, and there are millions of girls who never went to school, even for a day. We must understand that poverty is more than just a lack of money. It is also the inability to make a sound judgment. We could argue that poor judgment is the root cause of poverty.

One of the biggest challenges in nation-building is developing sustainable ways of living for its people. The Taliban must mobilize a fresh understanding of Afghanistan's responsibilities in the universal ecosystem and generate consensus for its stewardship of its people and environment through advocacies on changes in public policies and individual behavior to recognize humanity, ecosystems, ecology, health, and human rights as proper action. It is impossible to build a nation without the inclusion and consensus of women. The opportunity cost of less than balanced and fair empowerment and advancement of women is too costly for the development and sustainability of any community, culture, or country to bear. Alternative approaches such as repression and deprivation of women breed domestic conflicts as women worldwide continue to break traditional barriers of gender inequalities. The backlashes are worrisome in both domestic and international spheres.

It is essential to consider what type of precedence gender conflict sets for societies and generations to come when taking a stance on gender issues within the Fiqh or any government policy or constitution. The Taliban are not clear on exactly how they wish to govern. They are making it up as they go along. They have stated on numerous occasions that they do not want democracy. Iran offers a unitary Islamic republic with one legislative type of government. However, the Taliban would not adopt the Iranian Islamic system because it is Shi'a or for other reasons, but they have not explicitly stated their preferred alternative. Regardless of what the Taliban does, their Afghan women may lose some of those gains of the last 20 years, but they could never go back because society has transformed. The Afghan women love their country as much as the men do; they are determined to contribute to a positive change in their country. Human rights and gender equality set off alarm bells in the Taliban regime. However, gender harmony offers a solution to the Taliban problem.

The Taliban government must try to integrate gender harmony and women's empowerment into poverty reduction, democratic governance, crisis prevention and recovery, the environment, and sustainable development without compromising the integrity of one over the other within the context of Islam. They already practice this gender harmony initiative in health, whereby female healthcare practitioners attend to female patients. Or in religious practice, where women and men pray separately. It is probable to extend this practice across the board, including the parliament, government, and private sectors. The situation must culminate in women making decisions on women's issues, including education and justice. Education must include gender understanding and harmony.

The overarching goal in nation-building is to improve humanity, society, systems, performances, and productivity, enabling the sustainability of the unique Afghan identity and the prosperity of its people. For peace and prosperity to prevail, the transparent negotiation of harmony between genders is inevitable. The real meaning of gender harmony is the freedom to negotiate terms of engagement and cooperation between the genders. What is acceptable to men and what is acceptable to women are cultivated into the fabric of societal and cultural consciousness, including the penalties of violation according to Sharia.

People everywhere have decided to move towards progress in line with human civilization; emphasizing a 'comprehensive' approach to families' health and social life takes center stage in public discourse. It became clear that equal access, equal rights, equal opportunity, and meritocratic values culminate in harmony and peace in any society. Women should not be in the way of men reaching their fullest potential. Both genders cannot use the pretext of religion or contradictory views of self-determination to hinder the growth and opportunity of the country.

Since the Taliban are not yet on board with the concept of gender equality, the concept of gender harmony may help them see the harm in gender inequality and sex-based discrimination. The Taliban should organize a council of Islamic jurisprudence, including members of both sexes, to negotiate and find an agreement on acceptable political structures that do not represent Afghanistan or the Taliban as barbarous.

Achieving gender harmony—which acknowledges and appreciates the differences between men and women—requires educating both boys and girls about the fundamental rights of girls. Gender equality cannot be attained without first establishing gender harmony. The equality of women's and men's lives is not a condition. It is not enough to create space in the current social order for women to play their rightful role. Rather, the goal is for women and men to work shoulder-to- shoulder, each as the helpmate of the other—in the context of family, work, community, and international affairs—to construct a society that allows

for meritocracy and equity to flourish for all, irrespective of gender. The ultimate goal is to create a world where everyone has equal opportunities and treatment, regardless of their gender.

When there is gender harmony, the perspectives of men and women are recognized, balanced, and complimentary. The foundation of respect for men and boys is their right to it as family members, individuals, and members of the Islamic community. In addition, women and girls are treated with respect and are required to uphold such respect within the framework of Islamic culture, human society, and the family.

Peace in our hands mixed media from winners of the UN contest artwork on Peace 1st Ivan Huamani Lima, Peru 2nd Michelle Minzhi L, USA

Like in a harmonious dance, men and women can coexist peacefully in this faith, be even more productive and graceful, and have equal protection under the common law. Men and women can work together to strengthen each other's areas of strength and supplement each other's weaknesses to accomplish meaningful and fruitful tasks that are essential to nation-building and government affairs management. Gender harmony could lessen domestic abuse, lessen needless confrontations in public and professional settings, and increase understanding between the sexes. In the end, it might boost output and result in the desired sustainability and tranquility. In addition to assisting us in better understanding one another's viewpoints, or even assist in the assessment of emotional intelligence, or our nature, gender harmony allows us to work together to create a social structure that promotes the well-being of all.

The strategic solution that needs to be implemented in the curriculum of Madhhabs and Madrasas from elementary school to university level is the gender harmony project. The best way to achieve meritocracy, the purest form of Islam, gender harmony, and sustainable development goals is to have a basic grasp of how to coexist without violence, discrimination, abuses, and disputes resulting from gender differences. The Islamic world will now face this problem, particularly in Salafi and Wahhabi circles. The never-ending war is inside. The Taliban needs to get ready for gender-related discussions to understand and analyze the Fiqh's harmony-promoting objective.

The Taliban needs to communicate better with the public and provide the Afghan people with information that promotes gender education without sacrificing integrity for self-realization, acknowledgment, and respect for cultural diversity, as well as for the unrelenting pursuit of dreams, liberation from fear, and self-actualization. Therefore, women (mothers, daughters, aunts, and sisters) and men (fathers, sons, uncles, and brothers) have the same rights to worship, to engage in public discourse, and to make or have decisions that affect their families, societies, and futures. ' Ijtihad is necessary for proper Jihad. We are all from Allah, and we will all return to Him. Peace is Allah's cause.

The Messenger of Allah stated, "As you would have people do to you, do to them; and what you dislike being done to you, don't do to them." This assertion demonstrated how the golden rule permeates all ages. As stated in "The Forty Ḥadīth," "none of you [truly] believe until he wishes for his brother what he wishes for himself," according to Abu Zakaria Yahya Ibn Sharaf An Nawawi. "Seek for humankind, which you are desirous of for yourself, that you may be a believer," stated Sukhanan-i-Muhammad. The fourth Caliph of Sunni Islam and the first Imam of Shia Islam, Ali ibn Abi Talib, once observed, "Do not oppress, as you do not like to be oppressed." Treat people well because you want good things done to you. Think poorly of yourself, and you will think poorly of others as well. Reject the behavior of people that you would desire to be rejected by. Never say something to someone that you would rather not have said to you." The

Golden Rule—"We must treat others as we wish others to treat us"—was declared by the Parliament of the World's Religions in 1993 as the shared ideal among many different religions.

> *Why then would we wish for someone's mother that we cannot accept for our own? Why would we kill someone's sister and wish our own spared? Why would we deprive someone's daughters of what we encourage for ours'?*
>
> *If you want to know how civilized a culture is, look at how they treat its women." Bacha Khan*
>
> *"Comrades, there is no true social revolution without the liberation of women. May my eyes never see, and my feet never take me to a society where half the people are held in silence. I hear the roar of women's silence. I sense the rumble of their storm and feel the fury of their revolt."*
>
> *Women's Liberation and the African Freedom Struggle" The first step is to provide room for women in government. The government of Afghanistan must be inclusive of its gender and cultural diversity. — Thomas Sankara*

Can a bird fly with one wing? The exclusion of women is flying with one wing or one engine when there is an option for two. The war has left Afghanistan in ruins, and it has recovered. The United States rebuilt it. Now the Taliban needs to operate the affairs of the state. They did it before, and they were woeful at it. The Taliban government needs funds to run the affairs of the country. The international community understands this requirement, and no matter how stubborn the Taliban wishes to act, they could hold out not only on pledges but on Afghanistan assets in foreign hands. Arguments can be made that the Taliban government is not a legitimate representative government of Afghanistan.

The burden of proof is on the Taliban. This technicality nullifies that aspect of responsibility to the Afghan government in the Doha agreement and puts the Taliban at the mercy of the U.S. Therefore, the war is not over for the Taliban; the enemy is no longer the U.S. but their mothers, sisters, daughters, wives, and progressive men and women around the world. It is now the U.S. turn to wait them out.

Except, of course, that the Taliban takes new initiatives to form an inclusive government and fulfill its promise of a government system that serves all the people of Afghanistan without exception. This is not too hard to accomplish. Afghanistan has taken giant leaps before, and it can do it again under the Taliban's rule in the Islamic Emirate of Afghanistan. Some experts, however, believe that there is a plot to restore the splendor of the Durani dynasty. So, when the Taliban declares they will govern according to Sharia, they are effectively declaring they want to establish a sultanate on their own terms.

From 1980 until 1985, Anahita Ratebzad served as the Deputy Chair of the Revolutionary Council, which is the equivalent of the vice president of Afghanistan. No other woman has ever held such a prominent position in the nation. Her well-known tirade first appeared in the New Kabul Times on May 28, 1978: "Women should have equal access to health care, education, employment security, and free time so they can raise a healthy generation and contribute to the nation's future development." Government attention is increasingly focused on educating and enlightening women."

Anahita Ratebzad

Afghan women are reminded that a new revolution is imminent with the invocation of their spirits. This is the conflict over gender equality. This is not only an Afghan conflict. This is a conflict that transcends all Islamic sects and theological beliefs. The past and the future are at war with one another. The proletariat has always rebelled against the bourgeoisie in the Afghan civil wars. Though it has evolved into something far bigger, the Afghan civil wars have always been an insurrection of the proletariat against the capitalists.

Mary Akrami, director of Afghan Women Network; Laila Jafari, Afghan civil society and women's rights activist; and Fawzia Koofi in Qatar

According to a women's magazine, Ms. Women in the Room, article with Afghan Peace Negotiators Fawzia Koofi and Fatima Gailani's conversation with Renee Montagne on June 24, 2021, women are worried that after being victims of men's wars, they would become victims of the peace, echoing Anahita Ratebzad.

Koofi, a well-known women's rights activist and parliamentarian, was one of four women on the government team at the peace talks. Negotiating face-to-face with the Taliban, she said the Taliban seemed to be of the mindset that they could bring back the old ways. The negotiators sat with the Taliban. The women faced them and talked to them. Do they want what other people in Afghanistan want—a prosperous country? Gailani said that peace is not a lack of war; peace is to live happily with the Taliban and every other group. We do not want a peaceful prison. We want a peaceful country where everyone is free. We are all together, every ethnic group, every gender, every language, and every sect in Islam.

Both Gailani and Koofi knew that the Taliban taking power in the government was inevitable, as many Afghans do. Violence increased, including targeted killings of those best able to maintain the gains of the past two decades: activists, intellectuals, journalists, and government workers. Koofi has survived two assassination attempts, the latest this past summer, as she and her daughter rode back to Kabul from Parwan Province (a bullet shattered a bone in her arm).

When Montagne asked if the Taliban showed respect because they were sitting face-to-face with a worldly, highly educated, strong woman, Gailani said it was different because they knew her. She collaborated with them for 12 years as a neutral humanitarian president of the Afghan Red Crescent Society under the Taliban. She had witnessed villages destroyed and people killed children and women. So, quite frankly, they talked with all four women on the negotiating team with profound respect. They dealt, conversed, and argued the same way they do with male colleagues. So, this is particularly important. They see that women are the reality of a future Afghanistan. The inclusion and empowerment of women in decision- making processes is crucial for the development and progress of the country.

Koofi added that they classified the agenda as “easier” and “most difficult.” The Taliban put “cease-fire” as the most challenging agenda item for them to discuss. And just below "cease-fire," they put "women's, Islamic, and traditional rights." So, for them, it is the most challenging agenda to agree upon. For us, we have a constitution, which is our guideline, and that is why, moving forward, it has to be something that at least the negotiation team from our side should stick to, but this is going to be a matter for discussion.

women worry about their dignity being threatened as the Taliban returns.

The most conservative interpretation of Islamic women's rights has come from the Taliban. Additionally, there are more liberal schools of thought. Therefore, Islamic rights for women need to be at the forefront of political, not religious, discourse going forward, even within the framework of Islamic values, when there is no uniform definition or shared interpretation of them. We have to concede to the Taliban that while they are free to interpret things as they see fit, they also have to acknowledge that women are citizens of this nation in light of the significant changes in society. According to Gailani, women's participation in politics is difficult to reverse and cannot be done so. Because individuals have grown accustomed to their freedom of speech, it cannot be reversed. It is impossible to undo the current trend of young Afghans becoming more educated or the significance of education for both sexes.

Afghanistan in the present is not the Afghanistan of the nineties. Afghanistan's population is far more conscious of their needs. Afghanistan's people are resilient enough to be able to defend this. They are related. The world is watching and paying great attention to this era of social media, which did not exist in the 1990s. Afghan women are no longer as exposed as they formerly were. The Taliban puts women at risk of a radical rebellion. When these women rise, it will be to protect Afghanistan from the Taliban's dangers as well as to uphold their own dignity. They will not be silenced.

CHAPTER 32

The Fate of Faith

Innocent School Children that remain in Afghanistan

Afghanistan's future is in the hands of her children. The opportunities offered children in the broadest scope of society's needs and desires determine their development. This is one of the best arguments for the need for the liberation and advancement of women in Afghan society. This makes forecasting Afghanistan's future difficult because there are so many intricately linked and complicated variables that affect the course of the nation. Therefore, Afghanistan's future remains unpredictable after decades of fighting, with several possible outcomes depending on domestic factors and outside involvement.

Politically, the future of Afghanistan depends on the Taliban's governance and their ability to establish stability. If the Taliban can transition from an insurgent group to an effective governing body, there is a chance for a more stable future. However, this would require inclusive governance that represents the diverse population of Afghanistan, something the Taliban has struggled with historically. The treatment of women and minorities, adherence to human rights, and the establishment of diplomatic relations will be key indicators of the Taliban's ability and willingness to create a peaceful and progressive society.

Economically, Afghanistan faces significant challenges. International aid, which once supported a substantial portion of the country's economy, has dwindled, and the country is grappling with severe financial constraints. The future economy of Afghanistan will depend on the Taliban's ability to secure international support, combat corruption, and create a sustainable economic system that can support its population. The exploitation of natural resources, agricultural development, and regional trade could provide avenues for economic growth, but these require a stable political environment to attract investment and development projects.

Socially, much depends on the protection of human rights and the preservation of gains made in education and health services in the past two decades. The future could see a regression in social freedoms, particularly for women and girls, or it could witness the Taliban yielding to internal and international pressure to maintain and improve these social services and rights. Security remains a pressing concern, with the threat of ISIS-K and other insurgent groups challenging the Taliban's control. The ability of the Taliban to maintain security and prevent Afghanistan from becoming a haven for terrorist organizations will significantly impact the country's future and its relationship with the international community.

Afghanistan's future is therefore in a precarious situation, with the possibility of either a return to the cycles of tyranny and violence that have dogged its past or a more stable and productive way forward. The Taliban's activities, the tenacity of the Afghan people, and the involvement of the international community will all have a significant impact on Afghanistan's future. One of the largest airlifts in history took place during the Afghanistan evacuation. Between August 14 and 25, over 82,300 people, including U.S. citizens, Special Immigrant Visa applicants, and other vulnerable Afghans, were evacuated from Hamid Karzai International Airport. The evacuation of over 122,000 individuals from Afghanistan was a success. Upon arrival at Brussels' Melsbroek Military Airport on August 20, 2021, a little Afghan girl and her family were captured on camera bouncing joyfully into the air.

Viral Picture of an Afghan family, child skipping joyfully on the tarmac after landing in Belgium

The photo perfectly shows the elation of individuals who were able to escape before the deadline on August 31. Unfortunately, not everyone who sought to leave could do so. Many people have posted photos and called on countries to accept Afghan refugees so that the young people in Taliban-controlled areas can have a better and safer future.

Embassies from a few nations, including the USA, Germany, Saudi Arabia, the UAE, Canada, India, and Sweden, have been closed down. China, Iran, Pakistan, Russia, Turkey, and Qatar kept their embassies open. Sweden, Germany, and Finland are just some of the countries that have said they will no longer provide development money to Afghanistan. Efforts to help nationals of other nations leave Afghanistan have begun or been accelerated, and this includes countries with no diplomatic representation in the country. The Taliban's arrival has destabilized up to 6 million Afghans in the country. The United States government asked its allies to help with refugees' accommodations. Uganda, an African country, and Albania, Kosovo, and North Macedonia, European countries, are the first to open their doors. The U.K. was to resettle 20,000 refugees. Pakistan and Iran took in the maximum number of Afghan refugees and asylum seekers in 2020 and are now both dragging their feet. The United States is accepting people who have previously worked with the government in Afghanistan. Around 20,000 Afghan refugees fled to Canada. Tajikistan said it was ready to take in up to one lakh (100,000) Afghan refugees. Angela Merkel, the Prime Minister of Germany at the time urged her party that the country needed to admit about 10,000 Afghans at risk.

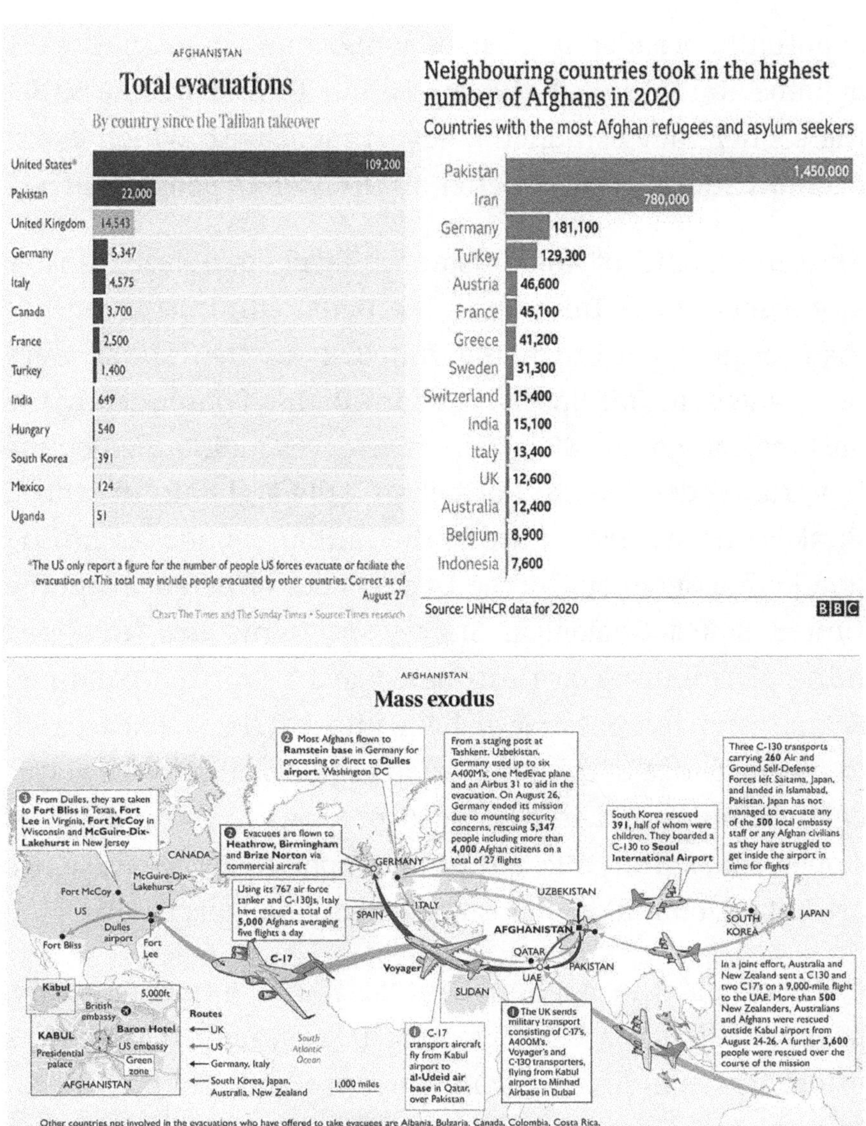

The former president of Afghanistan, Hamid Karzai, officially supported a seamless transfer of power and declared his intention to remain in Kabul, the country's capital, with his daughters. Karzai has stated his opinion that the current [Taliban] administration is just temporary and that it will eventually broaden its base of support and gain legitimacy at home. Karzai stated, "We advise our Taliban brothers that the sooner they establish a government with which every Afghan can identify, the better off the Afghan people will be."

The central bank of Afghanistan would not be able to transfer any assets to the Taliban, as the Biden administration has made clear. According to the United States, the Taliban were not granted the IMF Special Drawing Rights. Consequently, the vast majority of the $9 billion in reserves maintained by the New York Federal Reserve on behalf of the Afghanistan Central Bank is unavailable for use by the Taliban regime. According to a joint assessment by the Department of Defense and the United States Geological Survey, Afghanistan's untapped mineral resources are estimated to be worth $1 trillion. Afghanistan is home to over 1,400 mineral fields that are rich in a wide range of minerals, such as petroleum, natural gas, coal, chromite, gold, iron ore, lead, precious and semi-precious stones, salt, sulfur, talc, and zinc. Among the precious stones are rubies, emeralds, crimson garnets, and lapis lazuli.

Governor of the Afghan Central Bank, Ajmal Ahmady, proposed that the U.S. Treasury Department place assets under freeze in Afghanistan to put pressure on the Taliban to implement capital controls. Price hikes and a drop in the value of the local currency would result from that. The economic circumstances facing Afghanistan may force the future government to engage in negotiations. If not, the Afghan people will find it difficult to respect the governor. Still, the Taliban may need to retrain and reeducate its soldiers over the next ten or so years. Opposition and competition for leadership from other military factions are constant possibilities. Afghan women will be in the thick of things, no matter what.

Women for Afghan Women (WAW) addressed the UN on the terrible situation in Afghanistan, where the Taliban's takeover has resulted in the loss of millions of innocent lives and the forced migration of hundreds of thousands of people. WAW encouraged foreign friends to continue supporting the Afghan people during this trying time, and they begged all parties to preserve human rights and safeguard civilians.

Mixed Media: Effect of Taliban return on Afghan Women worry for the changes in common life.

The World Bank and the International Monetary Fund have stopped providing finance to Afghanistan since the Taliban took power, and the US has also frozen funds that were kept in reserve for Kabul. After 20 years of assistance to Afghanistan, donors had a "moral obligation" to continue aiding them because billions of dollars in aid had unexpectedly stopped flowing because of Western mistrust and hostility towards the Taliban. Fearing a return to the brutality that marked the previous Taliban regime from 1996 to 2001, U.N. chief Antonio Guterres felt that aid could be used as leverage with the Islamist hardliners to exact improvements on human rights. The U.N. secretary-general stated, “It is impossible to provide humanitarian assistance inside Afghanistan without engaging with the de facto authorities.” “Interacting with the Taliban at this time is crucial,” stated the secretary-general of the United Nations.

In the meantime, lively second-hand goods markets have sprung up in most major areas, and Afghans are turning to selling their household goods to raise money to pay for necessities. Last week, Ajmal Ahmady, the former acting governor of the Afghan central bank, tweeted that the nation was no longer eligible for approximately $9 billion in loans, assets, and aid. Former US Secretary of State Antony Blinken has cautioned that the Taliban would need to gain respect and legitimacy.

The chief of U.N. human rights, Michelle Bachelet, emphasized the concerns of the West. She said the Taliban had betrayed recent pledges when they ordered women to stay at home instead of going to work, prevented teenage females from attending school, and persecuted opponents who had previously supported them. “Dismayed by the lack of inclusivity of the so-called caretaker cabinet, which includes no women and few non-Pashtuns,” stated Michelle Bachelet, the main advocate for human rights at the United Nations. Secretary of State of the United States Antony Blinken has previously cautioned that the Taliban would need to gain credibility and backing following discussions with partners on putting up a unified front.

The strikes that left over 300 civilians dead and 28 military men injured during the evacuation of allies and expatriates from Kabul brought the Security Council together. approving Resolution 2593 (2021), which demands that terrorism be opposed, and human rights be respected and denounces the murderous assaults in Afghanistan. The resolution received 13 votes in favor, while the People's Republic of China and the Russian Federation abstained. The Security Council's fifteen members did, however, concur that no nation should be threatened or attacked from Afghan soil, and they emphasized how crucial it is to fight terrorism there. Stated differently, it demanded that more be done to support Afghanistan humanitarianly and that all involved parties grant access to the UN and its agencies, particularly to those who are internally displaced.

Resolution 2593 (2021) Malala Yousafzai, Deborah Lyons, UN Assistance Mission in Afghanistan, and Wazhma Frogh, Women and Peace Studies Org

Furthermore, by its wording, it obligated all international humanitarian actors and contributors to help Afghanistan and the main nations that host Afghan refugees. It continued by restating how crucial it is to protect human rights, particularly those of minorities, women, and children, and it exhorted all sides to work toward a comprehensive, amicable political agreement in which women would be fully, equally, and meaningfully included. The goal of the input is to emphasize the significance of protecting human rights, particularly those of minorities, women, and children, and to encourage all parties to pursue this goal with dedication and unwavering commitment.

The resolution, according to the US delegate, sets forth precise expectations. The resolution, according to the UK delegate, sets a precedent that the whole community will be closely monitoring. The Irish delegate stated that while her team would have preferred harsher rhetoric, we should assess the Taliban based on its deeds rather than its words. The Estonian delegate emphasized the significance of upholding international human rights standards, particularly regarding women and girls.

The Chinese delegate stated that any measures adopted by the Security Council ought to contribute to reducing rather than escalating tensions in the conflict, considering the precarious situation in Afghanistan. He emphasized that the recent disarray in Afghanistan is a direct result of the military's hurried exit and that this should be a period of introspection. The hegemonic habit of relevant countries imposing sanctions and deploying force at every opportunity should be changed. Moreover, such nations should not profess to be in favor of social and economic advancement while appropriating the riches of Afghans living abroad. It is also important to acknowledge the illegal actions of Australia and the United States that result in the deaths of defenseless individuals. It is essential to collaborate with the Taliban and provide them with direction to support Afghanistan's stability and bring about significant improvements. China also denounced the terrorist attack in Kabul, proving that the 20 years of its presence had not succeeded in eradicating these kinds of organizations. China thinks that successful counterterrorism initiatives require a well-rounded strategy.

Image: Afghans waiting at the airport attempting to flee the return of Taliban in August 2021

As with many other U.N.-led donor conferences, some countries injected more funds, while others highlighted commitments already made. German Foreign Minister Heiko Maas announced plans for Germany to pour 500 million euros ($590 million) into Afghanistan and its neighboring countries. Denmark pledged $38 million, and Norway promised $11.5 million. China promised $31 million worth of food and health supplies, and on Friday it said it would send the first batch of 3 million coronavirus vaccines. The United States pledged $64 million in new humanitarian assistance. Pakistan sent food and medicine, and it called for the Afghan assets frozen abroad to be released. Iran said it had dispatched an air cargo of aid. A total of $1.2 billion pledged in aid is double the $606 million requested for humanitarian causes. Amir Khan Muttaqi, the regime's acting foreign minister, told a press conference that the hardline Islamist group would spend donor money wisely and use it to alleviate poverty.

Image: Mixed media of US presidents that have been involved in the evolution of Afghanistan: Republicans and Democrats are evenly represented.

In his address to the country, President Biden stated:

> *"I accept responsibility for the decision." Some now argue that "couldn't this have been done in a more orderly manner"*

and that we ought to have begun the mass evacuations earlier." With all due respect, I disagree. In the midst of a civil war, imagine if we had started the evacuation process in June or July, deploying thousands of American forces and evacuating over 120,000 people. It would still have been a highly dangerous and challenging mission, with a rush to the airport and a collapse in government confidence and control. In summary, there is no evacuation from a war that can be carried out without the kinds of complications, difficulties, and dangers that we encounter. Not one.

Biden marks 9/11 with US former presidents, governors, mayors, and senators

In the following excerpt, President Biden helps bring closure to the United States war on Terror in Afghan. Remarks on the End of the War in Afghanistan, August 31, 2021, by President Joseph Biden:

Last night in Kabul, the United States ended 20 years of war in Afghanistan — the longest war in American

history. The assumption was that the more than 300,000 Afghan National Security Forces that we had trained over the past two decades and equipped would be a strong adversary in their civil wars with the Taliban. That assumption—that the Afghan government would be able to hold on for some time beyond the military drawdown—turned out not to be accurate. The fact is Leaving August 31 is not due to an arbitrary deadline; it was designed to save American lives. My predecessor, the former President, signed an agreement with the Taliban to remove U.S. troops by May 1, months after my inauguration. We faced one of two choices: follow the previous administration's agreement and extend it to have more time for people to get out or send in thousands more troops and escalate the war. That was the real choice—between leaving or escalating. Remember why we went to Afghanistan in the first place? Because Osama bin Laden and al Qaeda attacked us on September 11, 2001, they were based in Afghanistan. We succeeded in what we set out to do in Afghanistan over a decade ago. We delivered justice to Bin Laden on May 2, 2011 — over a decade ago. Al Qaeda was decimated. Then we stayed for another decade. It was time to end this war.

For now, I urge all Americans to join me in a grateful prayer for our troops, diplomats, and intelligence officers who conducted this mission of mercy in Kabul and at tremendous risk with such unparalleled results. We are going to continue to need their help. We need your help. And I am looking forward to meeting with you. And to everyone who is now offering or who will offer to welcome Afghan allies to their homes around the world, including in America: We thank you!

US troops praying after the terror attack during the evacuation from Kabul.

My fellow Americans, the war in Afghanistan is now over. We no longer had a clear purpose for an open-ended mission in Afghanistan. We have been a nation too long at war. If you are 20 years old today, you have never known an America at peace. Many of our veterans and their families have gone through hell—deployment after deployment, months, and years away from their families; missed birthdays and anniversaries; empty chairs at holidays; financial struggles; divorces; loss of limbs; traumatic brain injury; posttraumatic stress. And let me be clear: We continue to support the Afghan people through diplomacy, international influence, and humanitarian aid. We continue the push for regional diplomacy and engagement to prevent violence and instability. We continue to speak out for the fundamental rights of the Afghan people, especially women and girls, as we speak out for women and girls all around the globe. And it has been clear that human rights are at the center of our foreign policy. It is time to end the war in Afghanistan. Thank you.

May God bless you all. And may God protect our troops.

- President Joseph Biden

This book is dedicated to the brave women of Afghanistan, and my prayers are with them. They need the support of men to win the hearts of other women and men who do not understand or subscribe to the liberation struggle of women in Afghanistan. The liberation of women is the liberation of Afghanistan. Nowhere in the world and under no circumstances should men dictate the rights, institutionalize the abuse, or limit the freedoms for the advancement of women.

The goal of women's emancipation is not to harden women to become tough like men to benefit from masculinity. The goal is not to soften men to become like women and benefit from feminism either. Gender harmony brings about the necessary understanding of humanity, consensus for civility, and forging the path to enlightenment, peace, and prosperity without compromising the integrity of Islam. Gender harmony is like water. It reflects light, nurtures, calms, and breeds life. It simply means imaginative empathy, striving inclusively towards a brighter future for the society of which we are a part.

Gender harmony makes the constitution a sentient, sovereign, gender- sensitive instrument. I am committed to supporting the struggle of Afghan women for a peaceful and prosperous Afghanistan, and this book is a token of that commitment. Women in Afghanistan must ensure that provisions for women's rights are in the new Afghan constitution. If the constitution falls short of that, women and the international community must reject it.

This whole situation is the tragedy of the Dilemma in the US-Afghan Saga. President Joe Biden was right to withdraw. It was a difficult decision with lots of political consequences. We must applaud the President for his fortitude and wisdom in realizing that war is not the answer! Afghan women hold the key to peace in Afghanistan. They must stand their ground, and we, the world, must embrace all imaginable ways except violence to support them.

Women in Afghanistan must know that the entire world is with them, especially the men of Afghanistan. The successful suffrage of Afghan women is an enormous achievement for the world.

CHAPTER 33

The Women's Dilemma in Afghanistan

Image: from the movie The Swallows of Kabul depicting public scene under the Taliban rule

The U.S. exit from Afghanistan was a bold move and, ultimately, the right decision. The United States overstayed its welcome, and its continued presence in Afghanistan was unnecessary.

The Afghans wanted an autonomous democratic government with a measured progressive inclination, but they got a totalitarian dictatorship instead. They had three choices. Either corrupt democracy, protectorate occupation, or totalitarian theocracy. But they did not get to choose. Dictatorships govern without the consent of the people, and in totalitarian dictatorships, the power to govern extends to all aspects of life, which further worsens their living conditions and stifles any hopes for progress and democracy. The Taliban have forced the worst kind of governance system in modern civilization upon the Afghans, namely, a theocratic despotism that is dictatorial-totalitarian theocracy and gender apartheid. The Taliban is categorically headed by despotic religious fundamentalists. Despotism gives the ruler absolute, unrestricted authority. Through the application of a complex ideology, a totalitarian regime manipulates almost every facet of social life, including the economy, the educational system, the arts, science, and the morals and private lives of its people. With a narrow interpretation of Sharia as its charter, the group aims to achieve unbridled tyranny and total dominance over all facets of society by enforcing stringent laws and severe penalties for deviating from its inflexible viewpoints.

Despotism is the result of too much law. However, when a lengthy line of wrongdoings and usurpations all aimed at the same goal show a desire to subjugate people into totalitarian rule, it is their right and duty to overthrow such a government and install new protectors to ensure their security going forward. In the end, what transpired in Afghanistan was the political lumpen proletariat's takeover, which was brought about in a revolutionary sense by their perception of exclusion from the political system. In contemporary contexts, the term "political lumpen proletariat" refers to people who are susceptible to nationalism, populist rhetoric, or other ideologies that are detrimental to the interests of the working class or even to its overall development. Critics of this concept contend that it ignores the structural problems that led to these people's economic and political disenfranchisement and undervalues their agency. This makes sense considering the political and social revolutions that have occurred in Afghanistan in the past. Therefore, claiming the pursuit of divine power to use violence to deceive the populace or gain their favor is the simplest approach to explaining and legitimizing the usurp. Because of this, the Sharia is essential to preserving authority over the general populace. Women's subjugation becomes a necessary evil. The ruling elite, the Taliban, can then effectively manipulate and subjugate the populace in this way, ensuring their continued dominance.

The liberation of Afghan women was central to the story from the start. No outside force could ever take Afghanistan away from the Afghan people. Afghanistan has never been a part of any empire. In 1919, it established itself as a sovereign nation. That was 28 years before India and Pakistan gained their independence from the same British hegemony, making Afghanistan one of the earliest countries in the region to achieve sovereign autonomy. Two things make a law unjust: The first is the use of morally illicit methods. The second is if the law is not aimed at the common good. If rulers were to enact unjust laws or take measures contrary to the moral order, such arrangements would not be binding in conscience. In this context, we are dealing with the arbitrariness by which victims are chosen, and for this, it is decisive that women are objectively innocent, as it is a nature of being that is inalienable and entitled to certain human rights. They are subjugated for being what they are, not for a crime they might have committed. This is targeted tyranny. And when tyranny becomes law, rebellion becomes duty.' This is the women's dilemma in Afghanistan. As for Afghans, those who subscribe to the idea of government being a social contract between the rulers and the ruled and those who surrender their civil liberties in exchange for their safety and security, as well as those who benefit directly or indirectly from a tyrannical government, tend to have differing opinions on the role and effectiveness of their government. Some believe that their government is fulfilling its duties, while others criticize its actions and policies.

The idea of the right to revolt was famously articulated in the American Declaration of Independence, which declared that "whenever any form of government becomes destructive of these ends [life, liberty, and the pursuit of happiness], it is the right of the people to alter or to abolish it, and to institute new government." This statement reflects the belief in the people's power to challenge and change their government when it fails to uphold these fundamental rights. Mercy Otis Warren's book A Woman's Dilemma examines the traditionally limited role that women played in the American Revolution, highlighting their tenacity in the face of adversity as well as the conflict that exists between women's aspirations for equality and freedom and societal expectations.

Mercy Otis Warren was a pivotal figure in the political and social landscape of the American Revolution, using her sharp intellect and literary talent to advocate for independence and to shape the political discourse of the time. As a playwright, poet, and historian, Warren's satirical works and correspondence with influential leaders critiqued British rule and galvanized colonial opposition. Her advocacy extended to the realm of women's rights, where she implicitly championed the idea of women as equal participants in intellectual and political life, defying the era's traditional gender roles. Warren's extensive writings were not only instrumental in spreading revolutionary ideas but also provided a platform for expressing the potential of women as thinkers and leaders. Her three-volume history, "History of the Rise, Progress, and Termination of the American Revolution," was pioneering as one of the earliest narratives of the revolution from a woman's perspective, further cementing her legacy as an intellectual force in the fight for American independence and the advancement of women's societal roles. Her influence continued to resonate, inspiring future generations of women to seek active roles in their country's civic and political arenas.

Likewise, Qiu Jin, often hailed as a national heroine in China, was a revolutionary, writer, and feminist who became a prominent figure in the fight against the Qing dynasty's oppressive regime in the early 20th century. Her influence extended beyond her participation in armed uprisings; she was a vocal advocate for women's rights and liberation from traditional roles and expectations. Qiu Jin boldly challenged the status quo by unbinding her feet, a radical move against the entrenched practice of foot binding, and by founding a women's journal that addressed issues of gender inequality. Her enthusiastic poetry and essays inspired many and fueled a growing sentiment against imperial rule and for social reform. Although she was executed after a failed uprising, her legacy as a symbol of women's independence and a martyr for national liberation continued to inspire subsequent generations of Chinese revolutionaries, contributing to the eventual downfall of the Qing dynasty and the establishment of the Republic of China. Her life and work remain a powerful testament to the role of individuals in shaping the course of a nation's history.

As Afghanistan struggles with modern dilemmas, however, it continues to exhibit intense tribal and widespread economic hardship increasingly weakened the new government's support among the population. Corruption and nepotism are prevalent in the government. A major internal security factor has been criminal and terrorist activity associated with the prosperous drug trade. Drug- processing laboratories are located throughout the country, traditional informal financial networks launder narcotics profits, and some provincial and national government officials have been implicated in the drug trade. Afghanistan had the highest proportion of widows and orphans (respectively, 1 million and 1.6 million in 2005) in the world.

According to The Loomba Foundation's World Widows Report, widows in Afghanistan, Iraq, South Sudan, the Central African Republic, and Syria are most negatively impacted by conflict, as are those in northeast Nigeria, southeast Niger, west Chad, and north Cameroon by the Boko Haram insurgency. One in 10 women of marital age is widowed. The proportion is around one in five in Afghanistan and Ukraine. One in three widows worldwide lives in India or China, making it the highest concentration of widows in any country.

A significant portion of the crippled population and ex-members of local militias are likewise without access to assistance. According to data from The Asia Foundation, 17.3% of children between the ages of 2 and 17 and 80% of people in Afghanistan live with some sort of impairment (24.6% with mild, 40.4% with moderate, and 13.9% with severe). Afghanistan's female population is more likely than males to suffer from serious disabilities, which contributes to severe discrimination and other social challenges. This discrepancy feeds the cycle of marginalization and exclusion and exacerbates gender inequality.

Little welfare protection has been offered by the government. International nongovernmental organizations (NGOs), including Humanitarian Assistance for the Women and Children of Afghanistan, Afghan Health and Development Services, and the Afghan Women's Education Center, have been responsible for most welfare activities in the nation, along with United Nations agencies. NGOs also assist Afghan refugees residing in neighboring nations, particularly Pakistan. Human Rights: The 2001 Bonn Agreement established the Afghan Independent Human Rights Commission (AIHRC) to investigate war crimes and violations of human rights. Human trafficking and child labor are still widespread practices outside of Kabul. In conflicts between warlord forces, civilian casualties have occurred regularly. Poor conditions in overcrowded prisons have contributed to illness and death among prisoners. In the absence of an effective national judicial system, the right to judicial protection has been compromised as uneven local standards have prevailed in criminal trials. The government has limited freedom of the media through selective crackdowns that invoke Islamic law, and self- censorship of the media has been encouraged. The media remains government controlled.

Women's access to higher education and their ability to work outside the house, especially in politics, have once again been restricted. 25% of the seats in the National Assembly's lower chamber that were set aside for women under the 2004 constitution, which made a clear commitment to gender equality and women's advancement, are no longer applicable. Afghanistan's ongoing economic collapse following the Taliban takeover was a major factor in the country's humanitarian catastrophe getting worse in 2022. Throughout the year, more than 90% of the population experienced food insecurity, with tens of millions of people going hungry every day. The real war is a cultural war between the genders. It has always been the case. The war in Afghanistan is a proxy war for the normalization of traditions within Islam. We would lose the cause of our intended humanity if we called it the war of modernization or even the war of civilization. The Taliban war is a defiance to obey the universal laws enshrined in the Universal Human Rights Declaration. By excluding women from nation-building, they are putting the wagon before the horse, and this may explain why they are stuck. We can defeat apartheid. We have done it before. Women will win this war. They just have to decide.

CHAPTER 34

Lessons from Twenty Years of Reconstruction in Afghanistan: What We Need to Know

After the collapse of the Afghan government and security forces in August 2021, Secretary General Jens Stoltenberg proposed to the North Atlantic Council Organization (NATO)

to conduct a comprehensive assessment of its engagement in Afghanistan. The Afghanistan lessons learned process included both operational- military and political reviews, each covering the full timeline of NATO's involvement, from the terrorist attacks of September 11, 2001, and the invocation of Article 5 of the Washington Treaty, to the evacuation from Kabul. As such, it covered the UN-mandated International Security Assistance Force (ISAF) combat mission (2003– 2014) and NATO's Resolute Support Mission (RSM) to train, advise, and assist the Afghan security forces (2015–2021).

International Security Assistance Force and Afghan National Army strength & laydown

Troop Contributing Nations (TCN): The ISAF mission consists of the following 43 nations (the troop numbers are based on broad contribution and do not reflect the exact numbers on the ground at any one time).

Nation	Troops	Nation	Troops	Nation	Troops
Albania	255	Georgia	175	Portugal	105
Armenia	0	Germany	4415	Romania	945
Australia	1550	Greece	15	Singapore	40
Austria	2	Hungary	315	Slovakia	240
Azerbaijan	90	Iceland	3	Slovenia	70
Belgium	575	Ireland	8	Spain	1070
Bosnia & Herzegovina	10	Italy	3150	Sweden	410
Bulgaria	540	Jordan	0	The Former Yugoslav Republic of Macedonia'	165
Canada	2830	Latvia	175	Turkey	1755
Croatia	295	Lithuania	165	Ukraine	8
Czech Republic	440	Luxembourg	9	United Arab Emirates	25
Denmark	750	Netherlands	1940	United Kingdom	9500
Estonia	150	New Zealand	220	United States	47085
Finland	95	Norway	500		
France	3750	Poland	1955	Total	85795

The main findings and suggestions stated below are meant to assist NATO's military and political authorities in planning and directing their future crisis management initiatives:

Handling crises should continue to be a top priority for the Alliance. The goal of the international community extended well beyond eliminating terrorist havens; creating a stable Afghanistan proved to be quite difficult. As a result, allies should constantly evaluate strategic interests, be keenly aware of the risks associated with mission extension and try to avoid taking on responsibilities that significantly exceed their allocated responsibilities when organizing and carrying out future operations. In addition to seeking greater involvement from other international players who are better equipped to carry out those non-military consequences, NATO should set reasonable and attainable goals. Future operations by NATO to provide training, advice, and assistance should consider the political and cultural norms of the host country, as well as the society's potential to absorb training and capacity-building.

Nevertheless, the Special Inspector General for Afghanistan Reconstruction (SIGAR) was created during President George W. Bush's administration on October 4, 2008, for the primary purpose of conducting audits and investigations to oversee the use of U.S. funds allocated for reconstruction in Afghanistan. This agency was established as an independent U.S. government's leading agency with the mandate to provide recommendations to promote economy, efficiency, and effectiveness of U.S.-funded reconstruction programs and operations; prevent and detect waste, fraud, and abuse; and inform the Congress and the Secretaries of State and Defense about reconstruction-related problems and the need for corrective action. SIGAR's goal since its establishment the agency has produced studies that offered insight into reconstruction issues and held offenders accountable for defrauding the U.S. government through audits and investigations. The current Inspector General, John F. Sopko, was appointed as the Special Inspector General for Afghanistan Reconstruction on July 2, 2012, by President Obama, due to his more than 30 years of experience in oversight and investigations as a prosecutor, congressional counsel, and senior federal government advisor. His supervision effort has saved $billions of the US taxpayer war expenses since his appointment.

SIGAR began its Lessons Learned Program in late 2014 at the urging of General John Allen, former commanding general of U.S. and NATO troops in Afghanistan, former U.S. Ambassador to Afghanistan Ryan Crocker, and other senior officials who had served in Afghanistan. They alerted the

US to the need for a comprehensive review of its efforts in Afghanistan in order to improve similar efforts in the future.

Mr. Sopko often expressed his concerns about US inadequate oversight in Afghanistan since he started the job. He accurately predicted everything that went wrong with the reconstruction effort that forced the Marshall Plan for the abrupt exit from Afghanistan. Before Kabul fell, he summed up the reasons for the unexpected quick collapse of the Afghan government as the lingering problems of corruption, ghost soldiers, the dependence of the Afghan military on U.S. airpower, contractors, and other enablers, as well as the overall incompetency of the Afghan government.

Mr. Sopko argued that U.S. agencies made honest reporting difficult. Shortly after the fall of Kabul, the state department suspended access to all audits, inspections, and financial reports from SIGAR and other oversight agencies. The State department was afraid the information included therein would put Afghan allies at risk. However, there were concerns that, though the war in Afghanistan has concluded, that does not mean the American people, or its elected representatives do not have a right to know the truth about what happened in Afghanistan over the last 20 years. To that end, Congress has asked SIGAR a number of questions since the collapse of the Afghan government. They wanted to know why the Afghan government collapsed in spite of $146 billion and 20 years of reconstruction assistance; why the Afghan security forces collapsed suddenly; and what role the U.S. advisory and training efforts played in the collapse.

They wanted to know about continued reconstruction assistance, including contracts that are active or pending. They asked SIGAR to explain the extent to which the Taliban have access to previously provided government funding and equipment, particularly weapons left behind. Congress also wanted an explanation and document of the status of and potential risk to Afghan people and civil society organizations, including Afghan women and girls, journalists, educators, health care providers, and other nongovernment institutions since the Taliban took over. Congress wanted to determine whether Afghan government officials fled the country with U.S. taxpayer dollars, and Congress asked SIGAR to conduct a comprehensive, joint audit with the state and DOD IG's to look at the administration of the special immigrant visa program.

SIGAR reported that if the Department of State and Defense's restricted information had been released, the whole picture of August and all the warning indicators that could have foretold it could have been published. For instance, at the request of the Afghan government, DOD withheld information about the 2015 Afghan security forces' underperformance. Casualty statistics, unit strength, training and operational shortcomings, tactical and operational preparedness of Afghan leadership, a complete assessment of Afghan security forces leadership, and core operational readiness rates were included. Most of the information you would have needed to judge whether the Afghan security forces were a credible force or a house of cards waiting to fall was suppressed at the Afghan government's insistence. Given recent events, it is not surprising that the Afghan government and possibly some Department of Defense employees wanted to keep that information private, but it would have helped Congress and the public assess Afghanistan's progress and, more importantly, whether the US should have ended its efforts there earlier. Instead, SIGAR was forced to put all of this information in secret annexes, making it harder for Congress to obtain and preventing the public and press from discussing it.

SIGAR's lessons learned report was issued to coincide with the 20th anniversary of the US intervention in Afghanistan—ironically, it appeared just before Kabul fell. These matters are important. SIGAR's Twitter content was accessed 2.2 million times in August 2021, demonstrating that taxpayers not only deserve answers, but they demand answers. Families of Americans who lost their lives supporting that mission in Afghanistan must know that the cause for which their loved ones gave the last full measure was worthwhile and why the effort to build a strong and sustainable Afghan state failed so dramatically. The questions must be asked, and the answers must be revealed, no matter how unpleasant they may be.

As the President laid out in his speech on April 14, he made the decision based on four judgments: The president determined that it was not in our national interest to maintain U.S. troops in Afghanistan. In terms of Afghanistan and Iraq, there are four lessons to be learned:

Recognize the complexity of the local environment, including cultural, social, and political factors. A thorough understanding of the context is crucial for effective reconstruction and stabilization efforts.

Adapting to Changing Circumstances: Flexibility and adaptability are essential. Given the dynamic nature of conflict and post-conflict environments, strategies and plans must be able to adjust to changing circumstances. Rigidity can hinder progress.

Building and Sustaining Capabilities: Invest in building and sustaining the capabilities of local governments and institutions. This involves not only providing short-term assistance but also ensuring that there is a focus on long-term capacity building to enable self-sufficiency.

Ensuring Accountability and Oversight: Establish robust mechanisms for accountability and oversight. Transparency and accountability in the use of funds, as well as monitoring the progress of reconstruction projects, are critical to preventing corruption and ensuring that resources are effectively utilized.

Mr. Sopko criticized the Department's policy on classification, citing what Senator McCain said about classification, which is, that is basically used to protect against incompetency and other nefarious actions. It is the best way to hide screw-ups. The United States is a confident nation. However, as the adage goes, do not confuse fearlessness with competency. It may turn out to be incompetence, says Mr. Sopko. The government was making decisions and risk analyses based on inaccurate or inadequate information, and you are deciding based on inadequate or even false information.

Nevertheless, the US got hundreds of its ad hoc groups, mostly retirees, out of Afghanistan during the exit crisis. Note that for every Afghan that got out, there were five or 10 times as many who did not. These are Afghan journalists and teachers; if that can extend to other Afghans and those people, we are getting veterans every day who were shot to death, and this veteran population is still doing the bulk of the work to not only try to evacuate but also to try to raise money for people who are no longer getting a paycheck from the government of the Islamic Republic of Afghanistan. They cannot work. They cannot leave their homes. All of those people are running for their lives. All of the judges, female, or male, believed in the American way of democracy. All of the prosecutors, police officers, and Afghan special forces. Women and girls are in a special risk category of having to deal with the Taliban and losing a lot of the little advances made over the last 20 years. There were a lot of ghosts in the Afghan police and military. There were a lot of storages—soldiers that never existed—but there were a lot of honest, brave Afghans, especially in their special forces, but in other units that fought, that fought hard and died, and now they are all at risk. Every difficult issue Americans face is due to a whole range of government problems. The population is not designed or equipped to deal with all of the government's problems. The Afghanistan situation is complex and multifaceted. There are various reasons why some Afghans want the US out of their country. One of the main reasons is the desire for self-determination and sovereignty. Some Afghans felt that the presence of foreign forces, including the US, infringed upon their independence and national identity.

Additionally, there were concerns about civilian casualties and collateral damage resulting from military operations. Some Afghans felt that the presence of foreign forces led to instability and increased violence, impacting the safety and well-being of their communities. Furthermore, there were also cultural and ideological differences that contributed to the desire for the US to leave. Afghanistan has a rich history and diverse cultural heritage, and some Afghans felt that foreign influences, including American culture and values, were eroding their traditional way of life.

Furthermore, a few private American businesses that offer a variety of services—such as construction, logistics, security, and support for military operations—were well-known for giving a negative impression of Americans. Many well-known private companies are listed below: Triple Canopy, which offers security and protection services; Fluor Corporation, which specializes in providing construction, logistics, and life support services; KBR, Inc. (Kellogg, Brown & Root), a company that specializes in engineering and construction services for the government and military; Academi (formerly Blackwater), a private military company that provided security services; DynCorp International, which offered training, logistics, and support services for Afghan police forces; and more. A division of L3Harris Technologies called MPRI was conducting expert military training. Among the many services that Halliburton provides are engineering and construction. Raytheon offers equipment and technologies for the defense industry. Booz Allen Hamilton provided management and technology consulting services, while Lockheed Martin supplied defense and security technologies. These firms' involvement has been scrutinized and controversial, especially in relation to questions of accountability and the efficacy of their contributions to the mission in Afghanistan as a whole.

Terrorism and Human rights violations are actual U.S. national security concerns, just like corruption, and that is what the takeaway should be from Afghanistan. The real questions are: why did the Afghan government lose the support of its people, if it ever had any? Why does the Afghan military lose the support of the Afghan people, if it ever had any? And why did the United States and its allies lose the support of the Afghan people, if we ever had any?

Many people in the human rights sector argued that the US actually had Afghan support initially. However, they lost the support of the Afghan people years ago because of their indiscriminate bombing, indiscriminate night raids, and support for the ruthless warlords in Afghanistan. Every time the US army accidentally kills an Afghan, they create 10 more Taliban supporters. So, the answer to the question, How did the Taliban win is: They have the support of the Afghan people. They do not have magic weapons, drones, or f-16s, but they had the support of the Afghan people, and that is the question that the US and its' allies have to answer: why?

When a lauded and well-funded program fails, there should be accountability, such that those responsible should explain to Congress and the public. It was not transparent what type of information the ambassador was getting from the Taliban. Was he aware that the Taliban were going to be at the gates tomorrow and did not convey that information? And if he was not; we should ask the ambassador why he was not appraised or did not convey. Or he did convey the information, and somebody up the chain never briefed the president, because President Biden was clearly in the dark about what was going on or about the capability of the Taliban forces.

Ambassador Zalmay Khalilzad was the person that negotiated the US- Taliban accord and the US pullout from Afghanistan. Trump appointed him to serve as Special Representative for Afghanistan Reconciliation on September 5, 2018, remaining in the position under President Joe Biden until October 18, 2021. During that time, he oversaw the creation of Afghanistan's constitution, participated in the country's first elections, and helped to convene the country's first Loya Jirga (traditional grand assembly). Representatives from the United States persuaded Afghanistan's former monarch, 87-year-old Zahir Shah, to withdraw from consideration at the Loya Jirga to select the Head of State in June 2002, despite the fact that a majority of Loya Jirga delegates backed him. That move infuriated Pashtuns, who were concerned about the Northern Alliance's disproportionate power in the Karzai government.

When confronted by American journalist moderator Margaret Brennan on CBS News about why Khalilzad did not include the Afghan government in the deal between the U.S. and Taliban, he said, “Right.”

Margaret added, H.R. McMaster, a retired general and former national security adviser to President Trump, said you brokered a surrender deal. How do you respond to that? Khalilzad said, “The reason for the deal, according to my friend General McMaster and others, is because we weren’t winning the war. How long does General McMaster think we should continue losing ground each year? Why, why, was that the case after 20 years? With so much investment and so much loss of life, we were losing ground to the Talibs, and the alternative was either a negotiated settlement or more of the same. And people way above my pay grade decided more of the same was not acceptable anymore.”

Robin Raphel, a former senior U.S. diplomat with experience in Pakistan and Afghanistan, described Khalilzad as “an unrepentant hustler and a very skilled negotiator. Authorities in Austria were also looking into Mr. Khalilzad for possible money laundering and had frozen his wife’s accounts. The Austrian court later dropped the charges as a result of scavenger bloggers discovering the court documents in the general trash and leaking them to the public. Likewise, in an interview published on TRT World on September 21, 2021, Ahmad Wali Massoud, a Taliban foe who was also critical of Afghanistan President Ashraf Ghani’s government, accused Khalilzad of playing a part in organizing the Taliban’s return to power. Massoud believed that the Taliban lacked the military capability to regain Kabul without significant aid, and he questioned escalating US efforts to employ the Taliban to combat the terrorist group ISIS-K.

However, Mr. Khalilzad maintained that he was representing the United States to carry out the president's direction. Ambassador Khalilzad believed the Afghan democratic government were not serious, as they were depended on the US provisions and did not believe that the US could pull out. He says that his service was based on his professional assessment of the situation and points to his many past accomplishments in the country, including his roles in writing its past democratic constitution, establishing the American University of Afghanistan, and building girls' schools. "There's no way around the fact that Khalilzad was a highly esteemed and decorated senior US diplomat who masterminded the worst agreement in history, culminating in the US defeat and the eventual collapse of Afghanistan," remarked Eric Edelman, a former senior State and Defense Department official who collaborated with Khalilzad.

Before serving as the envoy to Afghanistan under the Trump administration, Mr. Khalilzad was a top State Department official during the Reagan administration, advising on the Soviet Afghan War. The Bush administration chose him as US Ambassador to Iraq, and he was credited with helping to negotiate compromises that allowed Iraq's Constitution to be ratified in October 2005. He advocated for President Bill Clinton "removing Saddam Hussein and his regime from power" with "a full complement of diplomatic, political, and military efforts." He argued for "trade sanctions" against North Korea, "improving US and South Korean military readiness," and "direct military attacks" in a 1993 document. He was also instrumental in the establishment of the American University of Afghanistan (AUAF), Afghanistan's first American-style higher learning educational institution, in 2004 and 2005. Mr. Khalilzad served as the U.S. ambassador to the United Nations from 2007–2009, during which he pushed for sanctions against Iran for helping the insurgent groups in Afghanistan and Iraq and its nuclear programs.

Mr. Khalilzad is a staunch republican, though he was born in Mazar- i-Sharif to an ethnic Pashtun from the Noorzai tribe, Afghanistan, and grew up in Kabul. He moved to America as a young immigrant looking for an opportunity to gain experience and he became a rare high- ranking Muslim-American diplomat who served as U.S. ambassador to his native country, as well as Iraq and the United Nations. Three different secretaries of defense have recognized Khalilzad's contributions to the government: Robert Gates awarded Khalilzad the Department of Defense medal for outstanding public service for his service in Iraq. Donald Rumsfeld awarded Khalilzad the Department of Defense medal for outstanding public service for his work in Afghanistan. Dick Cheney awarded Khalilzad the Department of Defense medal for outstanding public service for his time as an assistant deputy under the secretary of defense for policy planning from 1991 to 1992. Khalilzad has also been awarded the highest national medals by the presidents of

Afghanistan, Georgia, and Kosovo. In Afghanistan, he was awarded the King Amanullah Medal in 2005. The Georgian president awarded Khalilzad the Order of the Golden Fleece in 2016. Kosovo's president awarded Khalilzad the Order of Independence in 2017.

According to Mr. Khalilzad, with regard to terrorism, we have largely achieved that objective: "On the issue of building a democratic Afghanistan, I think that did not succeed. The struggle goes on. The Talibs are a reality in Afghanistan. We did not defeat them. In fact, they were making progress on the battlefield even as we were negotiating with them. And the reason we negotiated with them was because, militarily, things were not going as well as we would have liked. We were losing ground each year.

When asked, why wasn't there a better plan in place from the Trump administration or crafted by the Biden administration to execute what you put on paper?

Mr. Khalilzad stated that Gen. McKenzie has created a plan for the Defense Department and the Taliban approved the idea. However, absconding of President Ghani demoralized Afghan Army because the commander-in-chief has fled. However, this as concerns as it is questionable, that Ghani knew that the US has betrayed is people by negotiating with the Taliban. Anyway, it was all chaotic and as a result, the Afghan people panicked, resulting in the helter-skelter scenario at the airport. The popular reaction in Kabul exacerbated the situation. Fear and opportunity were both to blame. Fear, for a long time, everyone, including some officials, predicted a horrific war if the Talibs entered Kabul. Fighting on the streets causes damage to the city. That was one reason people were afraid. Second, the perception was generated that everybody who could get to the airport, regardless of whether they had documents or not, would be evacuated to the United States and Europe. This combination resulted in a flood of people arriving at the airport and causing the horrific scenes.

According to the UN, 70 percent of Afghanistan's population, or 29 million people, rely on donor-led humanitarian aid. Despite the enormous need, the UN's Humanitarian Response Plan had only raised 34% of its 2023 funding goal as of October 30. Although the United States remains the plan's largest donor, having provided more than $400 million in 2023, UN organizations have had to reduce help, and the World Food Programme has been forced to halt operations due to persistent human rights violations. The Taliban is guilty of human rights violations.

Since gaining power, Taliban officials have restricted education for girls past sixth grade and even third grade in ten provinces, forbidding women from traveling more than 72 kilometers without a male guardian and telling women to "observe hijab," preferably by not leaving the house; otherwise, a full coverage dress code is enforced. They have barred women from using gyms or entering parks in Kabul, halted women from working with the UN and other NGOs and limited the types of jobs available to women. This systematic discrimination is referred to as "gender apartheid." Sima Sami Bahous, UN Under-Secretary-General, called on the

Security Council in September to make gender apartheid a crime under international law. "Gender apartheid is similar to racial apartheid in South Africa or the Jim Crow era in America where the Black majority suffered atrocities." It is tough to think of a worse system than apartheid. Unfortunately, this is the situation for Afghan women, who are subjected to unfathomable abuses of their most basic human rights." Gender apartheid is the complete opposite of gender harmony.

These dynamics are still present under the Taliban's second government. Abuse of women is part of a broader disdain for international governance rules. The Taliban leadership has replaced the rule of law with its version of Sharia law, which includes stoning and public hanging as punishments. There is no specific advice regarding crimes that fall outside the scope of the Quran, and judgment is left up to the individual district court. As a result, the system becomes unpredictable and volatile, with no due process.

The criminal justice system is likewise volatile. Although Taliban leader Haibatullah issued a decree prohibiting detainee torture in January 2022, the United Nations Assistance Mission in Afghanistan (UNAMA) accuses the Taliban police, intelligence directorate, and prison authorities of committing 1,600 human rights violations between January 2022 and July 2023, including inflicting physical and mental suffering, using extended restraint and solitary confinement, and putting people to death, according to SIGAR.

The UN has made some grave predictions about what is going on in Afghanistan right now. On X, brave Afghan women like Lina Rozbih deliver daily news, analysis, and investigative reporting on Afghanistan. SIGAR's report is still being published. The Taliban are producing the toughest women the world has ever seen. Afghan women will outwit and defeat the Taliban. It is inevitable.

The Afghan girls attend virtual schools, and some are already doing it. They can communicate and coordinate with one another, and some are already doing that. There are videos of women being beaten in the streets, just demonstrating for their rights. Some people predict a civil war will happen. Be as it may, the lessons learned from the intervention in Afghanistan have implications for future military engagements, nation-building efforts, and counterterrorism strategies. There are complexities and challenges associated with interventions in regions marked by conflict and instability.

EPILOGUE

Humanity Triumphs when Empathy Prevails

Image: Mixed media from the documentary film, True story of Charlie Wilson - We won. Humanity Won. Empathy triumphed.

The Afghan conflict represents a clash of cultures. Neither violence nor external interventions will win the cultural struggle. Interventionists' successes rarely last because they are built on sand rather than solid bedrock. The US presence as an influence in Afghanistan is a good example, as is the Soviet experience in Afghanistan. A culture war is a cultural conflict between social groups struggling to dominate their values, beliefs, and practices. The Soviets did not fully comprehend this, and the Americans' intervention in Afghanistan's societal conflict and polarization of societal values made matters worse. The Taliban values are considered extremely conservative and are against those considered progressive or liberal.

People, mostly Africans from various parts of Africa, have asked me why I write about Afghanistan as an African. The response is straightforward. It is a responsibility. I write because I am compelled to carry out the essential obligation of conveying a specific message for a certain purpose. What happened in Afghanistan is an example of the reality of many conditions around the world. We simply need to look closely. The Taliban in power is comparable to Hizballah, Al Qaeda, Boko Haram, Alshabab, Boko Haram, Hamas, and other extremist groups using violence to seek political power and recognition around the world. The Taliban is a terror group that has successfully gained control over the nation of Afghanistan and is asking to be recognized as a legitimate government.

The U.S. once offered $10 million for information leading to the capture of the Taliban's leader, Mullah Omar, through the State Department's Rewards for Justice program, an effort designed to "fight against international terrorism." The National Counterterrorism Center also lists "Taliban Presence in Afghanistan" on its global map of "Terrorist Groups." Though the State Department has not designated the Afghan Taliban as an FTO, it has designated the group's sister network, the Pakistani Taliban, as well as the Haqqani Network, a group closely associated with the Taliban that was believed to have been actually holding Bergdahl for most of his captivity. It is believed that the U.S. State Department has not designated the Taliban as a FTO because of ongoing peace negotiations with the group. However, the U.S. government has faced criticism for this at home and abroad. It is clear that the Taliban has forced the U.S. to the negotiation table, demonstrating their influence and power in Afghanistan. Taliban's interest is in Afghanistan remaining stable and under their control, and they used terrorist tactics and guerrilla warfare to achieve their objectives. There is a lot to learn about the Afghanistan saga for the entire human society. It serves as a cautionary tale for the global community.

We have to observe all sides of the story. On the one hand, it tells the story of a people fighting for the right to self-determination on their own terms. On the other hand, it is a liberation crisis from gender apartheid. It is unfathomable for Nigerians to witness a notorious terror group like Boko Haram acquire power and govern. That is exactly what has happened in Afghanistan. These groups have many similarities. This is the nightmare the Afghans are living. On the other hand, the difficulties experienced by all Afghans strike a strong chord with me. I cannot help but empathize with their struggles and hope for a better future. It is crucial to recognize that gender equality knows no borders, and by supporting Afghan women, we are fostering a more inclusive and just world for all.

I worked extremely hard to tell this story as best as possible, using creative graphics and mosaic analysis to weave the story seamlessly. The materials used were sourced from the social media archives of various Afghans telling their stories to corroborate the news and documentaries available, especially pictures. I also discussed this with several Afghan scholars around the world and investigated many academic papers. I remain grateful to all who provided valuable materials. The story had to be told with pictures. Afghanistan is a unique country, and its story provides substantial clues to various dimensions of world development processes. I also investigated great history books on the topic, all of which are listed in the references. I became interested in Afghanistan in the late 1980s through an Afghan friend in Vienna. His name was Sassan Zadeghzahdey. Sassan protested daily at the UNO City Vienna International Center in the late early 1990s. He was a Mujahideen refugee protesting against the USSR occupation and foreign political exploitation of his homeland at the United Nations. I have encountered many Afghan women at the United Nations Headquarters during the annual Commission on the Status of Women (CSW) conferences in New York. Their stories of atrocities and conditions for women even under democratic rule are unbelievable, let alone under Taliban rule.

Afghanistan was quite different from the battleground it became in recent decades. Wars have changed people. Afghans need to heal, and the twenty years of American occupation and influence were not enough to repair the damage caused by both the Mujahideen and the Taliban.

I started to draft this book with the thought that none of us are free if some of us are not safe. That principle guided me through the journey and ensured my commitment to making this book a tool for justice. The idea of the book was serendipitous. After the Taliban stormed the Afghans' presidential quarters and the U.S. exit frenzy on August

15 and 16, I wrote a response on the African Views Organization's WhatsApp group that we call the Circle of Trust. My initial contribution was reactionary and in support of President Biden's decision to pull out. I had been following the story since 9/11. I was against the war. Vincent Lyn, who had authored a couple of books and traveled across Iraq, Syria, and Afghanistan, approached me to collaborate on writing an article on Afghanistan for Al-Jazeera. I agreed and started to do some research. The story was of great interest, given the background I had already cultivated in regard to Afghanistan. I realized that there are many pieces to the story, and only few would have an overview of the whole picture.

However, all along, I wanted to tell the story of Afghanistan from as neutral, objective, honest, candid, and courageous a perspective as I could. Charlie and Joanne Herring sowed the interest of Afghanistan to America. Although, Afghanistan was already a vital U.S. interest. The Carter administration had challenges in the Middle East. The Iranian Revolution (1979), which resulted in the removal of the US- backed Shah Mohammad Reza Pahlavi and the foundation of an Islamic Republic under Ayatollah Ruhollah Khomeini, was one of Carter's most momentous events. Iranian terrorists also took control of the American embassy in Tehran, resulting in the Iran Hostage Crisis, in which 52 American diplomats and citizens were held hostage for 444 days. The US Ambassador to Afghanistan, Adolf "Spike" Dubs, was kidnapped in Kabul in 1979 and subsequently killed during a rescue attempt. The incident occurred amid political instability in Afghanistan, leading to the Soviet invasion later that year. The Soviet Union invasion of Afghanistan prompted the Carter administration to respond with a range of measures, including boycotting the 1980 Summer Olympics in Moscow and providing support to Afghan resistance fighters, including the mujahideen. The 1980 United States presidential election saw incumbent President Jimmy Carter, a Democrat, lose to Republican candidate Ronald Reagan. The crisis in the Middle East was the primary reason for Carter's defeat, though Reagan had an appeal of his own to the American people. President Reagan utilized this opportunity quite effectively, and it turned out to be his noble cause. Reagan changed the world by convincing Michael Gorbachev to end the cold war between the USSR and the USA. Together, they changed the world by ending the Cold War. We must be cautious not to restart it.

We cannot afford to abandon Afghanistan because of its challenges. A positive outcome can be achieved, so we must continue to engage the Taliban government in international dialogue. Afghanistan is without a doubt the key to regional stability, but Afghanistan itself needs stability, and the key to Afghanistan's stability is to consider people's freedoms and ethnic participation in power.

The whole world should care about the status of women in Afghanistan because promoting gender equality and women's rights is a universal value that contributes to thriving societies, demonstrates empathy and solidarity, recognizes the interconnectedness of our world, and aligns with American values of democracy, freedom, and equality, ultimately fostering a more just and equitable global community.

This book was well considered with the hope that it clarifies the importance of Afghanistan as a crossroads for imperialism and starts the necessary discourse on the role and emancipation of women in Islam. This is the victory we have won—the realization and the knowing that war is never the solution. And this is a fight that the Afghans must fight themselves. This fight is not about conflict or even malice. It is about truth and enlightenment about the identity and values of a society. The defeat of ignorance can be delayed but inevitable.

In this case, the problem itself is the solution. It just takes courageous authority to see the will of God and separate it from the will of men. Therefore, Afghan women must lead this cause. There is no doubt that they will, and when they do, the world must stand with them. This current Afghan situation is almost poetic and relevant to the adage of opportunity in chaos. The contemporary has a cause, and if done right, the posterity shall look back on them with gratitude. The world is united behind the women of Afghanistan, and may Allah help them. After all, every part belongs to the whole; therefore, the whole belongs to each part, and there is a mutual interest to contribute to the development and optimum production capacity of every part for the benefit of the whole. May peace prevail on earth for the benefit of all, as we are all interconnected and rely on each other.

In the final analysis, religion is a human right, and so are women's rights. The question here is which one supersedes, and we have the right to debate this hypothesis. Human rights, including both freedom of religion and women's rights, are considered fundamental and should ideally coexist harmoniously. It is important to remember that human rights are not mutually exclusive; they are meant to be respected and protected in conjunction with one another. Balancing these rights requires open dialogue, respect for diversity, and finding common ground to ensure that everyone's rights are upheld. It is a complex topic, but promoting tolerance and understanding can help navigate these challenges. The first thing to recognize is that rights are not absolute and may need to be balanced against one another in certain situations. In order to find a balance, it is important to consider the context and potential consequences. One must also consider the principles and values underlying these rights. We must not regard religion as a collection of dogmas or competing denominations. It is right for any religion to be gender sensitive. However, it is wrong for any religion to promote gender inequality because it deprives individuals of life and liberty and goes against the principles of human rights. Gender harmony is essential for the progress of society.

RESEARCH SOURCES

PRIMARY RESEARCH SOURCES:

African Views: Afghanistan Country Profiles

U.N. Library: U.N. Meetings on Afghanistan

Library of Congress: Declassified records on Afghanistan

Wikipedia: Definitions and Biographies/History of Afghanistan

Council of Foreign Affairs: Analysis of Afghanistan

American Institute of Public Research: Institute of Afghanistan Studies archives

Academia, Research Gates: A Country Profile Compiled

Scholarly articles for google research.

National Museum of Afghanistan

Archives Unbound (Gale)

Joint Publications Research Service (JPRS) Reports (Readex, NewsBank)

Afghanistan 20/20: The 20-Year War in 20 Documents

BROADCAST MEDIA: Documentaries

NPR: History of Afghanistan

PBS: The Cold War/A Historical Timeline of Afghanistan

Youtube: Documentary: The True Story of Charlie Wilson

Documentary: Deutsche Welle (D.W.) Conflict in Afghanistan CSPAN

SECONDARY SOURCES: Historical and current News

Kabul Times: Various current and historical news on Afghanistan political events

India Times: Various current and historical news on Afghanistan political events

The New York Times: Current News on Afghanistan and the 9/11 Historical Archive/Soviet Occupation

Washington Post: Current News on Afghanistan and the 9/11 Historical Archive

AP News: Current News on Afghanistan

Aljazeera: Current News on Afghanistan and the 9/11 Historical Archive
Reuters: Current News on Afghanistan/Historical Archive
R.T.: Current News on Afghanistan/Historical Archive
Aljazeera: News on Afghanistan/Interviews (101 East)
Facebook: Family Archives and Charts
Bloomberg: Financial Analysis Charts
CNN: Reports on Afghanistan
BBC: Reports on Afghanistan and Charts
Factcheck: Afghanistan Reports

REFERENCES:

Wikipedia: Details on Various Afghan Persons and Validation of Definitions;
Chronology of Relevant Events: Who, Where, and When: USSR vs. Afghanistan resistance group (80% mujahideen)
Front: Mainland of Afghanistan, December 1979–February 1989
The Trump Plan R4+S. NSF Presentation Afghanistan By Bill Conrad
The Problem of Pashtun Alienation—Asia Report N 62 Kabul/Brussels/Afghan
Assessment: International Protection Needs of Asylum-Seekers from Afghanistan March 12, 2018, Vienna, Austria
Kapur Surya Foundation: Ethnicity, Power, and Authority: Emergence of Muslim Religious Elites in Afghanistan during the Socialist Regimes
An Unarguable Fact: American Security is Tied to Afghanistan and Pakistan: The American Enterprise Institute Senior Fellow and Director of the Critical Threats Project, Kagan

BIBLIOGRAPHY

A History of Women in Afghanistan Multiple sources
Vartan Gregorian, The Emergence of Modern Afghanistan: Politics of Reform and Modernization, 1880–1946

Thomas J. Barfield, Afghanistan: A Cultural and Political History (Princeton)

RAWA: an organization of Afghan women struggling for peace, freedom, democracy, and women's rights in Afghanistan.

The Soviet Afghan War: Breaking the Hammer and Sickle," Veterans of Foreign Wars, March 2002.

Afghanistan's Two-Party Communism: Parcham and Khalq, Lester W. Grau, and Ali Ahmad Jalali, "

"Women in Afghanistan: Pawns in Men's Power Struggles," Amnesty International Militant Islam, Oil, and the New Great Game in Central Ahmed Rashid,

The Taliban and the Crisis of Afghanistan, ed. Robert D. Crews and Tarzi The Politics of Gender and Reconstruction in Afghanistan, "Afghanistan Constitution, 2004.

Learning to Build an Islamic Republic of Afghanistan, Central Statistic Organization, 2010, http://www.cso.gov.af/demography/labor.html

A brief look at the contemporary history of Afghanistan Ataee, M. E. (2005, Kabul, Mayan)

Afghanistan is on the path of history. Kabul, Republican. Ghobar, M. G. M. (1978). Hashemi, S. S. (1982). Contemporary History of Afghanistan Kabul University Press Afghanistan in the twentieth century. Tanin, Z. (2005).

History of Foreign Relations in Afghanistan [1879–1928]. 2nd Vol. Kabul, Risallat; Tehran, Khawar. Zamany, K. M. (2014)

Afghanistan: No Country for Women

What the future holds for Afghan women Noorjahan Akbar

Al Jazeera and Rukhshana Media, an independent Afghan news agency reporting on women in prison. All images used in this book are in the public domain and available through digital images courtesy of Getty's Open Content Program and Google's open license. The author edited all the pictures and mixed media.

ABOUT THE AUTHOR

Nana Dr. Wale Idris Ajibade is an economist, a sociologist, and a modern philosopher. He is a professor of Sociology at Essex County College in New Jersey. He is the founder and executive director of African Views Organization (AV), a nonprofit with consultative status with the United Nations Economic and Social Council. The African Views Organization focuses on society's wellbeing by promoting cultural sustainability and harmony through scientific and social research, community assessment, resource mapping, and project development. He is the architect of the AV framework for comprehensively merging the U.N. Sustainable Development Goals (SDGs) and the African Union Aspirations.

He is an educator who teaches at the University, college, high school, and secondary and primary school levels. He created a new virtual parallel classroom concept for connecting children in Africa with children on other continents to learn together in real time. He developed and produced programs such as African Health Dialogues, advocating for establishing the African Center for Disease Control.

He designed global outreach for youth to encourage global perspectives and initiatives for sustainable development solutions. He coined the term gender harmony and is a staunch promoter of male involvement in the Anti-Violence Against Women Act (AVAWA) global campaigns. He defined and emphasized gender harmony as a strategy for peace. He advocated for African and Caribbean summits and visa-free citizenship for the African Diaspora as part of the reconciliation to the impact of slavery. He is the progenitor of the African Royal Kingdom (ARK) and the Royal Institute of Global African Cultures and Traditions for the Royal African Kingdom, with which he aims to use the power of cultures and traditions to re-unite people of African descent around the world.

Dr. Wale Idris Ajibade has given speeches at the US State Department, United Nations, African Union, colleges, and universities in the US, Europe, Africa, Asia, and Latin America on issues related to the role of cultures in peacebuilding, Sustainable Development Goals (SDGs), corporate social responsibility (CSR), gender equality, education, environment, health, media, and social and economic development. He has earned a Ph.D. in Economics, Public Administration, and Humanities. He is a Distinguished Professor of Sociology and Public Administration. He has a chieftaincy title, Nana Ankobiahene, from the Dwenase traditional district of Ghana. He speaks English, German, and Yoruba.

Image: Mixed media: Art by Lalla Essaydi

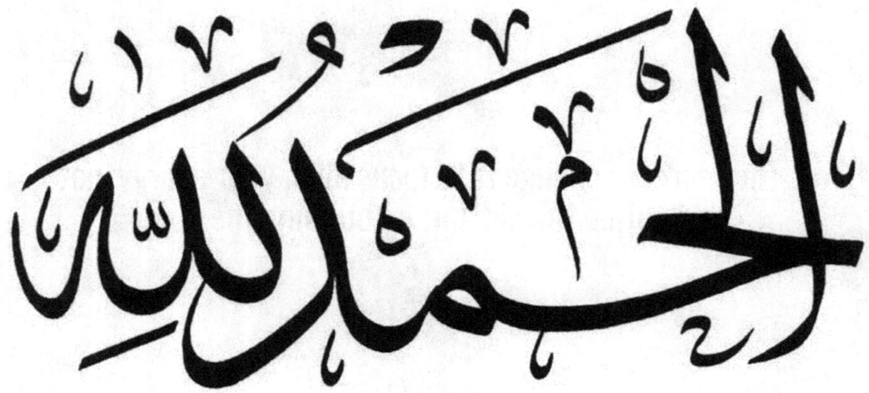

Alhamdulillah

رحمة الله علينا جميعا

Rahmat Allah Ealayna Jamiean

د هللا تعالی رحمت دې پر موږ ټولو وي

May Allah’s mercy be upon us all.

www.ingramcontent.com/pod-product-compliance
Lightning Source LLC
Chambersburg PA
CBHW032047020426
42335CB00011B/225

* 9 7 8 1 9 6 1 4 3 8 4 3 9 *